MW00850221

Transformative Negotiation

Transformative Negotiation

Strategies for Everyday Change and Equitable Futures

Sarah Federman

UNIVERSITY OF CALIFORNIA PRESS

University of California Press
Oakland, California

© 2023 by Sarah Federman

Library of Congress Cataloging-in-Publication Data

Names: Federman, Sarah, author.
Title: Transformative negotiation : strategies for
    everyday change and equitable futures / Sarah
    Federman.
Description: [Oakland, California] : [University of
    California Press], [2023] | Includes bibliographical
    references and index.
Identifiers: LCCN 2023000332 (print) | LCCN 2023000333
    (ebook) | 9780520386921 (cloth) | ISBN
    9780520386938 (paperback) | ISBN 9780520386945
    (ebook)
Subjects: LCSH: Negotiation.
Classification: LCC BF637.N4 F434 2023 (print) |
    LCC BF637.N4 (ebook) | DDC 158/.5—dc23/
    eng/20230407
LC record available at https://lccn.loc.gov/2023000332
LC ebook record available at https://lccn.loc
    .gov/2023000333Manufactured in the United States
    of America

32 31 30 29 28 27 26 25 24 23
10 9 8 7 6 5 4 3 2 1

*To those whose stories and wisdom fill
these pages*

Contents

Introduction

On a cross-country train trip from Washington, D.C., to Seattle, I met Nick, a chatty young man in his twenties. Over microwaved dinners in the dining car, Nick asked about my new job at the University of Baltimore, where I would soon teach negotiation.

"What are you gonna teach 'em?" he asked.

I told him a bit about my curriculum, which integrated the classic negotiation literature and lessons that I had learned through more than a decade of business experience.

"Yeah, that sounds cool," he said, "but it's not real. I can teach people what they need to know to save their lives."

Nick then shared stories from his childhood. When, for example, at the age of nine, his drug-addicted parents disappeared, he stole food to feed his siblings. He then talked about the physical violence he later navigated using his street-savvy negotiation skills.

"Wow," I said. "That does sound pretty different."

As the semester approached, I thought more about my conversation with Nick. Would my curriculum be appropriate for similarly street-wise graduate students from Baltimore? How different were our worlds? My experience was diverse, but in such a different way from theirs. I had spent a decade negotiating contracts all over the world. Based first in Manhattan and then in Paris, I had negotiated in French, Spanish, and English with companies in twelve countries, including in the Middle East. I had survived negotiations in small windowless rooms at

Googleplex and at a leading Chinese data company in Beijing, among many others. I hoped that having studied negotiation in the Key Executive Program at Harvard Business School and having a doctorate in conflict resolution would fill the gaps. But I worried, did I have the right preparation?

No, as it turned out, I didn't.

When it came to negotiation, Baltimore felt more foreign than Beijing. Most cities have at least one neighborhood struggling with poverty, crime, and drugs. But I had not spent much time in those areas. I wondered whether classic negotiation approaches might fail, or get people into more trouble, in these environments.

Baltimore turned out to be the perfect place to consider Nick's critique of my approach and the negotiation field more broadly. With just six hundred thousand residents, Baltimore has the second-highest homicide rate in the United States and ranks in the top ten U.S. cities for drug use. It also leads in overdoses, failed infrastructure problems, ongoing racial discrimination, and high incidence of excessive police force.[1] The vortex of problems seems to know no depths. In April 2019, federal agents raided then mayor Catherine Pugh's house while the FBI and the IRS searched her office for ill-gotten gains. By May of that year, the mayor was ousted. In June, Baltimore Symphony Orchestra members were locked out of their performance hall and denied health insurance while the management grappled with bankruptcy. By July, sports commentators joined in, questioning whether the Baltimore Orioles might be the worst team in baseball history.[2]

It's too easy to blame Charm City's challenges on those holding the guns, needles, and wads of ill-gotten cash. As in most struggling communities, however, the problems originate in multigenerational government policies and business practices. Baltimore's human history began with Indigenous tribes (namely the Susquehannock people) who hunted in the area. Later, colonists built the city to serve mainly as a fort. After a short period of coexistence, fighting broke out, resulting in the colonists claiming the land and ousting the original inhabitants.

Then came slavery. By 1808, the city had become the largest transfer point for slaves and cotton on the Atlantic coast.[3] The arts, hospitals, religious organizations, and schools flourished with the money that slavery made possible. Postwar share cropping and segregation deprived Black families, though liberated from slavery, of a livable wage and quality education.[4] Post-segregation discriminatory practices such as redlining prevented home ownership and access to the capital needed to launch businesses. While cities like Oakland and Detroit struggle with slavery's legacies, the slave trade does not define their historical landscape the way that it does in Baltimore.

The hundreds of groups and institutions continuously striving to pull Charm City from this cyclone of problems led *Baltimore Sun* columnist Dan Rodricks to christen it "Our City of Perpetual Recovery."[5] I wondered what, if anything, traditional negotiation strategies might contribute to this recovery.

TRADITIONAL NEGOTIATION STRATEGIES IN BALTIMORE

My concerns about the potential poor fit between my planned curriculum and my students' needs were confirmed immediately. The first week, Nevaeh asked me how to negotiate with the courts to get her kids back. She also wanted to know how to reduce late fees imposed by the IRS. Later that semester, Cornell asked how, as a six-foot-four, 240-pound Black man, he could avoid intimidating white people during negotiations. I had no idea what to say. The questions kept coming:

"How do I convince my brother not to use drugs before family dinners?"

"How should I reconnect with my birth father's family?"

"How can I get Geico [car insurance] to replace my stolen car?"

I had little personal experience with these problems, and the examples given in our class readings on negotiation discussed corporate deals, hostage crises, and debates between couples over how to spend their extra income. While the authors promised real-world solutions for "all readers," by the end of that first term, neither the students nor I were convinced. Matila said in class one night, "I just can't relate to these examples. I'm sorry they're having trouble with their million-dollar deal, or SUV, or whatever, but I'm not sure this advice works in *everyone's* world." Others nodded.

Many of my students lived in precarity. One, I later learned, had spent the winter term without heat or electricity. Several others struggled with post-incarceration challenges, and many carried significant debt. More than half could speak firsthand about domestic violence, homelessness, drug use, or life-threatening illnesses facing their families. Such urgent challenges needed—and deserved—better support from those who understood their lives, so I started having the students coach each other. One night, the class teamed up to help Aiysha with verbal harassment by her boss. Marsha suggested that Aiysha simply approach her boss directly and tell him that the situation was unacceptable. Aiysha thought about the suggestion and then said, "Well, maybe a white woman can say that, but not a Black woman." Aiysha was right to consider this difference. Research shows that if you are Black in the United States, your boss (Black or white) may hear a request differently than if it came from a white person.[6]

Learning this, I wondered about the ethics of teaching traditional negotiation pedagogy in Baltimore. The word *negotiate* derives from the Latin verb *negotiari,* which means "to do business" but whose roots mean "to give trouble to someone." Negotiations can be good trouble when people transform difficult encounters into opportunities for relationship building and shared problem solving. Might traditional negotiation advice, used in the wrong setting, set my students up for bad trouble? What if advice designed for white middle-class corporate environments could get my students fired or, if deployed in the streets, could lead to dangerous altercations? I turned to local experts for advice. Nawal Rajeh, named Baltimore's 2018 Peacemaker of the Year for the peace camp she cofounded, confirmed my suspicion: "I can't train [the kids] to be like me and my world. It might backfire for them. They have a different reality." To illustrate this point, she recalled a camper who complained about not getting her turn on the jump rope. Nawal said to me, "Now, I would have just asked the teacher to come fix it, but for these kids—out in life—there's often no one they can turn to. So, I told her 'Go get your turn. I don't know how you're going to do it but go get it.'" Sure enough, she did.

Context matters. The mismatch between worlds became increasingly apparent that first semester. The role-plays included with our textbook became almost comical as students negotiated for Pakistani prunes and pandas for a new zoo. They did not complain. They said they were used to this mismatch throughout their education. As a field, I thought the field could do better. No one suggests that the Palestinian-Israeli conflict might be resolved with tactics useful when purchasing an SUV, so why assume that negotiation tips useful for acquiring pandas for a zoo might help those emerging from cycles of poverty and disempowerment? Unless you teach negotiation from the perspective of the panda, I cannot see the connection. Neither could the students.

In addition to unrelatable examples, the existing literature often discusses people with New Testament names like John, Paul, Matthew, and Mary, whereas our students have names like Shakia, Le'Nesa, Deja,

Teisha, Kolby, and Enechi. The literature's prevalent examples refer to corporate contexts, whereas most of our students work in institutions that tend to be more hierarchical and rigid, such as government administration, social services, education, law, security, transportation, or healthcare. A student working for the military chuckled one night at the reading's suggestion to just ask for a raise.

Between terms, I continued to solicit feedback from students and other local experts. Students from California State University, Dominguez Hills, and Georgetown University broadened my perspective. These conversations sparked a curriculum revision that developed into a participatory action research project and, ultimately, this book.[7] Their lively stories and hard-won wisdom enable this book to achieve its four primary goals:

1. Help individuals move from precarity to stability.

2. Address significant blind spots in the negotiation field.

3. Introduce a new approach to negotiation that disrupts, rather than perpetuates, oppression.

4. Teach those with power how to use their power to create more equitable futures.

WHO THIS BOOK IS FOR

With these broad goals in mind, this book reaches several audiences. First, it is for anyone seeking social mobility toward a better life for themselves and loved ones. Anyone struggling with discrimination or marginality due to socioeconomic class, ethnicity, language, disabilities, non-cisgender identities, religion, precarious finances, incarceration history, or any other disadvantaging attribute will also find support here. While many of the examples emerge from Baltimore, anyone operating in volatile or fragile environments will find parallels in their own lives. People struggling in places as disparate as Appalachia, Tijuana, the *banlieues* of Paris, the lands of the Cree communities in Northern Manitoba, or even Sonapur migrant camps in the United Arab Emirates often have more in common with one another than with executives navigating corporate boardrooms just miles from where they live.

This book supports social change leaders from these communities. People who successfully rise from the margins can often handle the heat that leadership requires. CEOs, world leaders, and the ultra-wealthy can often get away with emotional outbursts and other behaviors that would cause many of us to lose our jobs or be thrown out of public spaces. Marcetta, who raised twelve children (not all her own), says no tantrum stops her from getting the job done. She has proof. One of her trainings as a correctional officer involves someone screaming horrible things in her ear while she completes a task. She has no trouble with it.

Not everyone can operate in these volatile environments. Negotiation books, however, often overlook these audiences, focusing instead on those in the middle who are bound by codes of civility. Will they be prepared to handle the intense emotional storms at the highest altitudes of leadership? Rosalind says she will be. A mother at age fourteen, she successfully graduated from college with an accounting degree. Unfortunately, she first used her accounting skills to help a drug lord and landed in prison. Now graduating with a master's degree, she says: "Those from challenging environments have the potential to be world leaders because we're flexible, civil, yet have the ability to be dog-get-down-and-dirty with the best of them." This book supports their ascent.

This book serves instructors of negotiation as well as of sociology, leadership, urban studies, and related courses. Negotiation instructors can now address some of the glaring gaps in the field. Instructors oriented toward social transformation and leadership will find actionable approaches that students can test out immediately. Instructors who assign the activities at the end of the chapters will have students returning to class with new insights and often surprising results. Many of my students paid for their semester with raises, new jobs, discounts, and newfound financial wisdom. Others repaired relationships with children, parents, friends, or exes. Students in their twenties had results, but so too did students in their sixties. It's never too late to start asking for what you need and want.

Current and aspiring managers who want to attract, train, and retain diverse talent will want to read this book as well. Many know the research showing that diverse teams tend to be more profitable.[8] But how does one keep these teams happy? Understanding the challenges faced by employees from historically marginalized groups prevents what psychologist David Ross called a "fundamental attribution error." This happens when we blame individual behavior on a personality defect rather than the context.[9] For example, when Karim stopped coming to class, I could have written him off as lazy or disinterested. Instead, I reached out every week, saying that we missed him and wanted him back. Two months later, he appeared in my office, hugged me, and said, "Thanks for not giving up on me." He described how he had been carrying the weight of his community and its problems. We found a way to get him back in school. Today, he draws on what he learned in class to increase the presence of youth voices in police training, create inclusive city monuments, and revitalize Baltimore's Black Arts District. Of course, managers cannot spend weeks chasing employees like I chased Karim. This book will help managers find approaches that work for their contexts.

When negotiating, for example, managers want to make sure they properly promote the diverse employees they hire. Business professor Paul Ingram notes that "workers who come from lower social-class origins in the United States are 32% less likely to become managers than those who come from higher social-class origins."[10] Those not being promoted suffer, but so do the organizations and nations. Ingram's research shows that countries with more managers from the lower classes have higher gross domestic product per capita. Ingram also refers to a U.S. military study showing that those with lower-class origins can be better leaders, in part because they are less self-centered, and a study of lawyers in the United Kingdom in which those from lower-class groups proved more proficient and had greater drive. Why would organizations want to miss out on these extraordinary people? My experiences in Baltimore lead me to agree with Ingram that those rising through conditions of socioeconomic adversity show tremendous "grit, courage, and a deep human understanding."[11] Value this grit in them and understand their challenges, and your organizations will thrive.

Public-sector leaders neglect these individuals' struggles at our collective peril. Many people from historically marginalized communities end up working in government or for various social service agencies. Michael Lipsky's seminal book *Street-Level Bureaucracy* urges us not to overlook the lower-level bureaucrats who collectively determine and deliver agency policy as well as decide who is a "criminal" or who is "mentally ill." They have tremendous discretionary power.[12] In Baltimore, graduate students help decide whether parents get their kids back; serve as recovery coaches, security officers, and halfway-house workers; and hold many administration positions. Our graduates have gone on to work for the Air Force, FBI, and National Security Administration, or pursued law degrees.

Those in positions of power will want to read this book for several reasons. First, being powerful does not shelter anyone from feelings of marginality. Yale University law professor Kenji Yoshino writes about how we all cover marginalized identities in our personal and/or professional lives.[13] Some of the pragmatic lessons may also be useful. A large salary does not necessarily equate to personal financial savvy, any more than having an email account means that we use email well. The book supports leaders who wish to generate equitable futures, serving the living as well as the unborn.

Finally, this book teaches the powerful about their power. Wharton negotiation professor Stuart Diamond finds that "the more powerful people are, the less attention they pay to the other side's needs."[14] If you want to understand your power, you will want to study those on the brunt end of it.[15] In other words, you may learn more about power from those working in Amazon's distribution centers than from those working in its corporate offices.

A BRIEF HISTORY OF NEGOTIATION

Today, if you want to learn about negotiation, you will find trainings offered through business and law programs. Bookstore staff slot negotiation books among the business-success literature, some by business school professors and others by independent trainers who boast of their sales or litigation experiences. Occasionally, a government or conflict program will offer a course in negotiation, but many do not. Most negotiation training resides in the business and law sectors. Here's why. At the end of World War II, those committed to preventing future wars, including the very real threat of nuclear war, believed in negotiated solutions.[16] Trainings influenced by game theory and mutual deterrence became the tactic of choice for long-term peacebuilding and de-escalation during the Cold War. Negotiations between Presidents Reagan and Gorbachev ended the Cold War between the United States and the USSR. The world exhaled a sigh of relief, but instead of bringing peace on Earth, the 1990s brought genocides in Bosnia and Rwanda and several African civil wars. Negotiation tactics alone could not halt the ethnic warfare. Those interested in interrupting these conflicts turned away from traditional negotiation techniques and studied the roles of culture, tribalism, values, identity, trauma, history, memory, religion, and gender in violence. These considerations informed the theory that supports practices of mediation, diversity education, problem-solving workshops, truth and reconciliation commissions, and local-level peacebuilding processes. Many scholars and practitioners interested in peacebuilding left negotiation strategies behind, finding them too static, thin, and impersonal to respond to entrenched, large-group hatred and conflict.

Peace and justice scholars further shifted away from negotiation after 9/11 and the subsequent focus on terrorism. How could you negotiate with a group whose identity was premised on your annihilation? Even if you wanted to, Western governments consider negotiating with terrorists a felony. Those interested in peace and social transformation focused less on negotiation and more on inner work, where power dynamics and beliefs about exclusion reside.[17]

Negotiation and peacebuilding grew apart. Negotiation flourished in business and law contexts, but often without the benefit of understanding transgenerational trauma, marginality, and structural oppression. This book reunites peacebuilding and negotiation to better prepare us all for the challenges of our time and those that will face future generations.

NEGOTIATING FOR SOCIAL MOBILITY

We cannot achieve positive social change without changing the personal circumstances of individuals. Negotiation skills can help improve lives. Successful negotiators can provide, for themselves and others, food, shelter, healthcare, and physical safety. When they are one of the few in their communities to do so, these changes bring new pressures.

For those on the margins, however, moving up comes at a price. In *Moving Up without Losing Your Way,* Jennifer Morton draws our attention to the emotional costs of mobility for those who must (or feel they must) leave to achieve. Teaching at the City University of New York (CUNY) in West Harlem, Morton became concerned as she watched students finding "success" while growing isolated from their communities of origin. Professional success can mean less time to support one's community physically and emotionally, yet new friends and expanded professional networks never replace one's community of origin. And when childhood friends and family members reject the person on the rise, this can leave the one moving "up" feeling guilty and lonely.

Catalina, the first person in her family to finish high school, struggled with this tension. Currently a criminology graduate student in Los Angeles, she described what happened when she read during a quiet moment of a daylong family event. Her cousin approached her and said, "You should have finished that before you came." Catalina tried to explain how much school reading she had, but he brushed her off. The books, the knowledge, and the growing possibilities for those on the move can be a painful reminder to those who feel left behind. If others in your life feel threatened by your changes, it can help to reassure them that you love them as they are. But that's not always enough. *Transformative Negotiation* takes seriously both the benefits of mobility and its social consequences.

In my search for people who rose without leaving their communities behind, I found Chris Wilson, a formerly incarcerated man and one of our star students. Chris tells people, "You're moving up, not moving out." His career took off first through his construction company and then through his memoir *The Master Plan: My Journey from Prison to Purpose.* He has an apartment and art studio in Manhattan but still maintains a residence in Baltimore, his hometown. Here, Chris funds local revitalization projects and mentors those reaching for more.

NEGOTIATING FOR SOCIAL TRANSFORMATION

When we have achieved stability and fulfillment, we can come back to free others. But if we negotiate ourselves into power and then use that power to oppress others, we become part of the problem. As business professors Julie Battilana and Tiziana Casciaro rightly warn, "Having once been wary of power is no guarantee that you will be immune to abusing it."[18] Too often, we see historically marginalized groups advocating win-lose pathways to power. Stacey Vanek Smith's 2021 book *Machiavelli for Women: Defend Your Worth, Grow Your Ambition, and Win the Workplace* provides an example. While the book offers many useful negotiation tips, building a framework around Niccolò Machiavelli's *The Prince* encourages women to become as ruthless as the patriarchies that held them (and others) back. *The Prince,* written in the early sixteenth century, directs those in power to maintain their positions through intimidation, brute force, and deceit. Machiavelli's famous assertion that "the ends justify the means" encourages followers to engage in any method necessary to achieve their goals—no matter how many may be harmed in the process.[19]

In contrast, this book offers a way to break glass ceilings without leaving everyone else under the shards. We do this by rebuilding trust rather than through domination. Conflict resolution expert Donna Hicks says that *dignity* plays a central role in rebuilding trust.[20] When we acknowledge, include, create safety, and give people the benefit of the doubt and the space to make their own decisions, we can rebuild trust even in the most violence-ravaged places.

Many of negotiation's core concepts remain relevant as we work to reunite negotiation with peacebuilding wisdom; they just need to be adapted for different contexts. Below, I outline some of those concepts.

Separate the Person from the Problem

Traditional negotiation training can show you how to focus on the goal instead of getting wrapped up in personal behaviors. For example, focus on getting your product to the client, rather than on your colleague's negative attitude. Organizations do best when members focus on solving problems rather than trying to change people.

What if we shift contexts to domestic violence? Here the problem is the physical abuse, not the person per se. Yet can you separate them? Sure, you can try to work with the partner to eliminate the behavior, but you also might need to leave.

Distinguish between Interests and Positions

Traditional trainings help us distinguish between what we ask for (our positions) and our deeper needs/desires (interests). We might ask for a $10,000 raise (our position) to meet our *interest* in paying for our child's college tuition. Staying focused on our deeper interests helps us be open to creative solutions and not dig in our heels.

As this book will show, for those in under-resourced communities, this teaching becomes even more critical, and ignoring it more dangerous. Where people feel forgotten, dignity is in short supply. Therefore, sticking to one's position can become a matter of pride. It's easy to lose sight of the larger goal. Safe Streets, an organization working to reduce violent altercations, helps parties in conflict make this distinction. For example, they remind an armed kid that while he wants his stolen cell phone back (his position), he also wants to survive the confrontation (his interests). In stressful moments, we can lose sight of the big picture.

Those navigating volatile contexts express concern that changing their position, even a little, can look like weakness. A reputation for weakness *can* make them more vulnerable. While we can help them see creative problem solving as a strength, those with whom they are negotiating might not see it that way. They need coaching on how to appear strong *while* being creative and flexible. This coaching ought to come from those with experience in these contexts.

Expand the Pie

This precept presents negotiations as opportunities to create more for everyone. Businesses look for mutual gains—say, getting access to clients in exchange for providing a technology. Maintaining this mindset can be challenging in resource-rich environments, never mind in contexts where groups experience a collective sense of scarcity. How can so little pie be expanded? Decades of failed projects and community efforts can leave people feeling despondent. Build trust slowly and use small wins to cultivate the community's hope in a better future. This takes time. Where chronic injustices have eroded trust, many will be suspicious of efforts to expand the pie. History has taught them that no matter what is promised, they will lose out.

Prepare

Negotiators benefit from preparation, whether this means research on the issues at hand or sorting out one's priorities. In the heat of the moment, we all can become derailed. Drawing on local experts, the chapters ahead show the kinds of preparation needed to move *into* the middle class.

Determine Your Range

The distance between your walk-away point and your ideal outcome is your negotiation range. When selling your car, for example, you determine the minimum you would accept and the amount you ideally want.

When looking for an apartment, Juanita knew that she would have to walk away from any costing more than $1,500 a month and any that did not accept pets; her ideal would be an apartment with lots of light, within walking distance to school. She knew her range, which is determined by one's personal situation and by the larger context: what one can get for $1,500 a month varies by city. The chapters ahead discuss contexts relevant to the socially mobile, rather than to those acquiring international companies.

Test Assumptions

Negotiation trainings encourage us to identify and test assumptions. This is a great practice. We might underestimate our counterpart's willingness to engage. We might be wrong about their interests. We can explore these possibilities through direct and indirect questions as well as by doing some research.

In chapter 2, I add a dimension to the issue of assumptions. Individuals from historically marginalized communities and/or impoverished households can internalize messaging that they do not deserve. In these situations, we want to first challenge what people believe they can have. I offer a way to engage in this process.

Have a Strong BATNA (Best Alternative to a Negotiated Agreement)

As we'll further discuss in several chapters, this tenet teaches that the more and better options you have, the more power you have in a negotiation. You're in a stronger position to negotiate for a raise, for example, if you have another job offer.

Those negotiating from the margins, however, must consider not only the best alternatives but those with the least *negative* consequences. Let's say a formerly street-involved person needs cash fast to pay alimony or court fees. He tried negotiating with his family for the money. They said no. He considers moving a little product (drugs), just enough to cover the legal and financial obligations, promising himself that he will only do it this one time. But is this the best alternative? Once he has reminded himself of the ease of acquiring money this way, it may be hard to choose a different path going forward. The best alternative might be to ask his employer for an advance, or get work in an Amazon warehouse for a week. It will be grueling and humbling, but sore feet and hurt pride will be better than jail.

Avoid the Past

Wharton negotiation professor Stuart Diamond finds that negotiating over past events often results in three outcomes: "war, litigation, and no deal."[21] But might these outcomes occur precisely *because* people cannot debate the past productively? When one side refuses to acknowledge and address past events, litigation, violence, or a refusal to negotiate becomes a way to be heard. Furthermore, overlooking the connections between today's problems and yesterday's traumas often leads to incomplete or short-term solutions. Creating long-term value often requires addressing longer timelines, especially for those seeking social transformation. Expanding negotiation's leading tenet of *win-win* will support these wider aims.

THE WIN-WIN-WIN APPROACH

The "win-win" approach to negotiation was introduced in Roger Fisher and William Ury's 1981 classic *Getting to Yes*. The seminal book has helped millions of people shift away from a win-lose approach to negotiation and toward mutually satisfying agreements that enhance relationships. The best negotiators, they say, find ways for all parties to achieve their goals. Those trained in this school of negotiation learn how to clarify their needs, understand the other party's needs, and work on creative solutions that address all concerns.

By discouraging harm to others for our own gain, a win-win approach deters Machiavellian-style leadership. This approach, however, attends to the interests only of the signatories, not of those who live out the consequences of the agreement. Take, for example, a construction company and a municipal government agreeing to a hydroelectric dam project. They leave the meeting thrilled with the new contract. But what about the Indigenous community soon to be forcibly relocated because of this agreement?[22] Is it a win for them? Did they have a voice?

Anyone from an under-resourced community can find further examples. In Baltimore, such exclusion from negotiation happened to Poppleton, a community with roots three generations deep. In 2021, the city and a development company sought to take 160 homes by eminent domain. The community circulated a petition saying that any revitalization project "must include the voices of and resources for all remaining residents."[23] Their unity and powerful campaign successfully challenged any so-called win that would harm them.

Shifting to a "win-win-win" approach offers another way forward. William Ury nods to the idea when he encourages readers to think about "the larger whole—the family, the workplace, the nation and even the world."[24] *Transformative Negotiation* shows us how we can do this and argues that personal fulfillment cannot be attained without this concern for the larger whole. A win-win-win model requires paying attention to those usually *not* at the negotiating table. In Baltimore, this means those living in zip codes where young men do not plan to see thirty, where mothers wait twenty years for the return of their imprisoned sons, and where many pray their addictions will not win them back.

The work of Baltimore native and renowned justice theoretician John Rawls supports this idea. Rawls employed the concept of a "veil of ignorance," asking us to consider: Would we be willing to be *anyone* affected by a given decision?[25] Let's say you wake up the day after your negotiation and find yourself in the body of someone excluded from but subjected to your deal. Would you still consider it a good arrangement? If not, you may want to rethink the plan. This simple exercise provides a morality test for all negotiations and even larger social problems. Justice advocate Bryan Stevenson says that we can evaluate the morality of an entire community this way: "You judge the character of a society not by how they treat their rich and the powerful and the privileged, but by how they treat the poor, the condemned, the incarcerated."[26]

This holistic approach to negotiation is not just a Candyland fantasy, but likely the only mindset suitable for leaders addressing our climate crisis, the expansion of authoritarian regimes, the opioid epidemic fueled by Big Pharma, and other ongoing structures of oppression. The advent of nuclear weapons taught us that win-lose can destroy us all. Today's crises show us that allowing elites to reap profits at the planet's (and its inhabitants') expense can also destroy us.

THE URGENCY

For individuals in precarity, the stakes could not be higher. Negotiation skills help them find shelter, avoid violent altercations, and convince loved ones to seek help for addictions. Parents and elders can influence youth to avoid the temptations of street life and practice safe sex. BIPOC parents can teach their children how to negotiate (or avoid negotiating) with police. For the ill and their caregivers, negotiation savvy can be a matter of life or death. Getting the right care in a stressed medical system requires persistence and vigilance, especially for those with reduced access to the system.

By placing these negotiations centrally, this book responds to the widening gap between rich and poor. Whether you define the middle class by level of education, violence, or financial precarity, the middle class is shrinking.[27] Psychologist Keith Payne calls this our "broken ladder," affecting everything from a family's economic situation to their physical and emotional health, as well as their trust in the government and its associated agencies. When people feel poor, they make riskier life decisions.[28]

Getting into the middle class can be nearly impossible for those facing structural barriers. University of Chicago professor Reuben Miller studied the post-incarceration lives of 250 incarcerated individuals and their families.[29] Many end up homeless because they cannot qualify for public housing, and staying with family could result in everyone's eviction. Even when they find shelter, court fees undercut efforts to pay for food and rent. Families step in to pay these costs, further impoverishing themselves and the whole community. Sarah Halpern-Meekin writes about the resulting "social poverty," defined by transitory relationships and more generalized isolation.[30] Many scholars and practitioners articulate the cages that keep people locked out of prosperous living. Using negotiation, this book charts an escape plan, aiming to knock down a piece of the wall on the way out so that the next person can get through more easily. Little by little, we grow the middle class.

CHAPTER 1

Imagine

OVERVIEW

In the children's board game *Hungry Hungry Hippos,* players smack a lever as fast as they can, trying to suck up the most marbles. Unfortunately, many people grow up and continue living life the same way, chasing what everyone else chases. Self-knowledge takes time, which is why most people just go for the marbles. When you reflect on your desires, you increase the chances that what you get will bring you and others happiness.

This chapter helps you take the following first steps:

- Discover what you want and why you want it.
- Liberate yourself from damaging influences.
- Create a vision for your life.

Taking the time to do this reflective work helps center and guide future negotiations for individuals as well as organizations.

QUESTIONS TO CONSIDER

What do you want? Why do you want it?

How will having this item or experience improve your life and the lives of others?

Clarity is your greatest power during a negotiation. If you don't know what you want, how can you get it? Sometimes what we want seems obvious. In a salary negotiation, we want more money. When negotiating for a new home, we want to pay as little as possible. Even a huge paycheck for a job that makes you miserable or a stately home you hate may only offer superficial, short-term gains. To thrive, we need to think more deeply about what we want and how we want to act in pursuit of these wants. How we handle these negotiations with loved ones impacts our lives as much as, if not more than, the amount of money in our bank account. When we lack clarity about what we want and who we want to be, we can fall into fruitless power struggles. By contrast, when we get quiet and reflect on what matters to us, we become more graceful (and effective) in all our interactions.

ROCK BOTTOM

Most of us live terrified of hitting rock bottom, but that can sometimes be the best place to think. After a knife attack destroyed his hand and his professional sports ambitions, Victor bottomed out. During his recovery, he remapped his life, choosing now to pursue a political career to support police reform and improve homeless services. His hell gave birth to a new life vision.

Incarceration, a dark spot for anyone, can be a turning point. Zoey met her guiding light there: "I was put in jail for a night after an altercation with my children. I had never heard God before, but standing in that jail cell, I heard, 'Sit down.' So, I did. Then, I heard, 'You need to get your life together and go back to school.' I have been in school ever since." Zoey received her master's degree in 2019.

Chris Wilson met his rock bottom while serving a life sentence for murder at the Patuxent Institution in Maryland. Even without hopes of release, Chris built a master plan for his life. This plan included travel, contribution to others, business success, and even owning a Corvette. Believing that an education would fortify his spirit and help him achieve his dreams, he traded two cartons of cigarettes for a spot in the vocational program. Fellow inmates mocked his pursuit. "Why bother, man? You're never gettin' out." Chris ignored them and soon took college classes remotely at the University of Baltimore.

After almost two decades in prison, Chris's passion and well-articulated master plan helped him persuade a judge to order his release. "I'll let you out," the judge said, "but you need to finish this master plan." Chris has since achieved almost everything on that list, including the Corvette. Now he's teaching others how to create and implement their dreams through a curriculum delivered to 520 inmates at Rikers Island. He encourages them to use their rock-bottom time in prison to think about what landed them there and what they would like to do differently on the outside.

COVID-related losses forced many to reflect and change course. Karim's father's lungs were so destroyed by COVID that doctors medically induced a coma. "It was surreal," Karim said. Thankfully, his father recovered—but COVID killed other loved ones, as did the street violence that increased during the confinement. Two young members of Karim's family were shot, one of them killed. Karim said, "The pandemic taught me how to sit with pain and conflict. . . . Before, I felt like I had to keep things in. I had been taking on everything and not getting anything done. [During the pandemic] I dealt with my shit and came out the other side." This included eating healthier and working out. His also found his calling: "I realized that I couldn't solve everyone's problems, but I could give them a voice." He started Voices of 21217 to "chronicle the experiences and imagination of youth in Baltimore City [living in that zip code], ages twelve to fourteen." His clarity of purpose attracted the Smithsonian Institution, which now provides equipment and training.

FIND YOUR QUIET

Luckily, you don't need a crisis to find direction. Laneisha said, "I book a hotel suite for a few days every couple of months or so and use it to just regroup." You can also spend time in a park, a library, a botanical garden, an empty stadium, or an art museum. Any quiet space that fills your soul can work. German philosopher Arthur Schopenhauer believed that only in this silence can we be our true selves and be truly free.[1] Find your quiet place and think about what you want and *why* you want it.

FIND YOUR "WHYS"

Studies show that we rarely know why we want something. We just identify a dream and make up a reason.[2] When you know your whys, you increase your chances of negotiation success. In *Getting to Yes,* William Ury and Roger Fisher distinguish between *positions* (what we want) and *interests* (why we want it). Negotiators who know their underlying interests can find ways to achieve them in unexpected ways.

Here's an example involving Karim, whom I introduced earlier. I wanted to connect him with the Baltimore Police Department to integrate youth voices into police training. Karim resisted the invitation because police had harmed too many people he knew. He courageously looked beyond this pain, realizing that if his project could reduce violent altercations between youth and police it would be worth it. He moved ahead. Today, Baltimore's police cadets learn directly from the local youth.

The deeper *whys* behind what we want can be tricky to find. Eric Ries, author of *The Lean Startup,* recommends going "five whys deep" to identify our deeper interests.

Here's what one student discovered:

POSITION: I WANT A NEW CAR

1. Why?
   Because I'm wasting time waiting at the bus stop.
2. Why does that matter?
   I have a lot of schoolwork and I focus better at home.
3. Why does it matter that you focus on your schoolwork?
   If I do well, I can get into a good law school.
4. Why do you want to go to law school?
   I want to help people who have been discriminated against.
5. Why does that matter to you?
   Because no one was there for my mother when she needed help.

Connecting to her deeper commitments will help her find a car that helps her achieve this goal and resist overpaying for it.

Here's another example.

POSITION: I WANT A FANCY WEDDING

1. Why?
   My friends all have fancy weddings.
2. Why?
   Maybe they want to impress me or because it is expected.
3. Why?
   Perhaps because they want us to remember their wedding.
4. Why?
   Because they think this is the most significant day of their lives.
5. Why?
   Because society has long taught women this and the wedding industry has a financial incentive to keep the idea alive.

Inquiry slows us down before a negotiation. Do we really need swans or a donut wall at our wedding? We may discover, instead, that we want a small wedding surrounded by loved ones and to save money for a home. Swans hate weddings anyway.

WHERE DID OUR WANTS COME FROM?

Having worked in advertising for over a decade, I know what goes into inserting desires into our minds and hearts. Millions of dollars directed strategically by many smart people tell us what to pursue. When we slow our pace and unpack our dreams, we become harder to manipulate. That said, some influences run deeper. Psychoanalyst Carl Jung said that the greatest psychological burden a child feels is the "unlived life of its parents." What did your parents (or caregivers) wish for their lives? Have you been pursuing their dreams instead of yours?

Culture also shapes our dreams. Linda Babcock and her colleagues studied college students at Michigan State University to explore how cultural expectations affect women's aspirations. They asked the female students, "Are you successful at getting what you want?" Almost every woman they interviewed said yes. When they dug deeper, they found that many women thought that they were successful "because they didn't want very much." BIPOC women limited their aspirations even more than white women.[3] Researchers hypothesized that women were socialized to have modest expectations for their success. That study, a couple of decades old now, might see different outcomes if replicated today. Black women, for example, are increasingly becoming entrepreneurs.[4]

COME AS YOU WILL BE

Sometimes we temper our own aspirations because the pursuit of greater things frustrates and pains us.[5] Play can help us break through the pattern of thinking small. At the end of each term, I borrow a game from *Chicken Soup for the Soul* author Jack Canfield and throw a "Come as You Will Be Party," where we dress up and act as if it is five years from now. Some show up "pregnant," others dressed in suits or beach clothing. People bring business cards, photos, and other symbols of their new life. It feels silly at first, but within a few minutes, the party starts to feel good. These games can be powerful. A year after she had completed the class, Michelle said, "Dr. Federman, you won't believe it! I got the civil rights job that I imagined at the Come as You Will Be Party. I never would have applied for it if we hadn't done that exercise!"

Throw your own party. You can throw a big bash for New Year's Eve or do it with just a few friends. Keep the props around you afterward. While a PhD student, I bought a graduation cap and gown and hung them on my bedroom door, so each morning I remembered my primary goal: "Finish!" After graduation, I passed them on to friends, who finished and passed them on to others. Play is powerful. This kind of play is not just for the young. Even retired folks have wisdom to share and chapters to enjoy.

HEALTH

Each term, more than half the class says that what they seek most is greater physical and/or mental health. They're right to start here. Historically marginalized groups and those living in financial precarity suffer disproportionately from mental and physical illnesses. Cultural norms that develop over time from social exclusion, reduced access to health education and healthy foods, and reduced time (and money) to exercise contribute to ill health. As does discrimination. In Baltimore, the correlation between health and wealth is crystal clear. Those born in Sandtown will likely not live past seventy, whereas those born in the more affluent Roland Park can expect to live until their mid-eighties.[6] That is a fifteen-year difference in the same city! The legacies of slavery, Jim Crow, and redlining all contribute to these problems, as do food deserts (neighborhoods without food) and food swamps (areas with only fast food).

Discrimination and collective trauma also affect health. David Williams, a professor of public health at Harvard University, studies the effects of racism on health. His team found that "racism is considered a fundamental cause of adverse health outcomes for racial/ethnic minorities and racial/ethnic inequities in health."[7]

Increasingly, researchers can document the effects of historical trauma. Scholars working with Indigenous communities in Canada often find that the distress contributing to suicide, drug abuse, and other mental health crises has originated in colonialism and its legacies.[8] Medical systems may treat individuals as dysfunctional because of this distress, when in fact their struggles have colonial origins. Working with a therapist who is informed about historical trauma can help. Cultural recovery can also serve as a form of treatment. Psychologist Joseph Gone, who has collaborated for twenty-five years with American Indian and other Indigenous communities to rethink community-based mental health, encourages Indigenous models of healing in these communities, rather than imposing Western therapeutic models. Other colonized or damaged communities might find similar strength in reclaiming traditions.

For those raised in under-resourced communities, setting your own standards for health becomes an act of power and even activism. We cannot instantly convince a grocery store to come to our neighborhood, but can alter our food choices, stop scrolling, and sleep, hydrate, and move more. These changes reduce dependency on medications with nasty side effects. Pharmaceuticals alone will not protect your health. Go ahead, the companies say, get sick, then you can take our pills forever. Their wealthy executives will use your money to host dinner parties overlooking the sea. In the morning, they will get up early, go for a long run on the beach, and make a nutrition-packed smoothie for breakfast. They know better than to become dependent on their own drugs. Answer the following questions to begin setting your own standards.

How long do I want to live?

In communities where people tend to die young, the answer to this question can set the direction of a person's life. Many young men in Baltimore do not expect to live beyond their thirties. As a result, they may amplify an already dangerous environment by making risky decisions. Chris Wilson, who grew up surrounded by poverty, gun violence, and addiction, says that these young men often have unprotected sex and father kids that they do not expect to live long enough to raise. Changing their behavior starts with helping them imagine their lives *beyond thirty*. Where would they like to live? What might they like to do? Hanging out with elders they admire can spark ideas.

How do I want to age?

Remember to declare *how* you want to age. Studies show that the age you *feel* affects how you age, both physically and mentally, more than your birth date does.[9] Wait, what? Yes, the age you *feel* affects the aging process more than your actual age. Feel twenty-five and your body will act like it is twenty-five. Aging well requires bucking cultural myths about how aging works. A 2021 study of 6,500 people published in *Science* magazine debunked the myth that weight gain is a normal part of middle age. Our metabolism slows in our sixties, not our forties.[10] This means that weight gain, for most of us, is not a natural part of midlife. Let me pause here and give voice to Alex, a former student who teaches me about fat shaming. Alex reminds me that weight is not the only way to evaluate health. So, instead of a number, think about what you want to be able to do and how you want to feel in your body. Do you want to be able to do a jump shot well into your sixties? Swim in the ocean with your grandkids? These dreams help us pursue our own standards of health, rather than accept cultural stories about how we must decline.

Who is my aging role model?

Find someone older than you whose well-being inspires you. Marcetta told the class about her idol, JoAni Johnson, who started modeling in her sixties. Robin told the class, "When we turned sixty, my friend and I ran a marathon to celebrate. This is something that would have been unheard of for my parents and their friends." Robin is one of my role models, as is Betty Holston Smith, a seventy-nine-year-old vegan who competes in one-hundred-mile races.

MONEY

Most people think of money when they hear the word *negotiation.* Anna Sales, the author of *Let's Talk about Hard Things,* compares money to oxygen. When you don't have it, it's all you focus on.[11] A certain amount of money helps us move beyond the oxygen problem, but how much will make you happy? United Nations World Happiness Reports show that greater national wealth does not always correlate to greater happiness. The United States, for example, has not yet ranked in the top ten.[12] Arthur Brooks, a leadership professor at the Harvard Kennedy School offers this tip to avoid being rich but unhappy: Use any extra money you have to spend more time with loved ones, not to buy more stuff.[13] Good advice.

Most people struggle just to cover basic costs. Chapter 4 shows how clarity around your finances, including a vision for how you plan to use money, increases your negotiation confidence and efficacy. It starts with knowing our numbers. When we know what we have and need, we make better decisions. Alternatively, when we *feel* poor (or out of control), we demonstrate more short-term thinking and take greater risks, such as gambling.[14] These efforts rarely pan out, leaving people in more precarity than before. Rebecca, who works with Baltimore youth on parole, observes this pattern: "Many of the men go after what they didn't have as a child, like the money, clothes, and status. What happens is that they go after these things in a way that perpetuates the cycle; they are arrested, incarcerated, and then absent as a parent." In the United States, the insatiable craving for consumer goods contributes to more than a million people going bankrupt each year.[15] Unless interrupted, the pattern passes to the next generation.

IMPRESSING OTHERS

Sunya confessed to the class that in her twenties, she sometimes wrote false checks on Christmas to be able to impress her friends with nice gifts. Research shows that this desire to impress others is somewhat hardwired.[16] We too often seek to be "positionally" better than others, instead of focusing on personal fulfillment.[17] In other words, we might not necessarily value (or desire) the Chanel bag or new Nikes, as much as we want to show that we can have, or give, them.

Wenling related to this topic. Her immigrant mother tried desperately to show others her success in America. Every year on Black Friday, the day after Thanksgiving, her mother would take the family shopping from 10 P.M. to 4 A.M. Wenling saw how buying respected brands as gifts made her mom feel successful, even if the family didn't necessarily want these items.

Men can feel pressure to prove their love and success by lavishing women with expensive gifts. Kolby used the class to negotiate with his girlfriend about the Gucci bag she wanted for her birthday. "I asked her if I could not buy her the Gucci bag but rather something more affordable. She agreed. . . . I showed her a Kate Spade bag and she loved it. Her emotions completely changed, and she started to agree with the idea that the Gucci bag is expensive." With this one negotiation Kolby paid for the negotiation class.

CAREER

When most people think of career-related negotiations, they think about salary negotiations or contracts with vendors or clients. But career negotiations begin within. Tiana thought that law school was her logical next step because she had been a paralegal for many years. When admitted to a law school in Boston, however, she hesitated. Moving to

Boston would require that her son move into her Baltimore home to take care of her mother. She asked herself, "At fifty years old, do I want to disrupt the family unit in this way?" After some deep thinking and quiet time, Tiana uncovered a desire to become a patient advocate for those in long-term care. The ongoing care for her mother helped her see how poorly our society treats the elderly. She wanted to be part of the solution. With this clarity, she could use her negotiation skills to land a job with a good salary. She could also use her skills to negotiate on behalf of elderly patients unable to fight for themselves.

Your Full Self

Another internal career-related negotiation is how much of ourselves we bring to work. Sometimes, when people say they cannot bring their full or "authentic" selves to work, they mean that they wish they worked with people from a similar background or in an organization with shared values. Or it might be an identity or past they feel a need to hide. The contracting company Chris Wilson launched after prison did well, giving him a chance to leave his past behind. When National Public Radio wanted him to share his incarceration and release story, he sought advice. His business professor advised him not to do the interview because he feared that Chris would lose clients. Chris spoke anyway and received a standing ovation from the live audience. His business tripled after the broadcast.[18]

When picking a workplace, you may be asked to hide, or downplay, your identity as a parent, caregiver, devout Catholic, climate activist, or political conservative, or hide your gender identity or some disability. Which of those identities are nonnegotiable for you?

MAINTAINING YOUR VISION

The clearer your life vision, the more effectively you will negotiate. Clarity also helps you ignore or move on quickly after engaging with people who don't support your aspirations. While incarcerated, Chris Wilson relied on what he called "positive delusion." To help, he made collages of girls in bikinis and the Corvette he wanted. "Keep dreaming, brother," the other inmates told him, mocking his efforts.[19] So that's just what he did. His clarity and focus eventually inspired a judge to release him from a life sentence, to go live the life he dreamed of.

Marcetta worked as a correctional officer in the Patuxent facility and watched Chris Wilson make this transformation. She also uses the visioning process. "I keep my future plans on the refrigerator in the kitchen and have faraway places as ever-changing screensavers on my computer at work. I have plans to see Gladys Knight in Atlantic City, Usher in Las Vegas, and Henry Louis Gates Jr. in Frederick, Maryland, in the coming months. Those goals are attainable and planned." I followed up with Marcetta four months later to see if she successfully negotiated for the time and resources needed to make it happen. She said, "Yes, yes, yes. I made it to all three!"

You can also use visualization by closing your eyes and feeling into your dream future. I cannot believe how well this worked for me. After college, I took a temp job at Wells Fargo Bank reading the fine print on the back of credit card statements. Nobody's dream job, but it paid well. Each night, I visualized my perfect day. Some days I added a small detail like a vase of flowers on a desk. One afternoon, riding the bus back from work, I saw a sign for "The Health and Healing Library." Something told me to hop off and go in. The library looked just like my evening vision! Big windows, plants, inspirational quotes all over the walls. A woman came out of her office to greet me. I asked if she had any jobs available. She said, "We've been interviewing people for weeks and haven't found the right person. I think you're the person we've been waiting for." That's crazy, I know, but it happened. I got the job and loved it.

MISSION STATEMENTS

Writing a mission statement and keeping it visible helps prepare you for expected and unexpected negotiations. Companies use these statements to maintain focus when handling daily challenges. Here are some of my favorites:

Sweetgreen (salad shop): To inspire healthier communities by connecting people to real food.

Patagonia (an outdoor apparel company): To build the best product, cause no unnecessary harm, use business to inspire and implement solutions to the environmental crisis.

Nike: Our mission is what drives us to do everything possible to expand human potential. We do that by creating groundbreaking sport innovations, by making our products more sustainably, by building a creative and diverse global team and by making a positive impact in communities where we live and work.

Essence (magazine): "Safe spaces" for black women to self-define themselves and articulate their lived realties. A critical theoretical framework allows uneven power relations to be examined and offers emancipatory perspectives.

See the activities at the end of the chapter to write your own statement.

"CURATE YOUR ORBIT"

Fulfilling your mission will require the support of others. Chris Wilson tells his mentees, "Find your first follower." By this he means, find the first person who believes in you. One good friend or supporter can help you face a world of naysayers.[20] For Chris it was Steve. The two partnered up and kept each other focused.

Then, Chris adds, "you have to curate your orbit." When Chris first left prison, he needed to avoid certain people, knowing that affiliating with them might draw him into situations that could land him back in prison. Curating your orbit can take time. If you find yourself alone, try this tip from makeup artist Takia Ross, who created an alter ego called Kiki Thunder. She says, "Kiki can do things I never would. . . . You need to be your best friend. . . . When no one else is around, can you talk yourself off a ledge? Can you self-motivate?" Name your alter ego and use it!

You can also curate your orbit by being intentional in your current relationships. Let's say you're about to spend the day with your sister. What's your goal? Do you want to relax, laugh, and enjoy yourself? If so, chill when she stops at the post office and drags you along on other errands. If fun is the goal, then make the trip amusing. Make her laugh, be playful with the cashiers. Bravo, you have just prevented drama.

VISION DIRECTS FOCUS AND EMOTION

Vision helps us use our time well. Author Eve Babitz wrote, "I know a bunch of people who don't consider the concept of fifteen minutes time at all. . . . Since I've started carrying a book everywhere, even to something like the Academy Awards, I've had a much easier time of it, and the bitterness that shortens your life has been headed off at the pass by the wonderful paperback."[21] After reading this passage, Catherine, a doctoral student, started carrying her tablet everywhere. She says, "It definitely helps me relax when I'm waiting as opposed to reading the news on my phone or scrolling through social media (things that can often cause *more* stress)." We can also use the time to build our expertise. While waiting in the doctor's office, we can listen to a relevant podcast. Savvy negotiators read about what matters to them and become experts in their fields.

Vision helps us navigate emotions like revenge, rage, and rejection that—if acted upon—can bankrupt us emotionally and materially. I practice and teach many techniques to help us manage emotions during negotiations, but I find this futuring practice one of the most effective. So does Nawal Rajeh, founder of By Peaceful Means, a free peace camp in Baltimore. They teach kids to regain their cool by reminding them of the bigger picture for their lives. To kids arguing, she may ask, "What do you want out of this interaction? What do you want long term?" These questions help kids practice pausing to think before acting, a critical skill for negotiating in a volatile city. For these kids, the stakes are high. When Nawal hears about them getting into power struggles with their school administrators over hall passes and other things, she worries. These arguments can escalate to suspension, activating the school-to-prison pipeline. Teaching them to remember their dreams helps them avoid these altercations.

Neuroscience supports this futuring approach to conflict. When enraged, we have less access to the part of our brains that can weigh the implications of our actions. During what is called an "amygdala hijack," right and wrong become more difficult to assess.[22] When we stop, breathe, and focus on the future, we regain access to the neocortex, which helps us make better long-term decisions.

Chris Wilson uses futuring questions to motivate change in adults. After prison, he worked first with a nonprofit dedicated to revitalizing Baltimore neighborhoods. He said, "I talked with gang runners who ran the soldiers on the corners. I didn't lecture them, and I didn't turn them in. Like in prison, I used the Socratic method, which means listening and asking questions to get them to think differently. What's your endgame? Where's this gonna lead? You're nineteen now, that's cool, but do you want to be out here when you're thirty?"[23] He said that while they often told him to mind his own business, another part of them thought about what he had said.

A CHANGING VISION

Your vision will keep changing and growing. Even if you have done this visioning before, do it again. So long as we are alive, our goals will continue to shift. We also adapt to new levels of success, health, fame, and even happiness. Students who do not do this work during the program often come back to me after the rush of graduation wears off, trying to figure out what is next. Start now. To those who are incarcerated or for some other reason unable to act on their vision immediately, Chris says, "Do the work, y'all. Read. Study. Act respectful. Earn every degree and certificate that you can. Make a master plan. Understand your endgame. Decide what success means to you, then figure out how to achieve it."[24] Getting this clarity is the deepest negotiation preparation you can do. In the chapters that follow, you will learn strategies and tactics that will support you in your pursuits.

SUMMARY

Negotiation skills help you get somewhere. You decide where. Developing a big picture for your life is the first step in all negotiation training (or should be). Otherwise, how do you know if getting what you negotiate for will make you happier? Vision boards, visualization, mission statements, and developing our orbit of support help us ensure that we negotiate in a way that aligns with our larger vision. When creating these visions, we want to consider goals for our health, career, finances, and relationships. This clarity grounds us during emotional and/or unexpected negotiations. Just as importantly, this visioning helps us negotiate with ourselves and others about how we use our precious time.

ACTIVITIES

The following activities will help you develop clarity about your priorities and serve as a guide to your future negotiations.

When You're Stuck

When we feel stuck, we can recall the words of poet Mary Oliver: "You only have to let the soft animal of your body love what it loves."[25]

Write down fifteen things, places, experiences, or people that the soft animal of your body loves. These can be silly as well as serious things.

Maybe you like glittery smartphone cases or time with your best friend. Reconnecting to what you love can help roll you into action.

Soul Goals and Ego Goals

This activity helps us distinguish between goals that will lead to lasting fulfillment and those that might lead to more fleeting satisfaction. Draw a line down a piece of paper. On the top of the left side write "Ego Goals" and on the right side write "Soul Goals." Ego goals include any objects, experiences, awards, or recognitions you want because you think that they will make you feel successful. They may also prove someone wrong about you—like, say, your parents or a teacher who didn't believe in a particular dream. Soul goals, in contrast, are those that will most likely lead to deep fulfillment and long-term satisfaction.

EXAMPLE

Ego Goal: Graduating top of your class from a leading law school.
Soul Goal: Using your legal training to help exonerate innocent people.

Sometimes we can have both. The important point is focusing on the goal that will bring you the most fulfillment and sustain your passion through the tough times.[26]

Your Mission Statement

Look up the Mission Statements of at least three companies whose products or services you like. Then write your own statement and post it near your work space.

You can also fill in this statement:

My mission is to use____ to help____ with____ in order to/so that____.
(skill) (who/what) (what problem) (to what end)

EXAMPLES

My mission is to use the power of graphic design to help small businesses market their services so that they can reach their consumers and flourish.

My mission is to use makeup artistry to help women experience their true beauty so that they have the confidence they need to pursue their dreams.

This Year

Free write for ten minutes on the question "If you could overcome just one conflict this year, what would it be and why?"

This will help you orient your time and negotiation energy toward the challenge most important to you.

What Kind of Emails Do You Want?

My inbox used to be filled with emails from angry clients or frustrated colleagues. Eventually, I decided that I would rather have emails from people saying how our work together improved their lives.

Write yourself five emails that you would like to receive in the next few years. Make them as detailed as possible.

Come as You Will Be Party

Organize a party or small gathering of friends and act as if it is five years in the future. Stay in your roles, talking, for at least three hours. Dress up and bring props to help you stay in the spirit. Talk about where you live, who is in your life, your work, your health, and anything that matters to you. Remember to bring the good things in your present life with you, such as relationships and good habits you want to maintain.

Staying Connected to Ourselves and Each Other

Daily check-ins help us stay focused. When Selena worked in a shelter for victims of domestic violence, residents began their day with these check-ins to discuss their feelings and goals for the day. "This encouraged the women to open up and seek help if they needed it."

Seeing how well it worked for the residents, Selena started to do these check-ins with her friends. They each write:

- a word to describe how they are feeling,
- their goal for the day,
- who they could ask for help in achieving that goal, and
- one thing that makes them happy.

Try this with friends, coworkers, or even your family over breakfast or dinner. Let us know what happens.

CHAPTER 2

Ask

OVERVIEW

Once you know what you want, you need to communicate your desires
to others. Otherwise, your dreams only live in your mind. And if you
cannot make requests, you cannot negotiate—full stop. This chapter
discusses the power of asking and helps you consider what stops you
from making requests. When you understand what blocks you, speaking up becomes easier. We start with practicing "low-stakes" asks to
build confidence and challenge beliefs and habits that keep you stuck.
Then we raise the stakes and prepare for important negotiations. Part of
preparation includes anticipating challenges such as hearing "no" and
even hearing "yes," which can result in mixed emotions.

QUESTIONS TO CONSIDER

Do you ask for what you need and want? If not, why not?

Who do you ask for help? Why?

Who do you never ask for help? Why not?

Once you know what you want, you need to make requests. Chevonie
agreed: "My mom used to always say 'closed mouths don't get fed!'"
Fernando, a second-generation immigrant from Ecuador, knows how
to make requests. His mother died of cancer and his incarcerated father

could offer little support, so he relied on ingenuity for survival. One night, I cashed in on the bold charm that he had developed to survive. Neither of us had much money, so we attended a free concert at the Kennedy Center in Washington, D.C. During the concert, Fernando kept looking at the people in sequined dresses and military uniforms waiting for their much posher event. When our concert ended, Fernando approached a woman taking tickets at a podium and learned that the USO was putting on a variety show to honor high-ranking military officers.

"Can we come?" he asked her.

I couldn't believe he'd asked. We were embarrassingly underdressed and not in the military.

"The event's sold out," the woman said, "but if you come back in about twenty-five minutes you might be able to buy the seats of no-shows. They run $125 apiece."

I thanked her and started to recoil. No way we would pay $250 to attend. Fernando smiled, thanked her, and insisted that we wait. After a while, he went back to the woman.

"Have any leftover tickets?" he asked.

"You know, we do," she said. "We have box seats open and we really have to fill them, or the theater looks empty when the cameras roll. I can give them to you for thirty dollars each."

We paid for the discount tickets and an usher led us to our seats next to a star of *Jersey Boys*, the night's honored veteran, and Miss America. When the music started, we started swing dancing in the space around our box seat. The head of the USO ran across the theater toward us and I was sure we were doomed. But instead of throwing us out she said, "You two are becoming the stars of the show." Thanks to Fernando's crazy request, I grabbed a peak life experience for thirty dollars.

So why don't we ask for things more often? Sometimes because we don't believe we deserve it. You may fear owing others or worry about rejection. You may also may fear a yes. A promotion, for example, can bring more responsibilities. This chapter will help you get beyond these fears to revive your natural inner asker. Practice in low-stakes situations prepares you for the more serious requests—whether for money, time, support, connections, advice, space, or even freedom.

Chris Wilson became a master asker in all areas. He created his life vision and then repeatedly requested that the judge reduce his life sentence. It worked. Once out, he kept asking big. He wanted to continue his education at the University of Baltimore but couldn't afford the classes. One day he ran into the dean, Darlene Smith. He told her about his love for the school, his accomplishments, and his admiration of her work. He knew that the university struggled to attract students from his neighborhood. He told her that if she helped him with tuition, he would help her get the students she wanted. She offered him a discount on his schoolbooks and help with other minor expenses. Chris replied, "Thank you, I appreciate that, Dean Smith, and I don't want to sound ungrateful, but honestly, I don't think I should have to pay for anything at this school ever again." She gave him a full scholarship.

Reflecting on that moment, Chris said, "Now, that was ballsy, I admit. But that's what it takes y'all. If you deserve something, ask for it. *With respect*. Don't be angry if you don't get it, but don't be too shy to ask."[1] Chris's vision prepared him to make his request when luck struck. Negotiations can happen at any time. Dean Smith did not expect to negotiate with Chris that day. If he had hesitated, he would have missed the opportunity.

We all hesitate at times. Maybe you speak up at home but barely make a sound in work meetings, or vice versa. Maybe you argue passionately with friends about a football game, but can't ask your mom to stop criticizing your girlfriend. We all have a different asking terrain.

Isaac, raised in Nigeria, has no trouble making requests of people in positions of power, except for his father. He says, "It is easier for me to write a twenty-page proposal to Bank of America for sponsorship of a community event than to ask my dad for twenty dollars."

Where do you get stuck?

We were not born hesitant. Most of us entered the world with a scream, and as soon as we could speak, the questions flooded out. A 2013 study conducted by Littlewoods.com, an online retailer in the United Kingdom, found that a four-year-old girl asks around four hundred questions per day, and a boy of the same age is not far behind.[2] Why do we slow down? Neuroanatomist Jill Bolte Taylor says that biology plays a role. When we go through adolescence, our brains direct our attention away from the world around us and toward finding a partner.[3] Do you remember when boys or girls became more interesting than bugs or the planets?

Biology isn't the only reason. Rejection, abandonment, or humiliation can shut us up, as can caretakers who discourage requests. Karen, a student in Los Angeles, says, "Being the youngest of six, my older siblings would always tell me to 'shut up.' Maybe this is why I have trouble speaking sometimes as an adult." Kids growing up in socially marginalized communities may internalize beliefs that they do not deserve success, inclusion, or self-actualization.[4] This can contribute to impostor syndrome, a feeling that we don't belong.

This chapter helps you reclaim your natural question-asking abilities. Your results may astonish you, as Damian surprised himself when, during our negotiation course, he convinced his boss to pay for half of his master's degree.[5] Brittany Ware says that her friends cannot believe her bravado since completing the exercises in this chapter. "They want to know my secret," she says. The answer? She has learned to ask.

Learning to ask can improve our lives in many ways. Research shows that speaking up for ourselves helps reduce anxiety and depression, while improving self-esteem and relationships.[6] Especially when we ask for support! Rehan Staton grew up in an unstable household. Teachers in school doubted his academic potential. After high school, Staton worked at Bates Trucking and Trash Removal in Maryland. By age twenty-four, wanting more, he asked his colleagues to cheer him on while he put himself through the University of Maryland. They did. Upon graduation, Rehan applied and was accepted to Harvard Law School. It's amazing what a little encouragement can do. Give this encouragement to others and ask for it when you need it!

Master askers also catalyze social and political change. In 1977, when Judy Heumann led 150 disabled persons in a twenty-five-day occupation of a federal building in San Francisco, her team had a very specific ask: Enact Section 504 of the *Rehabilitation Act*. This Act would require the government to provide federal services to those with disabilities. They succeeded, transforming the lives of millions of people throughout the country. In 2020, *Time* magazine named Heumann one of the most influential women of the century.[7] People today still benefit from her ability to ask powerfully and persistently.

WHY WE DON'T ASK

If asking is key to all personal and social transformation, what stops us? Let's start with the simpler reasons and then move on to the more complex ones. The first reason may be that you don't know what you want. If you need help finding clarity on that, revisit chapter 1 and do the activities at the end. Grab a friend and do them together.

Fear of Owing Someone

Numerous students told me they avoid making requests because they fear being indebted to others. One said, "I don't want to ask my sister for anything because I may not want to give what she asks for if she helps me." That's sad. The people who love us most want to contribute to our lives. Don't we want to contribute to the people we love? Janice discovered how asking for help from her mother helped them both: "I called my mother because I needed to get my hair colored and I didn't have time to make an appointment at the salon." Her mother agreed. "It turned out well," Janice said. "Exactly as I wanted. I also took this time to share some one-on-one time with my mother. Moments like that are few and far between." Don't rob the people in your life of the pleasure of supporting you. You may be surprised how much you enjoy supporting them.

We depend on each other, and our interdependency cannot be undone. When the class remains unconvinced, I ask them to look around the room and consider all the people involved in bringing these objects to us: the designers, manufacturers, distributors. Just watch movie credits. Success is a team effort.

Fear of Burdening Others

Sometimes we avoid asking because we fear burdening others. Yet the size of our need (or desire) is not necessarily equal to the effort required to satisfy it. Let's say you want to save money by finding cheaper parking options for work. Your colleague, Briana, knows about free parking. How much work is it for her to tell you? Not much.

During the semester, Noëlle discovered how asking helped, rather than burdened, a friend: "My friend has a clothing line, and we've been discussing how she can expand. . . . Since the weather is rapidly changing, I asked her to make a hoodie for me with her design on it. She said, 'Okay, sure!' She not only did it for me but marketed it on her website. She posted it as a new release yesterday!" Noëlle got her hoodie, and her friend expanded her business.

Perhaps you avoid making requests because you think the person dislikes you. According to conflict expert and renowned mediator Tammy Lenski, asking that person can make them *like you more*.[8] We do things for people we like, says Lenski. So, if we do something nice for someone, our brains tell us we like the person. Crazy, right? So don't fear asking.

Looking Stupid

Sometimes we avoid the asking that negotiation requires simply because we fear looking stupid. Kyle says, "Growing up, I was often the only Black student in otherwise white advanced classes. Fear of looking stupid caused me to hesitate to ask questions; and this fear was reinforced when teachers and peers took my questions as a sign that I did not belong in these 'gifted' spaces."

Some students told me they hesitate to ask questions because maybe the teacher answered it earlier when they weren't paying attention. Some older adults in our classes said they avoid asking because they felt they should know the answer.

What about those people who try to protect their egos by putting you down? Ignore them. During the pandemic, my husband and I needed an apartment in Montreal. Our first week in the building, the apartment manager snapped at me for not knowing the name of the owner, which she had never told me. Whenever her disorganization led to a problem, she rolled her eyes and somehow made it my fault. By the end, I found it amusing.

> When was the last time you held back a request because you feared burdening someone or looking stupid?

Fear of Consequences

Often, we keep quiet out of fear. Maybe we fear losing a job offer or straining a relationship if we make too big a request. Tamara, for example, feared asking her mother, who had dementia, to give up her car and move into elder care. Tamara already cared for her kids and an ill mother-in-law and worked a full-time job, so she couldn't provide the care herself. And she couldn't wait much longer to ask her mother to consider these changes. During the height of the pandemic, Tamara's mother drove to her childhood neighborhood in Baltimore, which over the years had become quite dangerous. Her mother roamed around looking for her old house, now replaced by projects, and got lost. Luckily Tamara found her. If her mother had continued to drive, she might have hurt someone on the road. Asking her to give up her freedom also represented a role reversal between child and parent, which can be uncomfortable for both. Tamara's fear of asking was understandable, but she persisted in facing it. She spent much of the semester using the course tools to navigate numerous uncomfortable conversations related to her mother's care.

Cultural Expectations

Sometimes we keep quiet because of internalized cultural expectations for our behavior. Linda Babcock studies this, specifically asking why women negotiate less often than men.[9] When she asks women why they avoid making requests, many say they were taught from a young age to focus on the needs of others rather than on their own. Chapter 7 looks more closely at these issues. For now, suffice it to say that cultural messages about your gender, ethnicity, or class likely influence how much you speak up.

Class

Class affects our level of comfort with asking as well. Sociologist Jessica Calarco studied what U.S. parents from different socioeconomic classes taught their kids about asking.[10] She discovered that middle-class parents encouraged their children to ask questions in school. They even coached their children on how to make requests to increase the chances of a positive response. A coached middle school student might say to their teacher, "I know you asked us to write a paper about bears, but can I write about foxes instead? We have a fox in our backyard. My family and I have been learning more about them." Calarco found that requests like these enabled kids to engage in assignments that nourished their curiosity. When stuck, they often asked for help. Through asking and receiving, they discovered that their desires mattered and their needs could be met. As a result, their love of learning grew along with their confidence.

By contrast, in the lower-class households Calarco studied, parents more often taught their children to show respect to the teacher by *not* asking questions. These parents feared that teachers would interpret their children's questions as challenging authority. Out of respect and fear of retribution, they taught their children to keep quiet. As a result, these students received less help on assignments and fewer accommodations for their interests. This affected their confidence as well as their grades.

Rodney, raised in Baltimore, noticed this difference. "Growing up, my very own classmates did not ask for the assistance they needed in class or outside of class. Whereas, in my lower-middle-class household, my mother, usually to my chagrin, was quick to reach out to teachers, guidance counselors or principals to ensure I got what I needed. And, although I acted as though I felt embarrassed by my mom's inclusion in the matters, I learned I could count on her to be a sounding board for me until I got older in high school where I would begin speaking up for myself. But it was her example that prompted me to use the voice I had, even when it felt uncomfortable for me to do so." Teaching kids to speak up respectfully can avoid the pitfalls of well-intentioned silence.[11]

It's never too late to start speaking up in classes. Raya, raised in Bulgaria, said, "It wasn't until I moved to Maryland and started attending a local community college . . . when I realized that asking for help when you don't understand something is completely fine, and that teachers have office hours specifically for this reason."

Teachers can help by not assuming that silence means that all is well. Some students silence their voices because they fear that their speech might reveal something about their social class or reinforce stereotypes about their intelligence. When a colleague of mine taught in France, he noticed that many students refused to speak. Privately he asked a few of them why. One student explained that as soon as they speak, they reveal their socioeconomic class. In the United States, scholars studying why some Black students kept quiet in class found that some professors and peers disparaged their way of speaking.[12] As teachers committed to the success of our students, it's up to us to create a class culture in which all students can express their needs.

Home

Growing up in violent or neglectful environments weakens asking muscles, especially when survival requires saying as little as possible.[13] Devon recalled some early lessons that taught him that speaking up made no difference. At nine years old, he showed his parents his hand swollen from an infected blister. They initially shrugged off his complaint. So Devon took a bus to a doctor—by himself. The doctor examined the hand and said that had Devon waited one more day, the hand would have required amputation. Saving the hand required surgery and a four-day quarantine in post-operative care to prevent reinfection. Devon recalls the doctor considering whether to call child services but hesitating. He says that had he known that child services could have removed him from the house, he would have asked the doctor to call. He didn't know that he could ask.

Growing up, what did you learn about asking?

Psychologists Christopher Peterson and Martin Seligman noted that "maladaptive passivity and emotional numbing" can occur because of traumatizing circumstances, leading to depression and other problematic conditions.[14] Devon admits that even today he has trouble making requests. For many people, trauma-induced silences become somaticized through various forms of physical and mental illnesses, including suicide.[15] Devon's brother experienced suicidal depression from the neglect, but especially from their father's physical abuse.

These silencing legacies can pass from parent to child and can also be passed down within groups.[16] For example, in Indonesia today, grandparents often remain silent about the suffering they endured in the 1965 genocide, fearing that speaking about their persecution would evoke it again or make their own families vulnerable. Their silence does not mean that they are at peace with the past.

When supporting those who may have experienced trauma, be careful not to mistake silence as contentment or passivity. Harriet Beecher Stowe made this error in her best-selling *Uncle Tom's Cabin* (1852), when she spoke of slaves having a "docility of heart."[17] Like many of her time, Stowe mistook deference as an attribute of enslaved persons, rather than as a symptom of brutal oppression. Individuals from historically marginalized groups can consider how resistance to asking might follow from the treatment of their ancestors. Discussing this with others of the same ancestry can help reclaim the voice that violence has repressed.

Being Foreign

When I was at home, I wasn't shy. I was the clown of the home, because I was loved.

It was in the outside world that I was judged, and I wasn't loved. . . . So I became very quiet.—Sandra Cisneros

As writer Sandra Cisneros notes, we can become silent when we feel like outsiders. Foreigners can be silenced by language challenges or because they believe they deserve less than local inhabitants do. To those struggling in a second language, I offer this advice: prepare your questions in advance. You might end up sounding more articulate and professional than native speakers! That might sound crazy, but the head writing coach at the American University of Paris told me that her foreign students often wrote *better* papers than native English speakers because they had fewer bad habits. A liability can ultimately become an asset.

Well-intentioned immigrant parents and grandparents may also discourage their children from drawing attention to themselves. Jack, a Jewish man who escaped from Poland just prior to World War II, said to his granddaughter, when he heard that she swam at a public pool, "You don't get in there and show off, do you? You just go in, quietly do your laps and get out, right?" To him, too much visibility meant danger. The message was to keep your head down and work hard.

Krish Vignarajah, the president and CEO of Lutheran Immigration and Refugee Service in Baltimore, says that many refugees fear retaliation for outspokenness. When President Donald Trump threatened roundups, "the playgrounds and churches were empty," she recalled.[18] Hiding becomes a way of survival for those trying to fit in. Unfortunately, hiding creates further marginalization. In hiding we cannot ask for help or expand our networks.

Positive role models can help. Look for people like you who have thrived. For example, the following NASA astronauts were born in Latin America: Franklin R. Chang-Díaz (Costa Rica), Fernando "Frank" Caldeiro (Argentina), and Carlos I. Noriega (Peru).[19] The following technology pioneers arrived in the United States on temporary visas: artificial intelligence innovators Andrew Ng and Yann LeCun and Alphabet (parent company of Google) CEO Sundar Pichai. These individuals enriched our understanding of the universe and revolutionized our communication technologies. Immigrants belong and should not be underestimated, and neither should we underestimate those from poor or forgotten communities.

Oppressive Regimes

Those who have lived in authoritarian regimes know the risks of speaking up. In the antebellum period, Frederick Douglass recalled a common saying among the enslaved: "A still tongue makes a wise hand."

Safety came from saying less. Douglass, who escaped from slavery, said that enslaved persons expressed contentment when asked how they were because slaveholders occasionally sent spies to identify those preparing (or even thinking) to rebel. Anyone who expressed anything less than satisfaction could be beaten, sold, or worse. The "docile heart" that Stowe thought she witnessed was a survival strategy. Oppression silences and can encourage false expressions of contentment.

Therefore, when teaching those who reside in countries whose governments imprison dissidents (real and perceived), I advise caution. In some places, asking can get you thrown into jail. Today in Saudi Arabia women can drive. Yet for over a year after the law granted this freedom, thirteen of the women who had advocated for this right remained on trial and four were detained. While in prison, Loujain al-Hathloul experienced torture, sexual abuse, and solitary confinement.[20] These women helped change the country, but at great personal expense.

Organized crime groups—trafficking drugs, people, organs, weapons, and other contraband—also discourage questions. In black-market economies, questions may be perceived as a challenge to status or pose a threat to livelihoods.[21]

Those with firsthand experience of authoritarian regimes may find the asking required by negotiation difficult. Distinguishing between high-stakes and low-stakes asks helps. Not every request is dangerous. The exercises at the end of this chapter will be especially helpful to those transitioning into a freer system. When negotiating with someone from one of these regimes, you may need to help them ask for what they need.

What stops you from making requests?

What opportunities might this silence cost you?

RELEARNING THROUGH PLAY

Acting and observing the results helps us distinguish between real barriers and maladaptive patterns. Testing ideas in the world has roots in Western and Eastern traditions. Tibetan Buddhists engage in Śūnyatā practices that treat all actions as experiments.[22] That means you act, see what happens, and learn from the outcome. Philosopher Karl Popper, in *The Logic of Scientific Discovery*, argued that ideas could best be "falsified" through testing.[23] Therefore, he encouraged us to evaluate the validity of ideas through experiments. The game presented in the next section takes its inspiration from these traditions.

Crazy Requests

In my class, we test through play. Students must make three *crazy* requests in one week and report back. These requests need to be low-stakes (low-risk) and something they might not usually request.

The results sometimes exceeded our expectations:

- Apple gave Bako a free iPhone upgrade. He felt so emboldened that he asked the woman next to him out on a date. She said yes.
- Justin, a deaf student, asked his favorite Mexican restaurant for a year of free entrees in exchange for making them a promotional video. Justin said, "It took a little back and forth, both of us explaining our reasoning, cost for food, et cetera, but at the end, I was able to get ten free meals!"

A few students used the game to speak to people in positions of power.

Lauren used the game to approach one of her role models, Assembly-woman Diana Richardson, during the Congressional Black Caucus Conference. "I felt very nervous and hesitant. . . . I didn't want to seem unprofessional and totally psyched myself out initially, but then I remembered the goal for the week was to just *ask*. Before I knew I blurted out, 'Hi! Can I bother you for a picture?' She smiled and responded, 'Of course, beautiful. You are not bothering me, and you are not bothering anyone by asking for anything that you want.'"

Lauren said, "This assignment was awesome. I never noticed how much anxiety I get when faced with asking a question. However, I have realized that the battle is primarily in my head and to just ask! The worst that could happen is you get a no, but the more you practice not asking, the less opportunities you create for a yes." The same week, Lauren also renegotiated her work schedule, enabling her to skip rush-hour traffic.

Some students had life-changing experiences; Jalen snagged his dream job on Capitol Hill:

I interviewed for a job that I really wanted. When I didn't hear back, I assumed I didn't get the position. . . . But then I received a voicemail from the person who interviewed me. When I called back, they said they selected me for the position. I was ecstatic, but they told me they were only offering me a part-time role. I knew that this would not be enough for me to resign from my current job even though it was something I really wanted to do. Thankfully we'd just been tasked with asking people three crazy requests. So, I just asked if they could make it a full-time role, and if not, then I couldn't take it . . . she got back to me and said they'd be happy to offer the role in a full-time capacity. I'm still in disbelief as I'm typing this message. I'm not sure if I'd be in this new role if I didn't have the courage to ask.

Play the game and let me know how it goes. There are just two simple rules.

Rule 1: If you ask for something, use it for the reason you expressed.

Wanita proudly told the class about her crazy request to a colleague to help pay for her university tuition: "She gave me $500 because she knows how hard I have worked to finish this program."

"Did you put the money toward your tuition?" a fellow student asked.

"No, I spent the money on clothes," she said unapologetically.

Wanita had used the game to scam a colleague. Even if her colleague never discovers the betrayal, she has damaged the relationship. Her classmates know that she did not honor her word and may hesitate to engage with her. In the long term, this approach to negotiation, relationships, and her word will not serve her. Even in a playful game like this, ethics matter. Trust is easier to keep than to rebuild.

Rule 2: The person can decline without negative consequences.

Use the game to practice using your voice rather than your authority. For example, do not ask your employee to work all weekend to finish a project. You have power over this person. No coercion, blackmail, or intimidation.

RAISING THE STAKES

Some asks matter more than others. In a medical setting, for example, an ability to make powerful and persistent requests can save your life. Kolby and other students who had been deemed "essential workers" during the COVID pandemic experienced this urgency. Kolby, a security guard, had no protective equipment early in the pandemic. His diabetes put him in the high-risk group.

"Most of the other employees were sitting around and taking it," Kolby explained. "There was no hazard pay or anything. The morale was really low, and the company has a bad reputation for doing things like this."

Kolby's request moved up the chain of command to human resources. But it was too late. He got COVID. He survived, but because he has diabetes, it was an especially scary time for him.

> What request, if granted, would have the biggest impact
> on your life?

Preparation

When done well, negotiations enhance relationships. This happens because good agreements result in all parties getting something they want. To increase the likelihood that your asks improve your relationships, build relationships before you need something. Do this by knowing the aspirations and struggles of the people in your life. Savvy businesspeople find out what keeps their prospects up at night. Then, they offer them solutions.

Knowing your colleagues' priorities can help you prepare your requests. Let's go back to Kolby. What does he need to know about the human resources (HR) department of his security company? Many employees (mistakenly) think that HR departments exist to help them. Senior HR managers in our program told their classmates that HR serves to protect the *institution* from lawsuits and unpleasantness, not to serve as impartial sites of justice. Mark, who worked for thirty-five years at the U.S. Department of Labor, urged me tell you, my readers, that this is also true for the Equal Opportunity Office (EOO). Employees would turn to the EOO after HR turned them down, misunderstanding that these offices often work together and often on behalf of the institution, not the individuals they supposedly served. Ouch.

Knowing that his employer wanted to avoid bad press during COVID, Kolby could research how better security companies cared for employees during the pandemic. He could add the data about his increased risk for serious illness due to diabetes. The more he could enter the negotiation process with objective data, the better.

Research matters in our personal lives too. What's going on behind the Instagram pics and LinkedIn updates of the important people in your life? The more you know, the more you can meet their needs. The more you can meet their needs, the more they will be able to meet yours *and* the richer your life will be.

Have a Plan B

Before entering a high-stakes negotiation, know your options. For this reason, Roger Fisher and William Ury teach negotiators to develop a "best alternative to a negotiated agreement," or BATNA.[24] The more options you have, the less power others have over you.

If Kolby had had enough savings, he could have walked away from the job. Without savings, his best option was staying there while applying for other jobs. Some negotiation experts believe that having a plan B distracts you from focusing on plan A. Find your balance here. Options decrease stress and prevent us from seeming desperate. In negotiation (as in dating) desperation, or as my students say, "being thirsty," can turn people off.

William Ury also encourages people to develop an *inner* BATNA, "a strong, unconditional commitment to ourselves to take care of our deepest needs, no matter what other people do or don't do."[25] Kolby's inner BATNA may be that no matter what the employer decides, he will do what he must to protect himself.

Asking Well

How to make the opening request depends on the situation. In 2007, writer Andrea Donderi sparked an interesting discussion when she shared an observation. The world is made up of "Askers" and "Guessers," she posted online. Askers speak up, she claimed, whereas Guessers read the situation and only ask when they anticipate a yes.[26] The results of the Crazy Requests game, however, showed that many guessed wrong. They got yeses in crazy situations. Our upbringing and cultural messaging can affect how we interpret our chances. Great negotiators read the room well *and* test their assumptions.

In every situation, we want to consider tone. Studies conducted by psychologist Peter Coleman and marriage expert John Gottman both found that *how* you begin a conversation affects its outcome. Start off snarky or critical, and the remainder of the conversation will likely take on that tone. Coleman also found that when we expect someone to be difficult, we act defensively, which can provoke difficult behavior. When we expect a positive interaction, we increase the chances that all will flow smoothly.[27]

Kolby knew that tone mattered when he wrote a letter to Human Resources about protective gear during the pandemic. Together we chatted about his strategy and settled on this structure:

1. A respectful introduction that includes his name, position, and request.

2. A paragraph that demonstrates his understanding of the company's challenges during the pandemic.

3. An explanation of the employees' concerns and why the company also shares these concerns (sick employees means a reduced workforce).

4. His request for a meeting to work through the challenges *together*.

When and where you make requests can affect the outcome. Generally, if you need to persuade someone, you go to them. This gives the person being asked a sense of control. You also want to pick a time when the person does not feel rushed. Jeffrey Fox, author of *How to Be a Rainmaker,* suggested scheduling sales meetings (or work asks) for Friday afternoons. People tend to be more relaxed, he said, feeling like the commitments of Monday remain in the distance. I followed his advice and advanced many contracts on Friday afternoons when I most wanted to be lazy. In some professions, early morning is best, before people are exhausted! Try both and see what works.

Emotions: Staying on Your Square

When you make your ask, stay steady. Negotiation experts Roger Fisher and Daniel Shapiro say that destructive emotions can destroy negotiations by either diverting us from our goals or damaging relationships.[28] Baltimore community organizer Karim Amin calls it "staying on your square." The Islamic teachers at his mosque teach this concept to help members stay focused on their goals and take responsibility for their emotions. Let's say Kolby's HR manager checks her texts repeatedly during the meeting. If Kolby interprets this as rude behavior, he may fall off his square. He might get angry and take the conversation in a negative direction. But if he is emotionally generous (maybe she has a kid in the hospital), he can keep his cool. Also, Kolby can also stay calm by reminding himself how his colleagues will benefit if he succeeds in getting protective equipment. A personal power struggle can cost everyone.

Sometimes we fall off our square when we feel intimated or vulnerable. To reduce the chances of this happening at work, keep a "what I did for my company today" list on your desktop. Add to it daily. Rereading this list before any important work meeting can help you stay steady.

Preparing to stay steady does not mean ignoring emotions. You *will* have emotions. Emotions can point to our values and to our unmet needs.[29] Destiny began the semester telling the class about her power struggle with her boss. By the end of the term, her boss fired her. Next semester, she had found a new job—but now she was struggling with this boss. I, and her classmates, began to see a trend. Rather than assuming she was the problem, I said, "Some of the greatest business owners are people who find working for others intolerable." I asked, "Might you like to run your own business?" Perhaps her anger and frustration reflected her inner entrepreneur trying to free itself. She had a choice: she could find new ways of working for others or run her own show.

Our emotions may be telling us that we are in a hostile relationship. Conflict expert Donna Hicks would call these the emotional indicators of dignity violations.[30] Lauren experienced dignity violations while working as the only person of color and the only woman in a law office. Her boss had a pattern of making mistakes, blaming her, and then being super-friendly. With total calm, she called him on it.

Lauren says, "I asked him to match my respect and my tone. I told him that I was an educated person and that talking down to me isn't the way I receive information." She asked for a time to discuss calmly what went wrong that led to the errors.

She shared with us throughout the semester how she navigated some challenging moments. She kept her cool and stayed focused on her future vision. She did not retreat. As a result, her emotions could not be used against her. By paying attention to our body language and tone, others can discern what matters most to us, something we may not want to reveal.

TEACUPS BREAK IN THE C-SUITE

The less you take things personally, the more powerful you will be. A colleague shared with me her concern for students who seem like "teacups," too fragile to receive feedback, hear the word *no,* or even challenge their own beliefs. These individuals, sometimes referred to as "snowflakes," crumble at the slightest upset and may attack anyone sharing information that makes them uncomfortable. Their emotional stability depends on everyone around them acting the way *they* want them to. They only want to hear information that affirms them and their worldview.

In my research for this book and an earlier book for which I interviewed ninety Holocaust survivors, I found that people from challenging environments seemed less fragile than those from more sheltered ones. In Baltimore, my students valued "being real" over being coddled. The idea of "safe spaces" seemed unrealistic to Monique, who wrote, "We all define 'safe' differently. What is 'taboo' to one, could be the path to liberation for another." Students resonated more with the concept of "brave spaces," in which people speak openly and vulnerably. I think that these students' desire to choose the real over the pretty will position them to become outstanding leaders. They can better handle the knockdown fights and crass attitudes that occur in high-level politics and business than those who have known only safe spaces. Teacups often break in the C-suite.

CLOSING

> Every performance has a finale to leave lasting emotions on the palate.—
> Lexy, student and dancer

As in theater and sports, how you leave a negotiation is as important as how you enter it. So think about your closing. If you negotiate a great deal, refrain from crying out with glee (at least until you get home). Looking too delighted can make the other party feel that they could have done better—and if they feel scammed, they may want to even the score. In sum, you want to set a tone of mutual respect, not "Gotcha!"

If you do worse than you expected, you might be able to renegotiate or pull out of the deal, but probably not right away. Lakeiska offered a job to a woman and then asked her preferred salary. The woman gave her a number and when Lakeisha accepted, the woman said, "Damn, I should have asked for more." While that was probably true, "Thank you" would have been a better response. End with mutual respect and gratitude, send a thank you note, and then regroup. There might be future opportunities.

LOVE THE NO!

When I first began in sales, I felt defeated by the seemingly endless string of no-thank-yous from prospective clients. My father, who loved sales, laughed and said, "You've got it all wrong. Negotiations *begin* with no!"

"How can negotiations *begin* with a 'no'?" I asked. "They just told me they don't want the product."

He explained: "'No' means you are in a conversation. The next step is to figure out *why* they said no. That's the hard part, but if you can get them to tell you that, then you can work on a way to address their objections." He said, "Go back and find out why all those people said no." I grumbled, then went about it. These follow-up calls felt like calling up every former boyfriend to ask why they dumped you. Useful, perhaps, but painful. Eventually I become more curious and less defensive. Many had a contract with a competitor, so I asked when it would be up. Others were in the middle of company changes and were afraid of adding new software to the mix. Some had heard critiques of our product. I asked about these critiques.

Invite the feedback. Get curious. Over the next couple of years, I found ways to turn many of them into yeses. During this process, I learned that *no* does not mean "never." It may just mean "not now," or it may reflect the person's first reaction or mood that day. It may simply mean that the person you asked lacked the power to say yes. Maybe their boss decides. You always want to find the name of the person who *can* agree to your desired terms in a negotiation. Next time you hear "no," ask why!

Forty-Eight Hours to Grieve

What dream did you abandon after a no?

Makeup artist Takia Ross says that when you get a hard no, "you only get forty-eight hours to grieve. Then you need to get out there, because in business forty-eight hours is a long time." She is right. I followed her advice. When an editor rejected one of my articles, I grieved for forty-eight hours. Then I pitched the idea to the *Harvard Business Review,* which published it. Huzzah!

Now I understand that if I'm not hearing "no" regularly, I'm playing too small. If you only get yeses, stretch further. If you have all you need, start asking big on behalf of those with less power than you.

If "no" scares you, practice in low-stakes situations. For the Crazy Request assignment, Janice wanted to practice getting comfortable with hearing "no." She said, "I asked my sister to come over to my house and wash my dishes. My sister and I live approximately twenty miles from each other. I was really hoping she would do this because I absolutely hate washing dishes. . . . The first thing my sister said to me was 'No,' and then she said, 'No way!'"

I told the class that asking for the extreme can help a smaller request seem more reasonable. Olivia tried it out. She asked her wife if they could start an animal farm. Her wife said, "Hell no!" Olivia proposed her real desire: "Well, then how about just one chameleon?"

"No" May Mean "No Fit"

If you stopped fearing "no," what might you ask for?

After my colleague Sadie received her PhD, she applied to 150 jobs, postdocs, and fellowships. Reflecting on that time, she said that while her ego took a hit every time she got a no, the five grants and opportunities she eventually won worked beautifully together, culminating in a full-time job that she loved. Even though it all worked out, Sadie received roughly 140 "nos"! So often, what we call personal "rejections" really just indicate a lack of fit—our needs and wants did not align with those of others at that time. No harm, no foul. Keep moving forward.

"NO" IS A COMPLETE SENTENCE

Learning to face no also helps us say no. When Takia Ross talked to us about starting her makeup business, she said, "In the beginning you feel you need to take every opportunity. After a while you realize that you cannot. 'No' is a complete sentence. When you allow others to respond to a request freely, you free yourself to do the same. They can say no without hurting the relationship, and now you can too!"

WHEN SUCCESS HURTS

While our negotiation class was usually fun and lighthearted, a few students shed tears. During a group discussion about the results of their asking exercise, Brittany teared up and started shaking. When I asked if she was okay, she said, "I never knew I could ask." She was thinking about all her years of needless suffering. Other students, too, could not believe how much more they could have had.

Conflict scholars write about "relative deprivation," which refers to a group's awareness of the gap between what they have and what another group has, especially after liberation of any kind. This sudden awareness can contribute to individual/group psychological stress.[31] We saw this play out on an individual level, as students observed the gap between how they have lived and what they now believe is possible for them.

Sharing these painful feelings with trusted friends and others experiencing the same discovery can help ease the pain. Friends can help us accept the past and focus on creating a fulfilling future.

SUMMARY

This chapter introduces *asking* as a critical step in negotiation. If you cannot ask, you cannot negotiate. If you cannot negotiate, you cannot escape from social marginalization or help others. Here's the bind: many people from historically marginalized groups or under-resourced communities have learned *not* to ask. They may have learned this from their parents or from messaging that they do not deserve. A violent or neglectful upbringing can also affect how comfortable people are with asking. Silence, a survival skill for kids navigating a dangerous household, can preclude social mobility later.

Practicing crazy requests and making strategic higher-stakes requests can help people break free. Even small successes show us that we can thrive despite troubled personal histories and ongoing inequities. If the world must become fair and kind before we negotiate for ourselves, we will have a long, uncomfortable wait. Through practice, we can improve our asks and get more used to hearing "no."

The next chapter discusses reciprocity. If we only ask and never give, our lives will not work either.

ACTIVITIES

EASY/HARD

Turn a piece of paper sideways. Make three columns and label them EASY, NEUTRAL, and HARD. Then, put names of people under the column corresponding to how hard you find it to make requests of them. Even if you have never asked them for anything, how much reluctance do you feel?

List as many names as you can. When done, look at the list:

- What do you notice?
- Are the HARD and EASY ones the same in all situations or just in some?
- Are your happiest relationships in the same column?
- What makes the HARD ones difficult?

Share your observations with others.

Crazy Requests

Make three crazy requests this week: low-stakes requests that people will likely decline. The idea is to ask for things that you need or want while being unattached to the outcome. See how it feels and get used to the awkwardness. Remember, don't threaten or risk a relationship or a job.

Understand the No

The next time someone says "no," find out why they declined. You can also do the exercise in pairs. Tell the other person who they are playing (your boss, mom, etc.) and to say no to what you will ask. Then ask them why. They can justify their reasoning however they wish to. See if you can address their concerns and move them toward a yes.

CHAPTER 3

Give

OVERVIEW

Great negotiators give *and* take.[1] Business and other competitive environments tend toward overtaking. That's why many negotiation experts urge their audiences to give—which will increase the givers' own happiness, too, they point out. A study across 136 countries found that buying things for others generated *more* joy than buying things for oneself.[2] In contexts of deep socioeconomic precarity, however, we often see the giving at the center of a harmful tendency: people forced to give beyond their means to make up for the lack of infrastructure and resources.

This chapter considers the art of giving in negotiation for those at most risk of emotional and financial burnout. The focus for these individuals becomes how to care for themselves, developing simple giving practices that serve others while also developing their social capital and expanding their social networks.

QUESTIONS TO CONSIDER

What do you give for free and what do you give for compensation? What is different about these gives?

During a negotiation, who might you trust more, givers or takers?

Do you think that givers get taken advantage of more than takers? Why or why not?

Unless you grow your own food and make your own clothes, you rely on other humans.

Even neglected kids have helpers. Andrew shared his story about growing up hungry because of the money going to his mother's drug addiction. To feed themselves, he and his twin brother went to the supermarket with empty backpacks, filled them up, and snuck out the back. Eventually they got caught. The security guard understood that they stole out of desperation. So, instead of turning them in, he told them not to do it again. Had the guard involved the police, the boys would have begun a criminal record that, in Baltimore, could have easily spiraled into prison time. Instead, Andrew finished college, received his master's degree, and became a semi-professional basketball player and a sports journalist. The security guard gave them the gift of looking the other way.

Our generosity (and the resulting networks we develop) shape how far we go and our fulfillment along the way. This extends well beyond money and includes the gifts of time, praise, freedom, and opportunities. Without boundaries, however, generosity makes us vulnerable to burnout. Our first-generation college students and many adult learners expressed the joys and burdens of caring for family and their broader networks. Many looked to the negotiation class to help them provide this care without sacrificing their own health and happiness.

CULTURE

There is no universally right way to give. Context matters. For example, if you gave me a camel for this book, I'd be flattered but bewildered. In Niger, that would be an exquisite, if overly generous, gift. We give successfully when we give that which is meaningful to others, and this varies by time and place.

In the 1920s, the anthropologist Marcel Mauss studied giving behaviors in Indigenous tribes in North America, Polynesia, and Melanesia. Within each of the tribes he investigated, leaders enforced their position through giving. This included physical gifts as well as banquets, military services, talismans, and even women and children who could be traded in payment of debts or given as gifts. Giving ceremonies help create alliances between clans, whereas "to refuse to give, to neglect to invite, as to refuse to take, is equivalent to declaring war."[3]

Willie Ermine, an elder and former First Nations University professor, says Cree "give away" ceremonies exist today. In these ceremonies, you are to "give away the things you cherish, your most treasured items. . . . The more you give the more you get."[4] Ermine says members judge each other by what they give more than by what they have.[5] This helps valuable items circulate.

In some traditions, giving poorly has profound spiritual consequences. For Hindus (Brahmins), early Romans, Maori, and some Indigenous communities, gifts contained the spiritual power of the individual, the gods, and/or ancestors. Hindu (Brahmin) culture teaches that not sharing food is "killing its essence." Similarly, Malay hospitality principles teach that he who eats without inviting his friend eats poison.

What are the giving practices in your culture?

In Baltimore, I discovered a practice of giving to others on one's birthday. Tiffany says, "On my birthday and on my siblings' birthdays I give my mother a gift. We celebrate the anniversary of our mother's willingness to gamble her own life to give us ours." Karah added, "My mom volunteers at a shelter every year for her birthday. I have always admired her for this."

Ebony, who works, attends school, and cares for her blind autistic son, shares her giving practices: "I give all the time. I give for selfish reasons. . . . Giving makes me feel awesome! Sometimes I will just pay for someone's groceries if they allow me. I give to the homeless all the time, I give to friends, strangers, etc. It's just what I do. I have been known to give my friends gifts on my *own* birthday. . . . Giving is what I know we've been charged to do by God. . . . I LOVE GIVING!"

Sandra, by contrast, lives in an affluent town in Canada. She keeps a record of the birthday gifts she receives along with an estimate of their cost. She uses the list to estimate how much others value her. If someone forgets her birthday, she will not contact them on their birthday. This practice yields poor results, and she admits to being lonely.

WOMEN'S WORK

When organizational psychologist Adam Grant studied the effects of giving on personal success, he found that over the long term, givers succeeded more than takers.[6] His findings encourage people in high-powered environments to give without "the fear of being judged as weak or naïve."[7] I wondered whether Grant's findings reached beyond business. What about the Ebonys of the world, who give massively to those around them and struggle with their health and professional direction?

Studies show that people who primarily give to others, without adequately caring for themselves, make *less* money, are twice as likely to be victims of crime, and are 22 percent *less* powerful than those who primarily *take* in relationships.[8] Caregivers, who are prone to burnout, rarely receive the financial bumps and professional respect of those giving in corporate contexts. In 2017, about forty-one million family caregivers in the United States contributed about thirty-four billion hours to provide unpaid caregiving. Analysts estimated that unpaid work equates to about $470 billion.[9] In 2020, caregiver estimates reached $53 million. Unpaid caregivers never receive compensation under national social security, health insurance, welfare services, or local resource schemes. Most of these caregivers are women of color and most are immigrants.[10]

Of those who receive salaries, child-care workers and personal-care aides are among the lowest-paid employee groups.[11] Cooks, maids of all kinds, and waitresses also made the list. These professions, often seen as women's work, reinforce a cultural belief that women provide less value than men or male-dominated professions. In the United States, immigrant women do many of these jobs, often without health insurance.

Then we have unpaid labor. Worldwide, women undertake 76 percent of unpaid work, whether direct caregiving or indirect care such as cleaning, cooking, and so on. This is three times more than men.[12] Homemaking remains the biggest profession in the United States. Jennifer Wolff of the Johns Hopkins Bloomberg School of Public Health studied over 1,700 unpaid caregivers of elderly family members in the United States. The majority of those providing aid experienced significant emotional difficulty, financial hardship, and reduced productivity at work.[13] Giving more does not make these women more financially or professionally successful. Instead, their work allows those in professional environments to earn more. If single, they do not necessarily benefit from these earnings.

Why do women give so much? Some say women are simply biologically programmed to care for others. True, many love to do it. Take Lisa, an elementary school teacher who is single: "If I know I'm going to buy groceries, I check in with my elderly neighbors to see if they need anything." It's no big deal, and she's happy to help them and chat afterward. She sees the broader value of these efforts. "Sitting on your porch talking to your neighbors while they're sitting on their porch is also building a healthy community." While happy to help, Lisa receives no financial remuneration for these efforts. Neither well paid as a teacher nor compensated as a community giver, she's left to figure out finances on her own.

Arthur Kleinman, a professor of medical anthropology and cross-cultural psychiatry at Harvard University, challenges assumptions that biological programming makes caring easier for women: "Often in our society, boys are raised to be careless, girls to be careful. It takes a long time for adolescent young men to learn to care about others and then become caring and at last give care."[14]

He is a minority voice. Many families see caretaking as women's work, rather than something exceptional that earns them respect or financial remuneration. Susan Sy and Jessica Romero's study of first- and second-generation Latina college students, found that family caretaking was an extension of their cultural identity.[15] The women below shared the family caregiving expectations in their cultures:

Judy, Chinese American, found herself expected to care for her aging parents. Each of her seven siblings, male and female, claimed that their own children and professional obligations made it impossible to tend to their parents. They saw Judy, single with grown children, as the obvious caregiver. So, Judy drove ten hours every other week to care for their parents. Neither her parents nor siblings expressed appreciation for her efforts.

Sophie, in Canada, can relate. As the only girl of four siblings, caring for their divorced parents fell to her. She sometimes drove to her mother twice a day to address her increasing dementia-related needs. She cared for her father extensively, even through his cruelty, like when he told Sophie that his housekeeper was "like the daughter I never had."

Laneisha, in Baltimore, talked about the strain of these responsibilities: "When my mother got really sick, my sister and I both had to take on the caregiving role suddenly until she passed away. Now I've had to begin to take on the caregiving role with my dad as well. It takes a toll because your life just suddenly stops, and you have to shift your attention elsewhere."

During the COVID-19 pandemic, caregiving demands skyrocketed. In May 2020, an estimated fifty-three million Americans cared for family, many giving up jobs they needed to do so.[16] Caregivers don't need to hear "Give more." Instead, they need support negotiating for themselves in a context that may judge them for resenting the work or struggling under its demands.

SELF-CARE/OTHER-CARE

Givers, by definition, sideline their needs to support others. Yet people with unmet needs experience more moodiness, anxiety, fatigue, and depressive feelings. Left unaddressed, emotional symptoms can develop into disease. In 2021, *Nature* published a shocking finding that "short sleep duration in midlife is associated with an increased risk of late-onset dementia."[17] Givers need to take care of themselves, and they can start by negotiating for more sleep.

For givers, self-care requires practice. I challenged students to find new ways to care for themselves. Nedra reported: "I treated myself to some peace and quiet by getting a hotel room overnight so that I could get some clarity on the direction I'm taking with my life."

Chevonie, who cares for family and does extensive community work, scheduled an appointment with a therapist: "My name was called, and I looked up to see a beautiful Black woman smiling at me. She extended her hand, which I shook, and she motioned me to her office. . . . For just over an hour, I spoke about my childhood, my marriage, what I love, what I wanted to work on, what I want to do . . . it was just about me. It was great! We laughed, I cried, and I shared."

I followed up with Chevonie three years later to see what changes she made. She said, "I'm not so accommodating as I used to be. Now I'll say 'I'm cooking dinner, if y'all want to come eat, great. If not, I'm not going to try to get you to come'. . . . I also say 'No' more often. They say, 'What do you mean, no?'" She stands her ground. Those around you might be startled by the boundaries. Explaining why you're doing it models self-care for others, especially children who learn by watching.

Note that people navigating discriminatory contexts need extra self-care. Those experiencing racism suffer more depression, anxiety, other forms of psychological stress, and poorer health than those not experiencing racism.[18] While we work on changing broader social attitudes, take care of yourself.

Sometimes people go too far in the self-care direction. During the height of the pandemic, Stanford University psychology professor Jamil Zaki warned that "self-care alone won't fulfill people's psychological needs as we rebound from the pandemic. After many months in relative isolation, we must reclaim connection and meaning. That comes not just from caring for ourselves but also from caring for one another."[19] For those who withdrew into themselves, he suggests adding "other-care" days to their "self-care" days.

When done in a sustainable way, giving heals. I learned this from a suicide prevention training and put it to use. After doctors physically saved my friend after a suicide attempt, I suggested that she use her time in the psychiatric hospital to write about the environmental issues she cared about. When the local newspaper printed one of her letters to the editor, she was hooked. The psychiatrist encouraged her to keep writing letters. Today she is a powerful advocate for the forests and wildlife. This work did not resolve all her pain, but it helped her reclaim a sense of purpose and power, and from there she could take on other life challenges.

VAMPIRES

The Christian value of giving to those less fortunate motivated many of my students. It's beautiful to watch their emotional and material generosity. For many, negotiation training becomes an opportunity to set boundaries, especially with "emotional vampires." Ally described them this way: "It's that person who on a phone call talks about themselves and by the time they ask about you, or switch the conversation to you, you're drained. It's hard to get away from that conversation let alone stand up yourself." At times, we all inadvertently suck energy and optimism from friends and family. But when this becomes a normal way of interacting, people start to pull away or get trapped in codependency— one needs to be needed, the other wants to be saved. Unwell people make poor negotiation partners. Unable to meet their own needs in a healthy way, they will be unlikely to meet yours. Encourage them to get the help they need.

How do you know if you are in a relationship like this? Watch how you feel after interacting with different people. If you feel constantly drained by certain relationships, wear some garlic, and ask yourself these questions:

Why am I continuing to engage with this person?

Am I staying out of fear, pressure, or guilt?

Is helping them a way of avoiding challenges in my own life?

How else might I use that time and energy?

What is the opportunity cost of hanging on to this dynamic? In other words, what happier, energizing relationships might I be missing out on?

After considering these questions, Jody used the negotiation class to help her leave a bad relationship. She said, "I've been in a toxic relationship for five years and I finally walked away. That was something I needed to do for myself. I had to give myself the gift of peace, sanity, happiness, and self-respect." Letting go of relationships we cling to out of a fear of being alone makes room for healthier connections.

SIMPLE GIVING PRACTICES

Have you ever done something nice for someone and they didn't appreciate it? It's possible you gave something meaningful to you, but not to them. When we practice presence, we become better at recognizing our needs and theirs. Then we can respond to the real needs, not the ones we imagine. Responding to people's actual needs is as useful in negotiation as it is in our personal lives.

Ashley discovered that her brother most needed words of appreciation: "My brother is the primary caregiver for his family. He's been juggling three jobs. He has a two-year-old girl and has a baby boy due in April. His wife cannot drive due to her vision. My parents complain to him about him not bringing his daughter around the family. . . . No one in my family takes the time to say they're proud of him. When I talked to him, I told him how proud I was of him, and how I admire him as a big brother. When I said that, he became quiet for a second, and he told me he appreciated it. . . . Overall, this made me feel happy as his younger sister."

To negotiate well, we need to become great listeners. It's easy to stop listening, especially to those we know best, because we think we know what they will say and what they want. Needs and desires change. When we assume that we know people, we miss these shifts and the distance between us can grow. When we tune out with new people, we miss all kinds of important information.

Who is the best listener you know?

When I asked my students to rate themselves as listeners, many rated themselves poorly. Scott admitted that after thirty-five years in the U.S. Department of Labor, he kind of stopped listening. People's stories started sounding the same, he said. "I wrote eighty-five grievances in my last year alone. I knew what they were going to say and how the process was going to go."

Jalen admitted to being what he called *a fake listener.* "People think I'm a good listener because I don't interject into the conversation much. I ask questions not because I'm interested but because I missed everything. I was probably thinking about my high score on a video game I was playing last night."

Leigh says that her work as a case manager for people struggling with psychiatric illnesses uses up her listening. After work, she forgets simple things like her wife's drink order almost immediately.

Mary said listening increases her anxiety. "I want to have a great response. I want the person to know that I care about them." So she now takes her dad's approach. He pauses and says, "I'm listening to you, and I am thinking about my response. That's why I'm quiet."

Then we had our selective listeners, like Toby, who said, "I'll pay attention when I think the information is valuable." I asked Toby how he knows if the information is valuable. Sometimes things people say prove useful down the line. Might there be value to listening to someone simply because you love them and care about what they have to say?

We all have our listening weaknesses. When do you check out?

Our disengagement affects others. Neglected children show decreased intellect, academic ability, memory, and executive functioning (planning) and increased emotional or behavioral disorders.[20] Parents working multiple jobs to keep food on the table often lack the energy to listen to young children fumbling with the language as they struggle to express themselves.

By becoming better listeners, we improve our relationships *and* communities. In chapter 1, I talked about Chris Wilson's job listening to community members about their needs. Many people said they needed work. So, Chris approached his boss about a new job-placement program. Luckily, she listened. He wrote up his proposal and she got it funded. His salary doubled and the program helped dozens of people get jobs: win-win-win.

Listening Techniques

How can we become better listeners? Breathing practices and meditation assist with listening and concentration.[21] By clearing our own minds, we make room for what others have to say. Reading helps by training our brains to slow down and grapple with new ideas. If you have a hard time focusing, set a timer for fifteen minutes. Read, then take a break. Or listen to podcasts or audiobooks without doing something else at the same time.

Good listening requires more than not talking. It requires fresh ears. As already mentioned, listening freshly can be most difficult with those we know best: we may think we already know what they'll say, or assume we'll have time to communicate with them again if we miss something.

The next time your sister starts ranting about her husband or your dad tells you that same story about high school, pretend it's the first time and ask new questions.

Because relationships crumble when people stop listening, marriage/couples' therapists offer a wealth of listening practices. One exercise, called the "Imago Dialogues," can be easily adapted for negotiation. First you repeat what the other person said, then you clarify. Let's say you are negotiating with your partner over how to celebrate his birthday.

He: "This year, I want to go out with my friends."

You: "What I hear you saying is that this year going out with your friends is important to you. Is that right?"

He: "Yes, I never see them anymore because our schedules are so different."

You: "Is there anything else that is important to you?"

He: "I'd like you not to be mad at me for hanging out with them."

You: "What I hear you saying is that you are worried that if you hang out with your friends that I will be mad at you? Is that right?"

He: "Yes, that's what happened last year."

You: "And that was frustrating for you?"

He: "Actually, I got angry. It's my birthday after all."

Without getting defensive, the listener gives the speaker room to express himself.

Once both people get to be the speaker and listener, the couple can work out how to create a winning birthday plan.

I challenge my students to do a version of Imago Dialogues with people in their lives. They must *ask five information-seeking questions with no agenda.* This means they can only ask questions to better understand the person's world, not to lead the person toward or away from a particular solution. Tobechukwu tried the exercise with his brother, who was diagnosed with paranoid schizophrenia. "He was discharged from the hospital on Tuesday after three months following his last relapse," Tobechukwu explained. "Yesterday I got on the phone with him, and we talked." During this conversation, Tobechukwu asked:

How do you feel?

How do you like the new medication?

How do we make sure you stay on the medication and go for quarterly checkups?

Would you talk to me whenever you feel like the drugs are not working?

Do you need anything?

"During our conversation," Tobechukwu said, "I realized how much he had been suffering. He possibly was not even on the right medications. As a result, most of his actions might not have been his own. I tried as much as I could to imagine myself in a similar situation, but, honestly, I don't believe I could possibly understand what he is going through. All I could do was reassure him of my commitment to him."

Robin reported on what happened in her household when she put the listening practices to use: "Over the past several weeks, I've made a conscious effort to listen to my husband and son at a deeper level. Instead of trying to multitask while listening, I am taking the time to actively listen when they are telling me something. This has proven beneficial for all of us." Good listening can reduce household and workplace tension, preventing conflict and making negotiations easier when they occur.

The "Unusual Give" Challenge

For relationships to flourish, we need to do more than listen. We must respond to the needs of others. Sometimes they need to be heard and sometimes they need a ride to the dentist. To expand our range of giving, I assign the "Unusual Give" challenge, in which students must give to someone new and in ways they are not used to giving.

For his Unusual Give, Kegan helped his friend prepare for a job interview: "I typically give gifts and other things that don't require too much of my time. The interview and debrief lasted about ninety minutes, but I didn't feel upset or as though I had wasted time. Instead, I felt truly satisfied about having given something that helped my friend in that moment. On Friday, they told me that they had crushed the interview, and I felt an additional sense of satisfaction because of their excitement. I felt proud at having taken time to give to someone else."

Mei-Ling used the assignment to support her mother: "My mother recently became a business owner at a nail salon. I already help her with payroll and official documents, but I don't typically help her beyond that. This week, I came to the shop during closing and told my mom I was going to help her clean up and go home early. It was something that felt good to say to someone who's sacrificed so much for me and still does. Everyone in my family knows how much time I need to study with three classes and work, so to take out time and give back to those that helped me get this far felt great."

Giving to someone who has hurt us or with whom we are angry challenges our giving muscles. Mormon took on the challenge: "For the task this week, I gave a networking opportunity to an individual I had a previous romantic relationship with. . . . Although a part of me wanted to be petty and not give the opportunity to my ex, I know that doing that would be incredibly pointless and not benefit me in any way, so I decided to just pass the information along to him so that he could potentially benefit from it."

When we give to others, we build trust; and with trust, communication flows more easily. Trust and communication improve the ease and outcomes of our negotiations.

YOUR REPUTATION

In work, as at home, your daily behavior affects whether negotiations become problem-solving sessions or power struggles. By treating people well, being honest, avoiding gossip, doing your job well, fulfilling promises, and supporting others you build your reputation. Robin, former head of human resources for Amtrak, stressed the importance of this: "It can take years to build a reputation and just a moment to ruin it." She built her reputation over two decades by consistently bringing a balanced and fair approach to challenges. Over time, colleagues increasingly turned to Robin for help. The process may feel slow, but when it comes time to negotiate at work, your good reputation increases the chances that colleagues will respond positively to your requests.

We strengthen this reputation by under-promising and over-delivering. When Krish became the head of the Lutheran Immigration and Refugee Service in Baltimore, she worried about winning the board's support. An employment lawyer advised her that "you create power every day by doing your job well." Krish followed this advice and developed a great relationship with her board.

You cannot always deliver. Sometimes your life or obstacles will thwart your efforts. When you cannot fulfill an obligation, acknowledge it and offer a fix. You're going to be late with a report? Follow these steps:

1. Acknowledge what you promised.
2. Say that you cannot live up to that promise.
3. Apologize.
4. Say how you will fix the problem.
5. Reduce the effect on others.
6. Keep excuses to a minimum.

It may sound like this: "I agreed to have this report ready by Thursday, but I will need until Monday to complete it well. I apologize for the delay. Thank you for your patience and please let me know if this causes any issues on your end." By taking responsibility and showing a team attitude, this practice helps preserve your reputation when you cannot fulfill a promise.

Gossip

Gossip—verbally passing judgment about someone when that person is not present—erodes reputations.[22] People enjoy talking about others because a shared enemy offers an easy, albeit costly, way to bond. While people tend to associate this practice with women, gossip expert Travis Grosser says men do it too, they just call it "bullshitting" or "blowing off steam."[23] Gossiping about colleagues may bring you closer to some people, but it harms the targeted person's relationships with others, harms the organization, and erodes your reputation. Remember that when you speak badly about others, listeners know that you may soon do so about them.

Gossip caused Catherine to quit her job:

> During undergrad, I worked three part-time jobs, one of them at a craft store as a sales associate. I worked hard and always picked up additional weekend shifts when I could. . . . One week, I was having a tough time juggling all my responsibilities; I was busy writing final papers and preparing for final exams while also working my three jobs. My mental health was suffering, and I made the decision to call my boss and tell him that I was unable to work my 3 A.M. shift later in the week. I could tell that he wasn't happy to hear this, but he also wasn't outright angry. . . . A week later, my coworkers told me that our boss had been saying nasty things about me during my missed shift.

I was mad and also lost all respect for my boss. After that incident, I began to pay more attention whenever my boss was around and noticed that he often gossiped about other staff members (and the female ones in particular). I worked a few more weeks at that job and then handed in my notice. I needed to escape the toxic environment.

Good choice, Catherine.

Some employers may treat you poorly no matter how much you give. Karah, a working single mother, agreed, "I have seen employees come to work sick, cancel vacations as well as other things for companies that treat them as if they are disposable." If you decide your workplace is toxic, while planning your escape, focus on serving your clients and colleagues while developing skills you can use later. Being great until the last moment can help you negotiate a better departure (leaving when you want, maybe getting severance) and increases the likelihood that you'll be able to use them as a reference for future positions. How you leave affects your reputation, especially in a small industry. Your departure will be the last memory many people have of you.

Reaching Out

We can also build our reputation by helping colleagues. Natassja used the Unusual Give assignment to try this out:

> This week I extended help to a coworker in need. . . . She is about my age and is also from another country. There is a slight language barrier, and she has a bit of difficulty with understanding both the clients and our supervisors. I noticed this and I thought I should offer to help her. After work, I started smalltalk with her and we started bonding over music, TV shows, and fashion. I then realized that we had a lot more in common than I thought. I then offered to help her, to coach her during our downtime, and even take one task off her plate. . . . She seemed so happy.

Showing this care for others and the organization, Natassja will likely be promoted soon. When she is, people will help her be a successful leader.

What if you like the job but one colleague drives you crazy? Do something nice for them. It sounds crazy, but it can change the relationship. Ashley took on the challenge: "This week I paid for my coworker's lunch. . . . She literally irritates me to no end. She often tries to critique my work ethic, and we usually debate on how to handle crises. . . . When I offered to pay for her smoothie, her face lit up. I can see she was surprised but confused as to why I bought her lunch. . . . This made me feel good, and I noticed how we did not have any problems for the rest of the shift." Rather than spending the rest of their shift negotiating about how to handle crises, they just worked as a team. Generate good will in your life and many of the power struggles that show up as negotiations will melt away.

Giving to competitors can also strengthen your reputation. Brandy gave a free business consultation to one of her competitors about different methods she could use to increase her sales. She says, "This is something I normally wouldn't do, not because it's a competitor. I don't believe in competition in a negative sense, there's enough money and opportunity for everyone; it's because I believe in getting compensated for my time and knowledge when it's being used to increase someone else's wealth. . . . I talked to her for about an hour, telling her [almost] everything I know. I felt really good about it, especially when she texted me a week later telling me everything that I shared with her worked and her sales had increased dramatically." In sum, giving builds your reputation.

Giving can be simple. Desha, who works in the criminal justice system, wanted to see what would happen if she gave some compliments at work: "I saw how excited people were. They really appreciated the compliments and it felt good to be the reason someone smiled. I also let everyone in my life know how much I appreciated them. I am not the most sentimental person, so, coming from me, it meant a lot and people knew it was heartfelt." Just a little thought and a decision to do something different can change a workplace.

Delivering, taking responsibility for not delivering, avoiding gossip, and reaching out to others builds your reputation. When you also reach out in difficult relationships or send someone to a competitor when appropriate, you create what I call "communities of good treatment." You may transform your current work environment or flow easily into a better one. Keep being great, and little by little you will build a happy world for yourself. Your negotiations will flow so much more smoothly, that they might not feel like negotiations at all.

SOCIAL CAPITAL

To build communities of good treatment, you need relationships. Yet many people negotiating from the margins have fragile networks. Sociologists James Coleman and Robert Putnam would say they lack "social capital." Social capital, according to World Bank social development specialist Deepa Narayan, refers to the "norms and social relations embedded in the social structures of society that enable people to coordinate action and to achieve desired goals."[24] Said another way, social capital is our connections and how effectively those connections help us make things happen.

Some people are born into communities and families with high social capital. They may float up into positions of power whether their talent warrants it or not. Hardworking individuals born into these communities can underestimate the amount those networks buoyed their success and provided safety nets. Many successful movie actors, for example, had parents with strong Hollywood connections. Some find the networks they need through plucky determination, but once in, they rely upon these networks to keep their success going.

Many immigrant communities build strong networks in the new country. I learned the power of these networks when my car window broke. My friend Fernando, of Ecuadorian descent, offered to take me to his "car guy." When I insisted on taking the car to the dealer, Fernando told me I was being stupid and stuck-up. I discovered he was right when the dealer asked $5,000 for the window and other "necessary" repairs. I agreed to meet Fernando's "guy," whom I'll call Jesús (for his healing abilities). Jesús fixed my window for $250 and said those other repairs were not necessary. Jesús then drove us thirty minutes to and from my home, so that we didn't have to wait while he worked. A few months later, when my car got crushed in a fender bender, Jesús fixed it for $750, allowing me to use the $6,500 insurance check to cover my rent while I completed grad school. Because a trustworthy mechanic is hard to find, some of you may write to me to get his real name. I might tell you. I might not. We'll see.

Networks matter, and underestimating their importance hurts those negotiating from the margins. Sociologist Joan Maya Mazelis, who studied women in Philadelphia living below the poverty line, observed how our culture of individualism discouraged people from reaching out to others and building relationships. She writes: "By convincing people that they as individuals are alone responsible for their place in the socioeconomic system and seeking to obscure the structural causes of poverty, it encourages avoidance of social ties and hindrance of collective approaches to poverty reduction."[25] Escaping poverty requires building and/or shifting networks. Networks determine whom you will negotiate with and the resources they have to offer.

Starting Again

Upon release from his twenty-five-year prison sentence, Ronnell was forced to sever ties with the few remaining relationships he had, even with his son. He did this, he said, because these individuals struggled with substance abuse and often had run-ins with the law. Had his parole officer seen him living among them, he could have ended up in violation of his parole. To stay out of prison, Ronnell needed a safe, stable environment. For a time, Ronnell said that his only network consisted of his case manager, parole officer, and boss at McDonald's. They "kept him grounded," checking on him every few hours.[26] Over time, Ronnell earned a good reputation and they, and others, started speaking on his behalf. From this foundation, he expanded his network by one: a girlfriend who believed in him and helped him pay for the parole and court fees that cripple many formerly incarcerated persons. Four years out now, Ronnell says he has become stable enough to reconnect with his son.

Transitioning networks can be painful, leaving people lonely and lost before they can return or find healthier connections. Latoya described her struggles:

> I don't want to hurt [my friend] Ramone's feelings, but I need to pull away. I love her but she's really into clubbing and drinking and I am starting to live a different lifestyle. I went to her house the other day for a barbecue, and I really didn't want to drink, but people kept saying, "Come on, have a drink." They kept asking and asking, and I eventually said yes. Then one drink became two. Then I had to go. I had my son with me in the car and as I was driving, I saw the police setting up a checkpoint to check for drunk drivers. Luckily, I drove by before they were set up, but I realized I may not have passed. I could have gone to jail!

Latoya couldn't make the changes she wanted while hanging around with people she had known for twenty years. "I was crying on the way to work this morning because I was feeling like I had to break up with my friends. I just want to tell them, 'It's not personal, I just need to step away.' It's nothing they did wrong."

I offered, "Rather than saying you're leaving, can you explain the changes you want to make and then ask their help in supporting you?"

She liked this idea. It may work, or she may have to leave for a time. If she chooses separation, she wants to tell her friends why and reassure them that she still cares for them. If you need to separate, do so gracefully: ghosting people hurts both you and them in the long term. People coming from resource-poor communities will especially need to connect with new networks to gain greater access to resources. Said another way, if everyone you know is poor and struggling, it's unlikely they can help you find your footing.[27] Mel, a student who reviewed this chapter, asked me to add that struggling people may not have contacts and career-specific information, but many can still listen and give good advice. Good point. Net worth is not your personal worth.

Building Your Tribe

So how do you build social capital? Baltimore makeup artist Takia Ross says, "You have to build a tribe." Takia grew up in a big tribe, a family of over a hundred people. She did their makeup for fun as a youth and soon discovered a real passion and talent for the art. She decided to professionalize herself, and while her existing tribe became her first customers, she could not continue to give to them and care for herself until she expanded her network. The university's business school helped this single mother of three win $65,000 in grants to launch Accessmatized. She now offers makeup from 4:30 A.M. to 11:00 P.M. and her artistry is highlighted in over sixty publications, including *Essence*.

Takia told our class about the kinds of givers we need in our tribe, which also points to ways we can give to others. She listed a number of things such a giver will do:

- Tell you the whole truth
- Be a nosy neighbor who checks on you
- Not let you play small
- Be a rock-and-roller (someone who runs with you to networking events, etc.—it's okay if it's your mom)
- Get on the floor and get social media pictures
- Do research (someone who knows the history and can tell you, "Back in the day . . .")
- Talk you off a ledge when you want to quit

Takia expanded on this last point: "Sometimes we need a marching band with theme music. . . . I quit my job two times a week. I've walked out on the boss many times and I'm the boss!"

Then give BIG to your clients. For Takia, giving means more than doing people's makeup well; it means listening to her clients. She explains:

People do business with people they know, love, and trust. I have no clients: I have good girlfriends. I treat my ladies like we're at Vegas—"What happens in the [makeup] chair stays in the chair." I know more about [my clients] than anyone in their lives. I try to know everything I can about people I know. In my business, I'm Google. For a long time, they knew nothing about me. It was all about them. The more you know, the more money you get. It's not just who you know, but who likes you. You will make big asks. You need your tribe to respond. I have three thousand followers on Instagram, but two hundred I talk to on a consistent basis.

Build this kind of tribe, Takia says, and "you'll get to the point where you don't market your business, your tribe does."

Rewind

Not sure where to start? Reconnect with wonderful people from your past. Reach out on social media and hit up every reunion. Divorced and in a career transition, Janice felt shy about going to her high school reunion, but she dragged herself there. At the event, she reconnected with Simon, a childhood friend. They fell in love and are celebrating their twenty-fifth wedding anniversary this year. Huzzah!

Reconnecting with old friends can even save your life. Tylis, a doctoral candidate, told me her story. Feeling deeply ill, she visited three medical specialists, who all disregarded her symptoms as a normal part of menopause. Because she was thin and ate a plant-based diet, they assumed that she was fine. Luckily, she had stayed in touch with a sorority sister who had become a gynecologist. Her friend looked at some of Tylis's lab reports and sent her to the hospital immediately. Tylis almost died because blood was not getting to her head and heart.

Friends with expertise in law, medicine, education, contracting, automobile repair, and so on can help you in many ways. Gain some skills so that you can give to them, too.

Giving to the People around You

You can also build your tribe by paying attention to the people around you. Betty saw Natasha, a fellow classmate, looking stressed in the library. When Betty asked what was wrong, she learned that Natasha could not finish her schoolwork because the library computers would not be accessible during the upcoming holiday. Betty offered Natasha her extra laptop. When they met again, Betty handed Natasha her old laptop with antivirus software her husband had added. Incidentally, Betty's husband did this during his tenth round of chemotherapy. He has since passed away, and Natasha will never forget their generosity.

Giving to Strangers

Giving to loved ones made some students feel vulnerable, so I challenged everyone to also give to strangers. La'Monica shared her experiment: "On my flight to Alabama, I decided to switch seats with an elderly woman who had recently undergone a total knee replacement. This was an unusual give for me because I looked forward to flying in the Delta Comfort section for my first time. . . . Because I gave my seat to her, the flight attendant called someone to upgrade my seat free of charge on my next flight with Delta Airlines. I was not looking for anything in return or any form of recognition. It was simply the right thing to do. Honestly, it felt amazing to be able to assist an elderly woman during a time of discomfort. Switching seats with Mrs. Gamble was the best part of my entire day."

Now hooked, La'Monica sought more ways to give:

> I gave ten blankets to ten different homeless people. My cousin went with me to the store to pick out the blankets. . . . We distributed the blankets to homeless women first, then to the men. As soon as people noticed what we were doing, several individuals started to slow down and hand us money. We assumed the money was to buy [the homeless] food, so we bought a family-sized box of chicken and each side item on the menu. We asked the KFC employees to separate our order into individual boxes, so we would be able to distribute the food with ease. The manager asked what we were trying to do, and we told him about the homeless. He gave us a second family meal free of charge. My cousin and I are both very emotional, so we began to cry. I never thought that distributing blankets to homeless people would turn into us feeding them as well. I felt even more blessed after putting a smile on so many different faces.

"Giving to several different strangers," she reflected, "was a humbling experience. Before distributing blankets and food to homeless people the other day, I was afraid of interacting with them. I know that sounds terrible, but they showed me that not all homeless people are trying to hustle people out of their money. The best part about giving to those I knew nothing about gave me an indescribable feeling. Not only was I able to give them something, but I was also able to listen to their life stories. Sometimes, that is all a person needs." La'Monica's give helped the homeless, but she also inspired her cousin, the passersby, and the KFC employee. *That's* how we change our world.

The outcome of Gabriel's give stunned him as well as the whole class. His friend in Nigeria located a family of two boys and one girl whose parents had recently died. Gabriel anonymously provided money to put them through high school. When told about the donation, the girl said, "No, you must put my brothers through school. I can stay behind." Gabriel's friend said to her, "No, the donor insisted that you go too." The girl broke into tears of gratitude. Hooked, Gabriel started putting more orphans through school.

Jamie gave to a stranger who annoyed him and learned a powerful lesson. For the class assignment he mowed the lawn of his neighbors, a couple whom he had never met, but whom the community did not like because they neglected their home. "The wife came to my house to apologize about her grass. She explained that she is the sole provider and is busy between work and running the household because her husband is dealing with post-traumatic stress disorder from his decade as a political prisoner in Burma. They ended up having children later in life due to his imprisonment and she is always very busy. Needless to say, I have cut their grass a few times since." A humbling lesson for us all. Instead of arguing with them or further isolating the couple, Jamie now engages with them from a place of compassion.

Tithing

In Baltimore, the Christian spirit of giving runs deep—and sometimes sideways. My first semester teaching there, a student who was also a minister saw me struggling and said, "If you want to understand your students, you need to understand the role of the church." So I agreed to go with her to church. I arrived early and tried waiting outside, but the welcomers ushered me in. I felt like an intruder. Black people, I thought, have to deal with white people all week and need this break. The warmth of the greeters assured me I was welcome and pushed me into the swaying crowd moving with the energetic gospel choir. By the time my student found me, I was holding hands with the people next to me and had tears streaming down my face. The energy, love, and possibility for renewal was unlike anything in my tribe.

While the pastor gave his sermon, a donation plate was passed around the room. During the intervening songs and performances, the plate circled around again and again, with people pulling out their wallets multiple times. When I asked my student where the money went, she said she was not certain.

Some people participate in the Christian practice of *tithing*, giving 10 percent of their income to the church. This practice takes its inspiration from Proverbs 3:9: "Honor the Lord with your wealth, with the first fruits of all your crops." Some have started to question, especially in regard to megachurches, whether the money gets to those who need it most or simply enriches the church and its leaders. Some churches now pass around credit card readers and offer seminars on how to continue to tithe while paying off debt.[28]

Giving 10 percent of one's income to those in greater need may indeed be an important spiritual practice and one that reaps abundance in the long term. But do some churches use tithing to prey on people who pray? I asked the students their thoughts. Karah said, "This is one of the main reasons why I do not attend church in Baltimore. It has become more of a business to exploit the community than to honor God. I refuse to give money to a church where the leader is driving a half-a-million-dollar car and living in a mansion and members of the congregation are struggling."

Shantell said that her grandmother, Ms. Carrie, was a faithful tither. "As Grandma said, 'Give and it shall come back to you, good measure, pressed down, shaken together, and running over.'" Shantell says,

> I admit, I have not done so because my income has not really allowed me to donate 10 percent without causing some financial distress, but I do give offerings to the church whenever I attend. I also give to the poor all the time, whether it's food, money, clothes, shoes, whatever I have. . . . I've taught my daughter the same. . . . A lot of people (friends and acquaintances) I know feel pressured to tithe. There are some churches where the members are living in poverty while the pastor is wearing designer clothes and driving luxury vehicles, so I understand why they don't want to give as much.

The question of tithing when you are poor affects folks Black and white, urban and rural. Minister Craig Ford, from Montana, struggles with how to advise his parishioners. "I was once helping a young man make a budget," he recalled. "He makes $18.50 per hour. He gives 20 percent to the local church. I felt like telling him to stop. I felt like scolding him. But I didn't want to discourage his generous heart."[29]

Selena shared her experience. When she and her mom moved to Hawaii, they visited a church that encouraged practitioners to work their way up to *50 percent tithing*. She says, "I almost screamed in church. I was so confused and a bit angry, considering that in one of their bathrooms they had *two* fifty-inch flat-screen TVs." For performances, she added, the church had smoke machines.

When the BBC asked readers to comment on the tithing practices they see worldwide, the feedback poured in. While some supported the practice, others expressed concern. These comments came from people living in African countries:

> The sad truth is that we are being milked like cows in the name of religion. The pastor, founder, general overseer, or leader is often as rich as Midas, [and] draped in a designer suit he exhorts us to dig deeper into our pockets and come up with more cash. . . . You don't need a middleman to worship God![30]

> *Abhorrent* is a more fitting term to describe the way unsuspecting church members are hoodwinked to part with their much-needed cash, that would otherwise contribute to alleviate household poverty, being channeled to "insatiable offering plates," which more often than not go to the pockets of pastors, who live in relative luxury while the rest of their congregation wallow in poverty.[31]

Scholars have chimed in too. Well-known American theologian Russell Kelly wrote a book in 2001 called *Should the Church Teach Tithing?* and has since become a public voice *against* teaching tithing as a Christian obligation.[32] He says that most tithing practices emerged in the United States after the 1870s. "Those of us who oppose tithing don't oppose supporting churches. We teach that tithing never was a part of the eternal moral law of God. . . . We teach that tithing was never commanded to the church after Christ's death and resurrection."[33]

Of course, you need to find your own path. If you tithe to support the poor, make sure the money goes to them, rather than paying for a smoke machine or strobe lights. Unfortunately, many people will happily take advantage of your generous heart for their personal gain.

SUMMARY

Yes, great negotiators give. Successful negotiations offer something to everyone involved. More broadly, giving builds our social capital and reputations. This chapter adds a caveat to this negotiation wisdom about giving: self-care and limits to giving can be negotiated as well, especially for caregivers. Caregivers often go underappreciated and their work underpaid. This happens because the work they do is seen as women's work and/or the work of the underclass. Even the most generous heart cannot continue when burnt out or lacking in material resources. We must replenish ourselves and learn how to give sustainably. The passing of humanitarian Paul Farmer reminds us of this. Known as the "man who could cure the world," Farmer tirelessly fought tuberculosis in

Haiti, Peru, and Russia. Some of those who knew him say he died of exhaustion. Please take care of yourself.

ACTIVITIES

Listening Exercise

Ask someone at least five open questions and offer no commentary. Practice understanding the other person's world without offering advice. Listen for their values, emotions, and beliefs. Just be curious.

For example, a colleague complains about a work situation. You could ask:

1. What is most upsetting to you?
2. How long has it been upsetting?
3. What would you like Person X to do instead?
4. Was it ever a good relationship?
5. Is there someone at work with whom you get along well?

Repeat what you understand them to be saying. Ask them if you got it right and if there is anything more that they want to add.

Unusual Give (#Blessed)

Give to someone you rarely give to and in a way that you are not used to giving.

Try with strangers and people in your life.

Reaching Out

Every week for fifteen weeks, reach out to one wonderful person you have not contacted for at least six months. That's just fifteen people. Keep the contact simple. You can just say hello, tell them you were thinking of them, and ask how they are doing.

Know Your Network

Steps:

1. Make a list of the people you interact with the most.
2. Circle the person you give to the most.

3. Put a square around the person who gives most to you.

4. Put a star next to the best listener.

5. Underline any relationship that feels tense. What could you do for that person?

6. Who, if you showed up more for them, could make the biggest difference in both of your lives?

Share what you discover.

Build Your Tribe

Make a list of everyone in your network.

Write next to them what skills and talents they have. If you do not know, put a question mark, and make it a point to know them better.

Is anyone an expert in something you need to know? Perhaps they know how to negotiate with a contractor, or how to negotiate with a car dealer. Ask them for advice.

Think of what expertise you wish you had. If no one in your network has that expertise, how could you expand your network to find someone with that knowledge or talent?

Self-Care and Other-Care Days

We replenish ourselves when we rest, and enrich our lives when we give to others. Pick two days in the coming month. Dedicate one full day to self-care and another full day to other-care. The self-care day might be a retreat day or time with friends. On the other-care day, you do something for others. Take someone on an adventure, volunteer, or offer to babysit your sister's kids. Or you could spend the day writing thank you cards to everyone who helped you in the past. Share your experience with others and the benefits you enjoy. Make this a regular practice and your negotiations, personal and professional, will go more smoothly.

Recommend Others

On social media, shine a light on people you know, and on LinkedIn write reviews for great colleagues. You can even recommend your professor! We all need each other.

CHAPTER 4

Money

Negotiation experts recommend certain preparations, such as research-
ing the salary range for your job, determining the market value of what
you want to sell, or learning about the other party. All great tips. But
how do you know what you can afford or what you need? Most experts
miss this point. Many people from historically marginalized groups,
under-resourced communities, or those who never learned basic money
management must pick up some key skills if they wish to negotiate well.
This chapter will help you

- drop the shame,
- get real about money,
- learn financial basics, and
- rule money so that it does not rule you.

Once we have laid this groundwork, we can turn to savvy experts'
negotiation advice for entrepreneurs, as well as for employees who are
eager to increase their salaries, status, or work flexibility.

QUESTIONS TO CONSIDER

How comfortable are you talking about money?

Do you know your monthly expenses and your total debt?

How often do you think about money?

MONEY AS OXYGEN

Many students say that the week on money proved the most important to them—and the most lucrative. Even those who began the term resisting the suggestion that money rules their lives eventually admitted how much it does so. Money buys time and freedom, funds dreams, and protects loved ones. The less you have, the more important it is. Investing mogul Warren Buffett compares it to oxygen: lose it for a few minutes and it's all over.

Money impacts our health by allowing us to purchase healthier food, access better medical care, and live in healthier places. Having money can even buy some happiness. Lara B. Aknin and her team studied 136 countries and found that even in countries as different as Uganda and Canada, using money to contribute to the well-being of others increased one's happiness.[1]

By contrast, those without money suffer more and must endure unhealthy situations longer. Eileen Chou and her research team even found a correlation between physical pain and economic uncertainty.[2] During the COVID-19 pandemic, Kolby's employer provided no protective equipment, even though his diabetes put him at high risk. Unfortunately, he lacked the savings to quit, and he got sick. Savings, or what freelance writer Paulette Perhach calls a "fuck-off fund," allows you to walk away from unhealthy situations and people.[3]

Our communities thrive when leaders care for communal finances and suffer when they do not. Baltimore cannot thrive, in part, because of financial mismanagement and corruption. In recent years, State's Attorney Marilyn Mosby, former mayors Sheila Dixon and Catherine Pugh, and the former police commissioner faced criminal charges for their misuse of funds. We all suffer when our leaders misuse funds.

Sometimes we confuse a huge income with good financial management. Mike Tyson, Nicolas Cage, 50 Cent, President Ulysses S. Grant, Mark Twain, and Kim Basinger all went bankrupt. Some were swindled out of their wealth and some mismanaged it. Fortunately, some rebounded. Many professional athletes have mismanaged their money, as have those in other lucrative industries. A financial advisor told our class about a client of hers who had a seven-figure salary but, because of debt, "at the end of each month doesn't have two pennies to rub together." Learn the basics, live by them, and lead others.

SHAME

If money management matters so much, why do people avoid mastering their money? Shame stops many from getting honest about their finances. Financial journalist Jean Chatzky says that we can reclaim our financial footing by first differentiating between shame and guilt. Shame is "I'm not smart enough, and I'm bad with money," and this often leads to hiding and to burying emotions with food, drugs, sex, more debt, or other forms of self-harm. The financial market collapse in 2008, for example, resulted in roughly ten thousand "economic suicides."[4] Guilt, on the other hand, is "I don't know enough about money, and I did something bad with it."[5] This feeling urges us to educate ourselves and make better decisions.

Cultural assumptions about those who struggle financially contribute to shame. According to Selena, a graduate student, people think that "poor people are poor, unhealthy, and/or addicts by choice. If they really wanted [more], they would work harder and do more. This ignores such barriers as food deserts, and lack of resources." Selena is right. In some Baltimore neighborhoods, people can find drugs more easily than fresh vegetables.

Wealthy people contribute to these biases when they attribute their success primarily to their financial savvy. Take King Charles of England. When his organic food company, Duchy Originals, eventually turned a profit, he told the British Embassy in Spain, "I'm a self-made millionaire, you know!"[6] Someone born as a future king, shepherded into the best schools, able to sell produce from a farm he inherited, with access to the best business advice, and who uses the monarchy's name in the branding has some advantages. Don't you think?

Gender and ethnicity also affect shame. In their study of more than 120 female managers across the United States, Ella Bell and Stella Nkomo found that white women experienced more shame around being poor than Black women, who had more experience with poverty and whose families and churches understood their struggles and cheered them on. By contrast, white women in rural communities, lacking this support, often withdrew.[7] Their community saw their poverty as a personal, rather than societal, failure.

Of course, not all Black women have this support. Sociologist Alexis McCurn discovered that in Oakland, California, many poor women struggle alone. The shame and pain of being poor leads many of these women to use clothing as a shield. They spend what little money they have on fashionable clothes—often resold stolen goods—to feel better about their difficult lives. McCurn saw women using food stamps dressed in expensive track suits, new Nikes, and designer sunglasses. Their children were often similarly dressed in name brands.[8]

McCurn's findings resonated with Rosalind: "In many urban communities, image is everything . . . who has the top fashions, the best car, who keeps their hair done, or has the latest phone. One time, I would be in that category myself. If it wasn't a name brand or a designer . . . I wasn't going to wear it. But since then, I've learned it's an inside-out thing. I've learned that I can wear something inexpensive, a three-dollar shirt, but I can feel good because what I wear is not who I am. [But] I grew up hustling. I was an Afro Girl, I mean I like my own money. That's what started me on the chase. It will take you places you don't want to go. That's how I ended up in prison. I was selling drugs—not trying to brag on it—trying to continue that lifestyle of having this, that, and the other. That's a kind of addiction and trauma itself you have to overcome."

Researcher Brené Brown found that sharing our vulnerability provides a pathway out.[9] Therefore, in class I give people space to share their money stories. Brittney G. shared this: "People see how hard I work and expect that I have some huge savings, but I don't. Only I know this truth. I get frustrated knowing that I am the only one to blame. . . . I work three jobs and still have nothing to show for it because I live paycheck to paycheck. I tend to overspend on my son because I am a single parent. I want to make up for the fact that I work so hard, which means I'm away a lot, and he doesn't get all the time he craves with me." Other single mothers told similar stories. They too found themselves overbuying to make up for the fact that their child had only one parent.

Neisha saw her mother struggle and wanted a different future: "When I was ten, my dad died of a stroke, leaving everything to my mom. . . . By the time I was in high school, it became more apparent that my mom was a struggling single parent. So, when I was sixteen, I started working and I haven't stopped since. The chase of stability and ability to buy things that I *want* [as well as need] became a driving force within me. I never felt stable and that's a terrible feeling for a child to have. . . . I want to set my children up for success. To do that, I need to have every aspect of my personal finance in order." The next section discusses how to learn the financial practices that will bring you and your family stability.

EDUCATION AND MISEDUCATION

Early money lessons affect how we negotiate our finances. Parents cannot teach what they do not know. Unless we educate ourselves, early teachings about money become the blueprint for how we interact with our finances as adults. This is fine for kids growing up in Scott's house. Scott worked thirty-five years as an economist with the U.S. Bureau of Labor Statistics. He began money lessons when his daughter turned twelve: "I taught my daughter about money, supply, demand, and residual value through Beanie Babies. She wanted a $100 bike. . . . At a Beanie Baby show she purchased Grunt the Razorback [Beanie Baby] for five dollars. On eBay we sold him for $125 and after eBay fees and freight, she had $110 to spend." She paid for the bike herself. Memorable lessons like these prepare kids for adulthood and give them a sense of control over their future.

Of course, not everyone grew up with a savvy economist who took the time to teach financial basics. Laneisha says, "I feel like I hold some resentment toward my parents because they didn't teach me about saving money or just being an adult in general. I feel like I was just thrown to the wolves."

Others talked about parents destroying their children's credit by opening accounts in their name and never paying the bills. Sade said, "My sister did this with my oldest nephew. I just wish she would be honest with him now that he's twenty-two. He's about to have his first child, so he needs to know. He talks about getting his own place and car, and it hurts me because I know he's going to have trouble and he doesn't deserve that at all." Digging out from bad credit can take years.

Some have unlearned bad money lessons. Moesha's family discarded bills and hung up on creditors. "It was only years later that I learned you could just pay them! . . . Over the last two years, I've been focused on eliminating debt and I truly watch every cent. . . . I have some family members that laugh at my money management style, but it doesn't bother me a bit." Her financial diligence has turned Moesha into a confident negotiator. She let me use her stories in this book only if I promised her two free copies and a book talk for her community! I agreed.

Like Moesha, Precious learned dangerous behaviors from adults around her. "Growing up, my family convinced me that the best thing to do is open tons of credit cards, get nice cars with devastating interest, and live luxuriously. . . . When I turned eighteen, that was exactly what I did. I now regret my financial decisions." Now her priority is becoming debt free. Many students struggle under the weight of credit card debt.

Paying the monthly minimum on a card with an interest rate of 16 percent can mean decades of payments. At 16 percent interest, everything you cannot pay off will double every four and a half years. Scott simplified it for the class, noting that "a five-dollar cup of coffee can ultimately cost twenty dollars if you try to live off your credit cards." Think of credit cards as being like a pet snake, friendly only if you feed it fully.

Payment apps like Affirm, AfterPay, Klarna, and QuadPay seem like a safer alternative, but watch out.[10] Some offer interest-free loans on purchases, but others charge up to 30 percent interest. Laneisha adds that "the downside is that on payday, most if not all of my money is going toward making payments on those open orders. . . . I am really not saving any money in the long run." Follow the golden rule: spend less than you earn and save the difference.

No Blame

Many self-defeating financial behaviors are a byproduct of structural oppression. Many problematic behaviors that students witnessed in their elders developed in response to discriminatory practices. From the 1930s through the 1960s, for example, Baltimore "redlined" predominantly Black and immigrant neighborhoods as ineligible for mortgages. Karah's grandparents lied to sidestep this discrimination. "When they purchased their home in 1982, they had to put on the mortgage application that they were white to secure the loan. It didn't matter that they were more than financially able. Race was still the deciding factor." Lying became a way of survival in a racist society.

While redlining is over, discrimination occurs in other forms. A 2018 Brookings Institution report found that Black homes were undervalued by an average of $48,000.[11] These realities contribute to a justifiable distrust of financial advice and banking systems. Unfortunately, opting out or lying often makes people more vulnerable. In 2016, the FDIC estimated that 40 percent of Baltimore residents are unbanked and/or underserved. Without a bank, many rely on alternative—often predatory—financial services such as payday loan services, pawnshops, and other high-fee services.[12]

Chris Wilson experienced the challenge of functioning without banks. Six months out of prison, he and a friend started a contracting company. They secured a $30,000 contract that required significant cash to pay for supplies. Chris explained: "Because of our prison records, we didn't have access to a line of credit [or credit card]. I made a mistake. I got an under-the-table loan. I'd get $3,000 immediately, but I'd have to pay back $4,500 within three months. I thought I didn't have a choice." His mentor Kyle discovered Chris's decision and said, "Be smart, son. Don't ever take a deal like that."[13] Kyle also taught Chris to add a 20 percent cushion to his estimates because things always go wrong.

Gambling becomes another response to ongoing discrimination and structural barriers. Some people gamble to close the cultural equity gap.[14] Unfortunately, Michael Callan and his colleagues who research gambling behavior find that people "only dig themselves into a deeper hole, which might instigate further gambling."[15]

Huge influxes of cash alone cannot resolve the equity gap. From her days in the drug trade, Rosalind learned that money creates more problems when people are not financially savvy: "In the 1980s during the crack/cocaine era [in Baltimore], there was tons of money in the city and people bought a lot of stuff really fast, then they had to protect and maintain it, which led to lots of fighting."

Even reparations for historical human rights abuses will not solve all problems. Elder Florence Allen of First Nations University of Canada talked about the compensation checks from the Canadian government to those forced to attend often-abusive residential schools. "I remember a lot of my relatives that got [compensation] money for residential schools and they gave it away. It was spent like water. They had it one minute and the next minute it was gone. So, there was nothing to fall back on."[16] In Baltimore, even if descendants of slaves received reparations, many could not cash them without paying huge fees because they are unbanked. Many students expressed concern that such money would disappear in their neighborhoods as it did in Elder Allen's community.

It's easy to fantasize about trust funds and huge salaries, but even they offer no guarantee of long-term financial security. Jonathan received a large inheritance in two payments: a million at twenty-three years old and another million when he reached thirty. He spent the first million in four years. At thirty, he spent the second payment within two years. Jonathan is now thirty-two, bankrupt and struggling to pay back loans.

Financial stability to me does not involve being loaded, it involves making great financial decisions.—Staci, student

God Will Provide (If You Sow)

Students often share their belief that "God will provide." Faith can give us strength in dark times and can reduce debilitating anxiety. We need faith. We also need action. Many Christians find their call to action in Ecclesiastes 11:6: "Sow your seed in the morning, and at evening let not your hands be idle, for you do not know which will succeed, whether this or that, or whether both will do equally well." You do not know from where your prosperity will come. When it comes, how will you treat God's abundance?

Katie Dudley of Jemma Financial sees many people negotiate for a higher salary, only to piddle away the new income rather than saving. She calls this "lifestyle creep." This means spending more when you have more. Then there's the issue of actually becoming a creep. I remember having dinner with a man—whose wife and parents were also at the table—who spent most of the meal talking about the increasing value of his $2 million home, his $500-a-week grocery bill, and the Rolex he wanted to buy (in addition to the luxury watch he already had). After dinner, when he realized that the server had put his parents' appetizer on his bill, he asked his father for the money. I sat in amazement as his father, who had just loaned him $20,000 for a new business, passed over a twenty-dollar bill. Will you become the rich person who charges his parents for an appetizer, or the one who demonstrates his success by caring for them?

STARTING AT THE END

Prepare for negotiations by planning your later years and legacy. Scott, our class economist, reminds his peers to think about their retirement: "Times have changed. Retirement is now your responsibility." He encourages us all to get "free money" from employers who match retirement contributions, which also reduces your taxable income.

Thinking about future generations can help us negotiate better today. Elder Margaret Reynolds of the River/Patuanak First Nation says, "I look after my grandchildren to make sure they're cared for. So, we make sure, my husband and I, we buy mutual funds, trust funds. Because I don't know what's going to be for my grandchildren years from now."[17] Keeping her grandchildren helps Elder Reynolds resist temptation.

Ironically perhaps, in facing death we may be entering the most important negotiations, both for us and our loved ones. Relationships can be destroyed when a dying person has not made their wishes clear. Alice, whose father died of COVID-19 in 2021, said, "I want to tell everyone to get a last health directive. This would have saved my mother so much anguish in the end." Without clear instructions, families must negotiate over how far to go to save someone's life. Do we try all treatments? Do we move to palliative care?

> If you ever want to see crazy come out, let someone die. It's the worst time.
> —Rosalind, student

Not planning for death can have a far greater effect on your finances than any negotiation. Ally says, "When my uncle died, everyone thought the home that he and my aunt shared would be given to her to pass down, but it wasn't, and she didn't know what to do and was left heartbroken and confused." State law passed the house on to his children.

I experienced this shock too. My father left most of his assets to his elderly partner, already a multimillionaire. This woman, who refused to sit with him during his chemotherapy treatments or attend medical appointments, lived in her own residence, leaving my dad hobbling around with oxygen tanks and struggling to feed himself. After he died, she scooped up the assets and moved on to another man in less than a year. Laws exist in France to prevent this well-known maneuver (often by women) to take advantage of lonely men.

I was so naive. My father and I had a relationship that many envied, so when he asked me what to do about his will, I just asked him to treat all the kids equally and make his wishes clear. I made the mistake of not asking about his plans. After sharing my story with the class, Michael said, "I never thought I'd share this, but the same thing happened to me." His mother remarried and left everything to her new husband. We talked about the emotional devastation. Those who love you cannot protect you from their weaknesses and the predators who prey on them.

A will is the last message you will leave in someone's heart.

Cultures vary when it comes to inheritance practices. Jen comes from a large Chinese American family with nine children. "In traditional Chinese families, all assets go to the first son," she explained. Her father decided he would "generously" split his money between the three sons, leaving the six daughters with nothing. Jen's sister said to their mother, "Mom, the will is the last statement you're leaving in everyone's heart. Do you want to tell your daughters that they do not matter?" Her mother convinced their father to include the daughters. He agreed, with one caveat: "Only those who gave me grandchildren! Not the ones who gave me nothing." Ultimately, though, he divided his assets equally among his nine offspring. After this experience, Jen made a will and showed it to her children.

If you care about anyone or anything, write an official will. A study of 2,500 Americans conducted in December 2020 found that two out of three people in the United States do not have a will that determines how their assets will be distributed after their death.[18] Those making more than $80,000 are more than twice as likely to have a will as those making under $40,000. Without a will, the small amount of wealth in these lower- and middle-class families is not passed on. Most offered two primary reasons: "I haven't gotten around to it" and "I don't have enough assets to leave anyone."

> Becoming a parent made me create a will. I hope I don't kick the bucket anytime soon, but making sure my daughter is secure means more to me than an uncomfortable conversation about death.—Karah, student

Elder Norma Jean Byrd, a prominent First Nations leader in Saskatchewan, Canada, teaches her community that a will can save them the thousands of dollars in legal expenses (and extra time) incurred by those who die without a will (called *intestate*).[19] Without a will, assets usually go to spouse and children, which law professors Reid Kress Weisbord and David Horton say may not be suitable for nontraditional families.[20]

Only finished wills count. Take the case of Aretha Franklin, who left behind three handwritten, contradictory wills that led to bitter fights between her four sons. Not sure where to start? Some employers now offer legal assistance with these documents. The book *A Beginner's Guide to the End: Practical Advice for Living Life and Facing Death* also encourages readers to create a "when I die file," which includes an advance directive (telling people what to do if you're unable to make decisions for yourself), a will and living trust, marriage or divorce certificate(s), passwords for everything, funeral instructions, and letters to loved ones that include the values and experiences you want to share with your family.[21] My grandmother did this, and her daughters treasure the letters.

TAKING CONTROL

Taking control of our financial lives prepares us to negotiate. When we know our financial situation, we can more accurately determine our aspirational point (what we want) and our walk-away point. We can also identify opportunities to negotiate. How do you gain control? Start calculating your net worth, which means your assets (what you have) minus your liabilities (what you owe). Britni said, "I always thought that having a net worth was for rich people or for celebrities. I thought because school loans made my net worth negative that there was not much I could do." Nope. Everyone has a *net worth,* and everyone can do something about it.

I have students calculate their net worth and review their credit card bills. Many report fixing leaks. Many cancel at least one subscription they never use or did not know they had. Yakini said, "I noticed that I spend more money eating out than I do buying clothes/shoes. . . . If I can go to the market and buy food to cook at home instead of eating out almost every day, not only can I pay down more debt, but I'll be able to save more money."

Once you clean up the waste, look for where you can negotiate. Karah, a single mom who works full time, said, "I renegotiate my bills once a year for lower rates. For example, I lowered my Verizon Wi-Fi bill by fifty dollars a month this year because they were offering a new promotion. Had I not called to inquire, I would have continued to pay the old rate." Smart.

Once you have a sense of where your money goes, keep an eye on it. For beginners, I recommend doing at least *one thing a day* for your money. You might pay a bill, cancel a subscription, listen to a finance podcast, or contact a lawyer about a will. Build up to *three things* a day and you will have claimed your power within less than a year.

The more you educate yourself about money, the harder it will be for others to swindle you out of yours. I like Suze Orman's books, as well as *Broke Millennial* (Erin Lowry), *The Financial Diet* (Chelsea Fagan and Lauren Ver Hage), *Start Late, Finish Rich* (David Bach), *In the Black* (Aaron Smith), *The Millionaire Next Door* (Thomas J. Stanley), and *Rich Dad Poor Dad* (Robert Kiyosaki and Sharon Lechter).

Financial experts can help you prepare for specific negotiations. My advisors help me decide how much to keep in savings and how much to invest. They also help me identify opportunities to save money. We communicate regularly to adjust. When it comes to investments, pick a *fidu-*

ciary who, by law, must manage your assets for your best interests—not their own.[22] Stockbrokers, by contrast, can place their well-being before that of their clients.

You don't need to be rich to start. Bonnie Stein founded Jemma Financial to help women with any amount of debt get their financial footing. Each semester, they save at least one student thousands of dollars. When Katie Dudley visited class, for example, Jenny asked if she could cash a 401(k) check she had received from her previous employer. Katie said no, she needed to roll it over into another retirement plan— or pay big penalties for withdrawing it early. This one question saved Jenny thousands of dollars. After class, Jenny told Katie, "I can't do this anymore. I can't live like this," referring to her debt. Together they developed a plan and discussed how to tell friends that she could not afford to eat out. Jenny said, "They started telling me that they should save money too!" Your positive changes will inspire others.

I DESERVE

> My daughter is asking the tooth fairy for $100, "because I really liked that tooth."—Mara Schiavocampo, ABC News correspondent[23]

Some students who grew up poor expressed their struggles to feel as deserving as Schiavocampo's daughter. Ginger, now a law professor, says, "When you've grown up accustomed to being broke, it can be difficult to wrap your head around what you're worth."

By contrast, others fell deeper into debt by living the way they felt they deserved. Yakini explains: "I felt I deserved to live somewhere really nice. That's how I got backed up with bills and had to move back home with my parents. Clearly, that is not the best idea. Living at home without having to pay rent, utility bills, and a cable bill is a blessing. Although I now had the extra money to save, seeing that extra money made me think I had more to spend." Yakini defaulted on her car payments: "They came and took my little Altima." She depleted her emergency savings to buy it back, and, Yakini admitted, "I filed for bankruptcy."

After finance week, Yakini said, "I've opened two additional saving accounts. One savings account is for my 'new home furniture,' so when I purchase my home, I can use that money to furnish my home. My second savings account is for my 'new home repairs,' so if anything goes wrong in my new home, I will have the money to cover the costs." She learned the hard way but is now on her way to becoming a good money steward.

STUDENT LOANS

How you manage school loans can affect your wealth more than any salary or used-car negotiation. The U.S. Student Debt Relief Plan will provide relief to many, but stay vigilant. Hasan Minhaj's show *Patriot Act* warns viewers about school loan sharks and other predatory practices. It's worth watching.

Talk to experts. Financial advisor Bonnie Stein told me, "No one tells these students that if they end up with $60,000 in student loan debt and plan to work as a social worker, they will be paying that off for a very long time." It can be a shock. I saw a student crying during her graduation. When I found her afterward to inquire about the cause of her tears, she said, "I think I'm crying because I have $100,000 in school loan debt and a degree in creative writing." That *is* scary. Even bankruptcy will not free you from these financial obligations.

Financial aid director Zhanna Goltser talked to us about common mistakes:

- Students avoid the financial aid office.
- Some wait too long to start the process and find that funds run out of money, whereas early applicants can become eligible for multiple programs.
- Students take multiple loans to pay living expenses. "It seems like easy money," Zhanna warns, "but then you have to pay them back with interest." Those who do not finish their programs struggle to repay these loans without a degree.

In sum, seek help, start early, and don't be seduced by what looks like easy money.

Students offered these additional strategies:

- Maryann's daughter put her tax refund each year toward the interest on her school loans. When she graduated, she owed only the principal.
- Jamal negotiated with his employer to pay for half of his master's program.

- Earl said to ask potential employers about student loan repayment assistance: "I've been in meetings where Human Resources is told *not* to mention the student loan repayment assistance unless the candidate mentions it." Mention it!

- Scott suggested attending community college for two years and then transferring to another university. "You end up with the same degree as someone who paid double!"

- Nafeesat talked about "thrift groups" in Nigeria. People transfer money monthly to a trustworthy person and then, when it's your month, you get the money. The money helped her settle into Baltimore during her master's program. This runs on the honor system, so it comes with risk.

Ginger wiped away $90,000 in law school loans with the Public Service Loan Forgiveness (PSLF) program. If you work in public service and make 120 months of qualifying payments, the remainder of the debt is forgiven. She says, "That could equal tens of thousands of dollars once you factor in all the interest you pay over the life of a loan. The process is complicated and cumbersome and requires consolidation and regular employment certification, so you have to stay on top of it, but for me, it's worth it."

Ginger went on to say, "One common mistake many of us made as new lawyers was to put our loans into deferment or forbearance for a period. It was tough to make $1,000-a-month payments on a $50,000-a-year salary. Some people played the deferment/forbearance game for years. Now they owe more money than when they graduated fifteen years ago! In hindsight, we all wish we would've eaten more Ramen in the early days. If it's at all possible for you to make your monthly payments when you graduate, please do it. . . . My friends would've saved tens of thousands of dollars had they prioritized student loan payments." Paying off your school loans well matters for your financial success and reputation.

YOUR FINANCIAL REPORT CARD

How you pay off your debt (school loans, mortgages, credit cards, car payments) determines your financial reputation. In the United States, you can see your reputation through your credit score and credit report.

These reports, rather than your negotiation skills, determine the interest rates on loans, so they matter. These scores can also affect your ability to land a job or get promoted. Katie Dudley says that "in finance/banking, almost all companies will run some sort of credit check/credit history inquiry. Accounting firms, mortgage companies, and many retail firms (employees handling money) will also want to know about a candidate's financial background. This can even affect your security clearance for government jobs. Same with TSA agents." Although they cannot run these reports without your permission, if you want the job, you must grant permission. Brittney, who works in defense, can attest to this: "I didn't understand the value of a credit score until I bought my first car. . . . I also now have a [military] security clearance that takes my credit score into account." Government and military agencies find that financially stable people are less susceptible to bribes or blackmail.[24]

STARTING FROM NOTHING

What if you have no money? Start small and know that people who start from nothing can develop a better understanding of finance than those who always had money. Career coach Lakeisha Mathews's early financial struggles help her weather financial storms: "When I hear that the university is going to make cuts, I don't freak out because I've had to tighten my budget before. I've done this."

Get help. Elder Rose Bird of Thunderchild First Nation says, "When I got out of jail and I got my own place, my mother came over and stayed with me and said, 'Where's the money?' I put it on the table. She said, 'Do you have any envelopes?' Her mother took the envelopes and distributed the cash into one for rent, others for food, cigarettes, and utilities, and so on. When finished, her mother said, 'Go hide it where you won't think about it. Whatever money you have left, then you can go to Bingo.'"

Rosalind, who mentors returning citizens and people recovering from substance abuse, says, "I go with them to the store and show them two offers for toilet paper and ask which deal is better. With meat, they just see the price. I teach them to look at the price 'per pound.' They say, 'I never thought about it.' Then, when their kids ask them for lots of gifts, I tell them to tell their kids to pick two things and then we work to find the best deals on those two things." This helps them gain skills and confidence.

Just monitoring your money closely can guide you to stability. Lisa shared, "When my husband and I separated . . . I had to take care of all the bills all by my lonesome. I'll be honest, I was TERRIFIED!! I don't make enough money, but I learned quickly in my case, it's not how much you make, it's how you manage what comes in. So, I sat down and looked at every penny and managed to pay every bill on my income without working a second job." Lisa did this, in part, by canceling unused services.

Immigrants have their own challenges. During the 2007–10 economic recession, Latin American immigrants were most likely to lose their homes.[25] Why? Because they did not understand the differences between reputable and predatory lending practices.[26] Negotiating well in any society requires knowing the system. The knowledge, once acquired, can be passed down within families and shared with friends. If you have knowledge, please share it.

TALKING ABOUT MONEY

Because money connects to our sense of security, freedom, and worth, many find the topic painful. Yet if we cannot talk about money, how can we negotiate? Mentors and money buddies can help us practice talking openly. My money buddy and I read finance books and check in weekly about our financial activities. Financial therapy pioneer Bari Tessler suggests that people (especially couples) set up a recurring "money date."[27] This puts boundaries around the subject and avoids periodic upsets throughout the week. It also interrupts dangerous silences and maladaptive strategies that can compound problems and travel from one generation to the next. I asked Earl, who grew up in Baltimore, how he thinks local families might respond to such meetings:

> I can say that in the traditional African American family a "meeting" of sorts concerning financial boundaries is awesome in theory but it's not as realistic in practice, especially for the child or member of the family who is nine times out of ten the first generation to go to school or even bring attention to the bad generational financial habits. These meetings often cause tension. I've literally witnessed them cause rifts in the family, as some would see this as "he/she thinks that they're better than us" or have the mindset of "why can't we just do things the way that they've been done?"

I'm glad he pointed this out. We do not want to create rifts between people. Harvard negotiation expert Daniel Shapiro suggests preparing for difficult conversations this way:

1. Identify the taboos.

2. Create a safe zone for talking about them.

3. Figure out whether you will accept, chip away at, or tear down the taboo.[28]

Chipping away at it might look like this: Share your positive changes casually over time to develop an atmosphere of safety. When you go deeper, highlight what your family does well regarding money. Communicating your love and respect can decrease the negative charge around these topics. Come in gently, like financial advisor Mimi Makowske. She begins by asking permission to have the conversation: "Can I ask you about your salary?" "Can I ask you about your debt?" This might be the first time the person has spoken these numbers out loud. Throughout the process, reassure people of your intentions not to shame them but to care for their legacy as well as for the family's well-being.

Putting boundaries around how much we give others creates tension and can ruin friendships. Nafeesat struggles with friends and family in Nigeria who constantly ask for money. They do not understand that her U.S. student visa prevents her from earning money. "How do I let people know that I now have a car because it is a necessity here and not a luxury as it is back home?" People think she is hoarding money or giving it to someone else. "Gradually, your reputation changes from good to bad," she explained. Scheduling conversations to educate friends and family could help reduce the pressure. In those conversations she can reassure them that she loves them and wishes she could do more. This is no easy feat. Negotiation studies show that we expect great deals from our best friends and family.[29]

La'Monica experienced these raised expectations from a former roommate. "I agreed to allow Tiffany, my college roommate, to move into my apartment while she attended summer classes. I told her that she would be responsible for paying the utility bill, and I will continue to pay the rent and the cable bill. She agreed. Two weeks before the utility bill was due, I asked when she would have the money."

"Uh, I'm not sure," Tiffany said. "I just had to spend my money on a family emergency." Eventually, she admitted using the money for a cruise coming up in July.

"So, when will you pay me back?" La'Monica asked.

"At the end of August when I receive my student reimbursement check," she replied.

"That is unacceptable," La'Monica said. "This means you're not planning to pay either the June or July utility bill. You're going to need to move out. I'm not going to allow you to keep living off of me for free."

La'Monica offered a blow-by-blow of the fraught negotiation that unfolded.

"What if I pay in installments?" Tiffany said.

"No," La'Monica said. "You have already lost my trust."

"But the bill is just too expensive."

"It would have been smaller had you just paid it the first of every month."

"You are so selfish. I wish I never asked to stay at your place during the summer!"

"How am I selfish? I let you live in my apartment."

They agreed that Tiffany would pay by August 15 or Monica would call her mother and tell her about Tiffany's behavior. "Tiffany paid me the money a few days before the fifteenth of August. We are no longer friends because of the situation, and I haven't spoken to her since she gave me the money. I've learned to never allow someone to live with me without a written agreement of what they will pay."

Negotiations with friends and roommates do not need to ruin relationships. Tusmo and her roommate successfully negotiated food purchases: "We came to an agreement that one month one of us buys groceries, and the next month the next person buys groceries that equals up to the same amount as the other. This negotiation honestly saves both of us money, and we are both happy with it." Domestic negotiations do best when we create an atmosphere of trust, nudge open taboos, and work together as a team.

FINANCE AT WORK

Salary Negotiations

You can follow your budget and never overspend, but if you are not making enough money to sustain you, then you will continue the poverty cycle.—Karah, student

When many people hear the word *negotiation,* they think salary—though, as already noted, other personal negotiations can be more important. That said, let's make the most out of salary negotiations, because most do not. A 2020 study found that 60 percent of the 1,200 women interviewed had never negotiated a salary.[30] Over a lifetime, this can add up to a million dollars of lost income.

Career development expert Lakeisha Mathews provided the following salary negotiation tips. Shanae paid attention during class and later put these tips to use. She increased her salary by $40,000!

Tip 1: Talk money *after* the offer.

Talk about money only after they offer you the job. Once they do, the conversation has now shifted from *search* mode to *hiring* mode. Let them offer a salary, and avoid sharing your past salary when possible. Some state laws protect you from needing to share your previous salary.[31] Federal government jobs are an exception.[32]

> The hiring company had seen my previous salary and offered to double it. At the time, it looked great to me. But as time went by, I realized I could have gotten more if I'd negotiated better.—Nafeesat, student

Lakeisha tells students to remember that managers don't have a magic money bag. Furthermore, employers pay taxes and benefits on top of your salary, so you cost more to them than your salary. If they ask you for a range, give a reasonable range based on the position.

Lakeisha sees students asking $88,000 for an entry-level job.

Yakini says, "This makes me think back to my younger days when I first started out in the legal field. I was requesting the same salary that someone with five-plus years of experience would request. I had no knowledge of exactly what the employer needed from a qualified candidate, as I failed to do any research before my interviews."

Salary ranges can often be found on the internet.[33] Getting the range right matters. By law, some human resources departments in government agencies must give the job to the equally qualified person who asks for the lower salary.

Tip 2: Take time to think.

Remember not to accept the first offer. Chris Wilson, who negotiated the end of his life sentence, told me that when Penguin offered him a book deal to write about his prison experience, the publisher proposed paying him $150,000. Chris confessed to me that he got it up to $600,000. That's amazing.

When they offer you the job, Lakeisha advises saying something like "Thank you so much for the offer. I'm very excited about the opportunity of working for your organization. I would like some time to consider it." Employers know that you must consider your financial situation and discuss the offer with your family. This also helps you not look too desperate. Negotiation expert Ron Shapiro calls this the "I'll get back to you" strategy.[34] If you don't plan to take the job, respect their time by thanking them and declining.

Tip 3: Build relationships.

Lakeisha says that "the salary negotiation is not a sale. . . . This is a time of relationship building where you show how you'll be as an employee. . . . Employers don't like when people show up and it's all about them. People are interviewing you to help their company, *not* to fund your lifestyle."

When you return, you can say something like "Thank you again for the offer. I am interested in the position. I was hoping for X. Is there anything we can do to get closer to that?"

Then shut up. Don't talk too much. They may need to get back to you. If they need more reasons, "talk about what you will do for the company and any experience you have that supports the claim that you can do this work."

Do *not* tell them that you would like more but will take the job for less. One of Lakeisha's new hires made this mistake, asking for her ideal salary while admitting that she would take the job no matter what. Lakeisha said, "Why should I offer her more if I can get her for less?"

Tip 4: Look beyond the salary.

"Negotiate well," Lakeisha says, "because if you get a job and don't get paid what you're worth, you're not going to stay, but remember that other benefits will matter as well." Healthcare, retirement matching, teleworking, vacation, and flexible schedules all affect your happiness. She says that if you have kids, you might seek a work environment where people are supportive of those with families. And if you see "Other duties as assigned" on the job listing, ask what that means exactly.

Working with happy people in a functional environment also matters. A great place to work may be worth a small reduction in salary. While Nafeesat regretted not negotiating for a higher salary, she stayed because of the great benefits, "and the work environment was the best. I looked forward to getting to the office. My colleagues became my family, and we had fun while moving the company forward." Your happiness has value.

Tip 5: Get it in writing.

When negotiating a new job, get all promises in writing. Things change. The person who negotiated with you may leave, or the institution may fall on hard times. During my own hiring process, a director explained that every faculty member receives $1,200 per year for travel to conferences—but I didn't ask that this be included in my contract. As soon as I started, the institution froze all travel expenses—except for faculty who had it listed *in their contract*. Please, learn from my mistake.

Remote Jobs

For remote work, Lisa Rangel, founder of Chameleon Resumes (a Forbes 2013 Top 100 career website), offers the following tips. Don't accept a salary reduction because the work is remote. Find out if the company wants a remote worker to save money or because their local talent pool is limited. If the company turned to remote workers to save money, they may have less wiggle room. If they need your talents, you may be able to increase your salary.[35]

Promotions

Promotions offer a chance to renegotiate salary and benefits. Ask your employer when salary reviews occur, and don't ask for a raise after three months on the job, like some of my students who wanted more money because the job proved harder than expected or they thought they had negotiated a poor deal initially. Often, asking for a raise too soon will backfire. If you want a promotion, do a great job.

Chris Wilson mentors people entering the workforce after prison. He sees many do a "half-assed" job on small projects, with an eye to getting the money as fast as possible to pay for court fees, diapers, rent, food, alimony, and/or transportation. He knows their desperation but tells them that money will come when they do a great job. Being reliable will earn them a great reputation, he says, which will bring more opportunities.

Know what matters to your employer. Richard, who owns a security company, told us about an employee named Mike who was doing a poor job, yet asking for a raise. Mike told him, "From now on, I'll work for forty-five dollars an hour. Izzy's making that much, so that's what you need to pay me. I have more experience and more training."

First, Richard knew that Izzy was making forty dollars an hour, *not* forty-five dollars. He did not appreciate Mike manipulating the numbers.

Richard responded, "True, you have more experience and more certifications, but Izzy makes more than you because he's much more available. You're in school. Izzy works sixty hours a week."

Mike responded, "You just want a 'yes' man."

Richard agreed. "Yes. Guys who are more available are more valuable."

Mike didn't get his forty-five dollars an hour, or even forty dollars.

Had Mike asked Richard why Izzy made more money, they could have explored ways for Mike to get his increase and Richard the help he needed. Instead, the relationship eroded. Manipulation makes it harder for the other party to trust you.[36] So do not lie about rates, having another offer, or what you were paid in your last job—people can check the data. Be real, no cap. If the other party seems shady, think carefully about doing business with them.

Do your research. Once on the inside, you might ask colleagues what they make. Millennials seem more comfortable with this transparency than older folks.[37] Behavioral economists attribute this comfort to social media and the shared pressure of school loan debt. I encourage skeptical older employees to try being more transparent.

Note too, that promotions are not always a gift. Simona's husband received a promotion offer that included a move to Boston. Before countering with a salary request, the couple calculated the cost of living in Boston compared to Baltimore (at least double). They decided the salary increase must both cover the cost-of-living difference *and* go beyond his former salary to be worthwhile. Simone and her husband had a good BATNA (best alternative to a negotiated agreement) because they liked Baltimore.[38] When the company declined the amount requested, they politely declined the promotion offer.

WINS!

Natassja used these tips to increase her salary from $24,000 to $42,091:

> Prior to taking this course, I would have been happy just being considered for a promotion. After doing some research, however, I discovered that people in my position could potentially make between $38,000 and $45,000. I

would have been okay with making $40,000 but, as we learned in class, it doesn't hurt to ask for more. So, after receiving the offer, I thanked my supervisor for considering me for the promotion and then submitted a counteroffer of $45,000. My supervisor said she would get back to me within a couple of days. She returned, informing me that they could not accommodate the full $45,000, but they were, however, able to offer $42,091. She also offered me flexibility in my work schedule to accommodate my school schedule. I was more than satisfied with that offer but, to not seem too eager, I told her that I needed twenty-four hours to consider the offer. I returned the following day and accepted the offer. For the first time ever, I negotiated my salary, and to my surprise I got what I ultimately wanted. This class has truly been so helpful in providing excellent tools for negotiating.

When I asked how she thought this negotiation might affect the relationship with her supervisor going forward, Natassja said, "I think it helped it. She respected me more."

Entrepreneurs

Even though they have no boss, entrepreneurs negotiate all the time. The better they know their numbers, the better they can negotiate. Yakini shared her experience: "I am in the process of creating my own cosmetic line and have been searching for the perfect lip gloss tubes. I've researched different tubes, so I know that type of quality I want and the cost. I ran into a vendor with the tubes I wanted. They had great customer service and a great rating for delivery speed. However, they wanted three times more than the average vendor. I negotiated with the vendor and provided them with my bottom-line number. . . . I informed the company that their pricing was higher than the average. It may have just been my luck, but they agreed! I felt like a bad and tough businesswoman after that sweet deal!"

Entrepreneurs also need to decide what to charge their clients. Takia Ross, founder of the makeup company Accessmatized, talked to the class about rates: "We're afraid to say the cost out of our mouth. But if you're not breaking even, then something must give. You will either have to cut costs or raise your prices."

"Do you lower your rates if someone cannot pay that amount?" a student asked.

"No, I have a standard rate. If you cannot pay it, you can make an appointment with someone who works with me. If you give one person a discount, then others will ask for one. Plus, I also don't have time to chat with people about their personal financial situation. The negotiation itself costs me money," Takia replied.

She talked specifically about the pressure to offer people of color a discount. If she gave a discount to every person of color, she explained, she wouldn't be able to sustain her business. Learn to hold the line.

CONCLUSION

When you know your numbers, fewer people can negotiate you out of your senses. Standing in your financial truth also helps you avoid power struggles, game playing, and the need to manipulate others. With so many benefits, why do people avoid their financial reality? Usually out of shame and fear. Among those brave enough to look, many find that they have more income than they realize—it just slips away through leaks and mismanagement. Even a humble salary can pay off debt and build a retirement nest egg. Those who build this stability are less likely to make financially risky decisions or accept a bad deal. For example, a savings fund (aka "fuck-off fund") allows us to walk away from abusive partners, employers, landlords, and even tyrannical national leaders.

Start where you are, knowing that your financial situation may be impacted by legacies of oppression and ongoing inequity (ethnic, gender, or otherwise) or family dynamics. Release the embarrassment and map a path to liberation and justice by using the lessons in this chapter. Once you do, cash will no longer rule everything around you.

ACTIVITIES

Financial Biography

Write your financial *future* story, which includes how you wiped away debt and became financially independent. Write about how you feel in relation to money and how you use your money to help yourself and others.

Money Buddy

Find someone who, like you, is committed to taking control of their financial life and start supporting each other. You can read money books and talk about what you are learning and the changes you plan to make. Sometimes it's easier to start with someone *not* in your family. This also helps you practice talking about money.

Mentor Yourself

Negotiation scholar Linda Babcock discovered that women advocate more powerfully on behalf of someone else than they do for themselves. Pretend you are your own mentor and write a letter to yourself offering advice on how to negotiate and manage your money.

Money Date

Take Tessler's advice mentioned above and schedule a money date. You can also have one alone. During her money date, Tessler reviews her cash flow while eating her favorite chocolate and listening to her favorite music.

Stretch the Dollar

With your partner or roommate, pick a month and see how far you can each stretch your money. Maybe you shop at yard sales for children's clothes or take in a matinee movie ticket. The person who saves the most wins their choice of what discounted movie to go to!
(Thanks to Scott Paris for this idea.)

One Thing a Day for Your Money

If taking hold of your finances feels overwhelming, start by doing at least one thing for your money every day. Over time, this builds comfort with money and financial competence. Here are more than a few ideas:

1. Pick up a penny.
2. Pay a bill.
3. Organize the bills in your wallet.
4. Use a coupon.
5. Set up automatic savings with your bank.
6. Cook instead of going out.
7. Shop around to get the best deal.
8. Ask for a discount.

9. Read about finance.
10. Sign up to meet with a financial advisor (a fiduciary!).
11. Write down everything you spend.
12. Review your credit card bill.
13. Look up the interest rate on your credit card.
14. Use points to buy gifts.
15. Go for a walk with friends instead of eating out.
16. Look for a cheaper phone plan.
17. Meet with an accountant.
18. Make a will.
19. Buy a fireproof/waterproof box for your important documents.
20. Post your money goals on your mirror.
21. Dry clean at home (there are easy at-home kits).
22. Look up the salary range in your chosen profession.
23. Open a Roth IRA.
24. Find out the maximum retirement contribution you can make.
25. Find out if your company has a matching program for retirement.
26. Get a book at the library instead of ordering it online.
27. Ask a friend to be your money accountability buddy.
28. Talk to kids about money.
29. Swap money-saving ideas with friends.
30. See if you can return a product that you don't use.
31. Bring your own coffee.
32. Go through one hundred unread emails (money tends to hang out in there).
33. Follow up on reimbursements.
34. Before you buy something, ask yourself why you are buying it.
35. If you cannot pay your whole credit card bill, at least pay double the minimum.
36. Attend a free event.
37. Sign up for a rewards program.
38. Organize a clothing swap.

Take Stock of Your Finances

To negotiate powerfully, we need to know what we have and need for stability.

What is your monthly income?

How much do you owe?

What are your monthly expenses?

Can you survive on your savings for six months?

Do you have retirement accounts? If so, what will these accounts likely generate by the time you retire?

Good Money or Bad? (Class Activity)

Some people keep themselves from having money because they believe that you can become wealthy only by exploiting others. In class, play "Good Money or Bad?" Put up pictures of wealthy people and discuss the ethics of their wealth accumulation. I used author J.K. Rowling (*Harry Potter*), Beyoncé Knowles-Carter, Patricia Bath (pioneer in blindness prevention and treatment), Yvon Chouinard (environmentalist and founder of Patagonia clothing), and Steve Chen (YouTube founder).

CHAPTER 5

Digital (#Facepalm)

OVERVIEW

Digital communication technologies influence *how* we negotiate as well as *what* we pursue. Other people's social media posts shape what we want for ourselves, as do the ads. These digital tools affect our relationships when we stop meeting face-to-face and pursue followers instead of investing in real friendships. This chapter first considers the broad impacts of new technologies, then discusses best practices for negotiating over email, instant messaging, and video. These tips will help you use communication tools in a way that serves your life, rather than detracting from it.

QUESTIONS TO CONSIDER

What was the last thing you negotiated over text or email?

What were the benefits and drawbacks of negotiating this way?

How might a face-to-face meeting have changed the tone and/or outcome?

Stranded during the pandemic, I needed to rent a car. Seeing the insane cost of rentals, I posted an ad online. A young man replied via email, offering his car for $200 a month. We moved to text and then spoke over the phone to discuss the details. We would meet only when he handed me the keys.

Increasingly, we negotiate over multiple platforms and may not recognize these exchanges as negotiations. Figuring out when we meet, who will take out the dog, and who will host Thanksgiving are all negotiations. Their outcomes affect how our daily lives unfold and, as important, whether we build or harm our relationships in the process. Technology also offers advantages for negotiators. New technologies enable us to shop around for competitive pricing and alternatives, thereby making us less desperate. Email and text chains record what was said, allowing us to readily return to a previous promise. Those negotiating in a new language have time to translate their intentions and needs correctly.

Negotiation experts Noam Ebner and Anita Bhappu say that online negotiations can even help with unconscious bias by giving folks with "lower status" or those from historically marginalized groups more of a voice on an issue. In email, people react less to your job title, age, gender, skin color, clothes, or size and more to the quality of your ideas. If you think there may be bias at play, digital negotiations may be your best bet.

But because instant messaging encourages reactions rather than thoughtful responses, in our haste, we can easily misinterpret others' needs and emotions. Those who become more present and savvier in their use of these platforms, however, can strengthen their networks and find workable solutions to digital media's disadvantages.

OUR DIGITAL LIVES

This book appears during a still-unfolding revolution. In the words of Sherry Turkle, MIT professor of the social studies of science and technology, "We have not assessed the full human consequences of digital media."[1] We do know *some* of the consequences, however. Shalini Misra, who researches the psychological impacts of digital stress, says that "cyber-based overload" affects our ability to process information and our sense of well-being.[2] Other researchers, studying the psychological effects of Facebook and Instagram on roughly 130 women aged eighteen to thirty-five, found that "the frequency of Instagram use is correlated with depressive symptoms, low self-esteem, general and physical appearance anxiety, and body dissatisfaction."[3]

Smartphones can numb deeper feelings of loneliness. Have you ever scrolled through TikTok for more than fifteen minutes?

"EVERY SINGLE NIGHT!" blurted Laneisha.

"Guilty!" admitted Briana.

"More than I want to admit," said Lexy.

When you scroll too long, TikTok reminds you to live your own life or at least take a break and get some water. These apps stimulate parts of our brains but satisfy just one small part of us.

Influencers struggle too. Journalist Jenni Gritters interviewed twelve mega-influencers who each said that "they felt tied to a static, inauthentic identity."[4] People let their posting override their thinking so much that now, more people die from accidents during selfies than from shark attacks. In 2018, more than 250 selfie deaths occurred when people fell to their deaths, were electrocuted, or were eaten.[5]

Nafeesat told me how social media affects foreign students like her. She knows people from Nigeria who, when in the United States, "project a kind of flamboyant lifestyle they do not have. This confuses those at home about the reality of living abroad. There is nothing wrong with having a social media presence, as it helps people ease stress, but people have to learn not to communicate the wrong message just to chase clout." Research shows that Nafeesat is right: when we post more realistic photos and follow fewer strangers, we tend to experience less depression (aka #instasad).[6]

Cost to Relationships

Negotiations flow most smoothly when we develop trust and presence. When we stop and listen to others, we communicate care and respect. Unfortunately, digital technologies erode this presence. A research team at the University of Texas at Austin discovered that the mere presence of our cell phones (even in our pockets!) diminishes our focus and cognitive resources.[7] Shalini Misra discovered that regardless of your age, gender, ethnicity, or even mood, having your smartphone *visible* during a conversation decreases the *quality* of that conversation. It makes people less empathetic and less friendly.[8]

"Phubbing," or phone snubbing, means looking at your phone rather than the person in front of you. Studies show that the more you phub, the less people enjoy their time with you.[9] They feel the disconnection. Looking at your phone while with people, even at home, weakens bonds and increases feelings of jealousy.[10] Studies in China, Turkey, and the United States all show that phubbing contributes to loneliness and depression.

Maryann says, "On my first date with my husband, we went to a restaurant, and he pulled out his phone as soon as we got to the table. I said, 'If you have other things you need to do right now, we can reschedule.' He put his phone away!" She carried these strong feelings to their family life, "For the last twenty-one years, I strictly enforced 'no technology at dinner.' I believe this helps recharge yourself and your family. . . . Sometimes, it was very quiet, almost uncomfortable, but that was okay. Most of the time, you end up chatting about something. These times have produced some of the best conversations, whether there was happiness, sadness, or anger." Unless you're waiting for an organ transplant, put the phone away.

When negotiating, phubbing reduces the exchange of information, decreases trust, and can make your counterpart think less of you. And yet I have heard more than one story of people texting during job interviews! Put the phone away. Selena said, "I spent a few hours talking with my mom about my career and academic plans, some fun facts, and this chapter, all completely without my phone. I can honestly say it was one of the best conversations we had because I unplugged!"

When reading messages, slow down. Skimming messages too quickly can make a conflict out of nothing. Britta shared two technology misadventures: "This week, I misinterpreted a work email as something way worse than it was—I thought I was getting taken *off* a project when in fact I was getting more responsibilities!" Thank goodness she did not send a snarky email to her boss. Britta added, "I also had a very heated text exchange with my partner, who was working late all week. We both misinterpreted each other by including little to no tone in our texts when we were both feeling a little neglected." She could have harmed both relationships by hastily shooting off snarky responses.

Parents will want to think carefully about how they mentor children in regard to these devices. Sherry Turkle asks, "If children don't learn how to listen, stand up for themselves and negotiate with others in classrooms or family dinners, when will they learn the give-and-take that is necessary for good relationships, or, for that matter, for the debate of citizens in a democracy?"[11] The stakes are high.

Phones before Food

Phones have become a status symbol. Jenny, who works for a large tech company, chuckled at my cell phone's protective case. She said that in

San Francisco it's a status thing *not* to have a case because it shows that your company will replace anything you break. Staci, a student, talked about the tragedy of poorer people trying to keep up. She told the class about her job in a Baltimore cell phone store where she often saw visibly poor individuals spend hundreds of dollars on cell phones. Her breaking point came when a woman bought a $700 phone while her child stood shoeless and hungry at the counter. Staci left the counter, bought the child a McDonald's Happy Meal, and quit her job. Don't let these seductive tools negotiate you out of your senses.

> Americans check their phones roughly one hundred to two
> hundred times a day. How addicted are you?

I Could Be Anywhere

This book offers negotiation strategies to help you live your best life as well as improve the communities in which you live. Technology, while providing useful tools in these pursuits, can erode our neighborhoods in subtle ways. Talking on the cell phone while walking, for example, makes us walk slower and miss important cues (like a bus coming).[12] We're also less friendly to passersby. It seems small, but multiply this detachment by millions and you change the vibe of an entire city.

Selena says, "My favorite thing about my time in Cuba with no access to my phone other than music, I got to truly experience everything around me. I would go on hour-long walks through the city and meet people, see art, dance with strangers, and take in the beauty. I felt truly free and connected to everything. It was amazing."

Putting down our phones not only helps us live fully, it can keep us from dying. The CDC says that reading or sending a text while driving fifty-five miles per hour is the equivalent of driving the length of a football field with your eyes closed.[13] In 2019, roughly 40 percent of teens reported texting while driving. For whatever reason, white teenagers tended to text while driving more than African American or Hispanic teenagers. If you have a teenager at home, talk to them about distracted driving. Lexy says, "My mom had my whole family download an app that turns off notifications when we drive and informs people that we are driving but will get back to them as soon as it is safe to do so." If you get hit or hit someone else, you will spend your time negotiating with doctors, lawyers, and insurance companies. Probably not your dream.

Get Your Head Out of Your Apps!—Street sign, Victoria BC

When Negotiating, Monotask

Research increasingly shows that we cannot multitask as well as we thought. Digital distraction expert Gloria Mark and her team at the University of California, Irvine, found that an interruption took people about *twenty-five minutes* to recover from.[14] Yikes! To compensate for interruptions, people often increase their speed, which increases frustration and stress.[15] This means that we make more errors.

Most of us need to practice focusing. Jeremy Readleaf found a way to use technology to help many of us focus better. A few years ago, he rolled into his therapist's office stressed out about his inability to focus on his film projects. He told the therapist he needed a "cave day," meaning a day in which he could hide in a cave and work. Caveday was born (see https://www.caveday.org). What began as a few friends monotasking—working on one project at a time—in Manhattan cafés boomed during COVID, and now hundreds of people convene each day online. Right now, I am in one of Jeremy's caves with my phone hidden and my email closed. Companies like Facebook, Instagram, and *The New York Times* also turned to Jeremy and his team for help. Managers find that their employees live in fear of missing something or getting into trouble for not responding to everything immediately. Eventually they burn out. For better relationships, more career success, and less stress, *monotask!* This will make you a stronger negotiator.

In an age of distraction, presence is a superpower.

Your Social Media Persona

Recall that smart negotiators do their research. This means that a client or potential business partner might scroll your social media postings before doing business with you. I search people's social media pages before renting them my apartment. Karah says, "This is why I keep my social media private. . . . I do not give someone who does not know me personally the chance to judge me based on my social media posting." Filling your feed with duck-lip selfies may not be what you want to show a potential employer, buyer, or future investor. Posting only self-glorifying images may communicate to others that you think mostly about yourself. This can be a turnoff to potential partners, both personal and professional. People prefer to hire givers. Go scan your social media postings. How might you look to a potential employer? How might you look to someone who is about to do business with you?

NEGOTIATING ONLINE

> Bargaining over the internet is like flying a plane without any radar.
> —Scott, student and retired economist

Trust builds when we express our thoughts, share personal details, and even unconsciously reveal ourselves through our clothes and body language.[16] Gauging people's emotions and needs becomes difficult without the visual cues that help us understand others and determine how others respond to us.[17] We do not know whether our message comes off as mean, arrogant, cold, apathetic, or insincere. Of course, we can communicate without being next to each other—humans have written letters for years. What has changed is the speed. In the mid-1700s, a letter took two weeks to travel from Philadelphia to New York. Today, we have grown accustomed to instant feedback and can too easily freak out when we do not hear back immediately. Improving our online negotiation skills begins with managing expectations around response time.

Managing Anxiety

Waiting for a reply after you send a message, how long before you worry that maybe the person doesn't respect or value you? How long before you become angry? I asked students how they react when someone doesn't respond immediately.

Briana: "I automatically think the worst."

Natassja: "I freak out if I don't hear from my boyfriend one day."

Matthew: "Wow, your boyfriend is lucky. My wife freaks out if she doesn't hear from me in two hours! Once I was taking a nap and she actually drove home from work to find out why I wasn't responding to her messages!"

Are these reasonable expectations? Is responding immediately a sign of respect, and is waiting a sign of rejection?

Many people take silence as rejection. John and Julie Gottman, renowned for therapeutic work on marital stability, help us understand why. In happy couples, bids for attention receive responses. For example, if I say to my husband, "Ugh, this is so frustrating," while working on a task, I feel acknowledged if he responds, "What's up?" If I continue to express frustration and he says nothing, I may feel ignored. No big deal if it happens occasionally. Couples headed for divorce, however, regularly ignore bids for attention.[18] New technologies extended this immediate bid-response expectation to all kinds of personal and work relationships.

Expectations differ. Do not assume that others operate on your timeline.

Natassja said, "I view it as being inconsiderate and rude when someone reads your text and takes six hours to respond back. . . . When negotiating, I think it is important to respond back within the first thirty minutes of when the last message was sent."

Karah disagreed. "Thirty minutes! That's not enough time. Personally, I give someone twenty-four to forty-eight hours to respond. After that, I will send a follow-up."

Managing your own anxiety is critical to online negotiation.[19] People take time to respond for many reasons. Lexy gave the example of working ten-hour shifts at Target, where she could check email only once a day. Some people need more time to think.

When you feel anxious about a lack of response, try this strategy offered by author/philanthropist Tony Robbins. When someone doesn't behave the way you expect, ask yourself, "What else could this mean?" Then think of five possibilities. You can make some of them silly.

Maybe your boss didn't respond because

- she binged on ice cream last night and feels too gross to respond,
- she is having gum surgery,
- she is caught under a heavy object, or
- her dog died and she's scrolling through her photos reliving the good times.

Thinking about the other person's world—even in ways that make you laugh—softens you. When they do respond, you will be less angry and more curious.

Laneisha said, "As someone who has a lot of abandonment trauma and needs a lot of reassurance, I resonate with this [discussion]." For people especially sensitive to abandonment, I suggest posting a note where you can see it that reminds you, "Delay Is Not Abandonment."

While waiting, use the time productively. Prepare better for the negotiation by learning more about the company or service.[20] If job searching, apply for another job. Options will decrease your anxiety and make you feel less dependent on that person or opportunity. You can read more about your field to increase your expertise. Or, you can make a list of everything you said you were going to do but haven't yet done—and do it. When you hear back, you won't come off as desperate. Chill, breathe, and don't decide what silence means. If you have not heard back in several days or a week (depending on the situation), you can inquire again.

Use the time.

Now, with our anxiety in check, let's turn to the potential and perils of email, text, and video for negotiation.

EMAIL

Accurate and persuasive email messages can elevate your work life and even your love life. Alan Dennis of Indiana studied seventy-two college students and found that people had more emotional investment in email than in voicemail, even when it came to romantic messages.[21] So, how can we bring out the best in ourselves and others over email? Negotiation expert Stuart Diamond encourages us to think of email as "sort of like tofu—it takes on the flavor of what the recipient is feeling at the moment."[22] By this he means that the mood of the recipient affects how they interpret the email. So choose your words carefully. When possible, use email to continue a relationship rather than start one.[23] Phone calls (video or audio) make connection and empathy easier. Even when negotiations shift to email, call occasionally, and meet in person when possible, to keep communication flowing well.[24] The moment the email tofu starts to taste bad and the exchange becomes tense, back away from the keyboard. Downward spirals can be hard to correct online, so move to the phone or meet in person if the tone changes.[25] After speaking, send an email summarizing what was discussed. This helps everyone stay on the same page.

The Opening

When you cannot speak or meet before the negotiation begins, the *initial message* becomes critical.[26] Stuart Diamond recommends starting with something personal.[27] Maybe you just moved and are surrounded by boxes. Or you just had a major life event. Or think space and *time*. If it's Monday you can say, "I hope you had a nice weekend." In

January, wish the other person a "Happy New Year." If you are in the same geographic location or know something about events in their location, say something locally relevant, such as "Those wildfires have been really devastating. I hope you and your family are safe." You can also say something about where you are. "Dear Zita—Greetings from sweltering Oakland."

If you are connected via social media, you can also ask about or comment on any recent posts. If they say their son graduated, congratulate them. But then let it go unless they bring it up again. Demonstrate your care and interest for the person beyond business. Keep it general unless they offer more. Tiffany, for example, does not like it when strangers or acquaintances say that they will pray for her or her family. Use your judgment to make sure that your comment feels appropriate for the context.

People increasingly use ChatGPT and other artificial intelligence tools to write professional email and save time. While these tools can be useful for tone and grammar, do not skip the personal touch. The more you can build an authentic connection, the better able you and the other person will be to handle conflicts as they arise.

Body of the Message

Now for the content. Research shows that people more often reach a good agreement if someone says in the initial email that you have an intention to pursue a mutually beneficial outcome (good for both). For example, if you see a used car you like, write an email to the seller saying something like "Dear Karim, I saw your ad for the 2019 Honda. It looks like a great car. The asking price is a bit steep for me, but I think we can find a price that works for us both. Would you be willing to chat with me?" This message has an optimistic, team-player attitude.

Emmanuel "Manny" Forge, a former Mercedes Benz car salesman, offers additional tips for using email to negotiate the price of a used car. Because car sales are a month-to-month business, Manny says communicate that you plan to buy soon. He says to write the salesperson something like "I'm interested in buying a car in the next two weeks," rather than "I'm interested in one of your cars." Then tell them your alternatives, which could be a car at a different dealer or even sticking with your old car. He encourages you to have options, because the more you commit to one car, "the more they control the negotiation." Finally, he advises including an offer (what you're willing to pay) and the date you want to move ahead.[28] This gets their attention. Because different nego-tiations have different norms, find someone with experience in that kind of negotiation.

Negotiation expert Noam Ebner encourages us to avoid sarcasm, cynicism, and even humor in email negotiations. Unless you know the person very well and have laughed together before, avoid clever com-ments. People may not recognize the sarcasm or humor, or they may take you less seriously. When it comes to the details of the negotiation, being "basic" (unoriginal) is a good thing.

When negotiating via email, be basic.

Responding

Given how anxious people can become while waiting for a reply, make a habit of telling them that you received the message and when you plan to get back to them. You can just write "Thanks for your message. I will respond later this week." Give yourself some space. Use the time to seek advice or do some research.

Natassja rightly encouraged her peers to "read messages fully and multiple times" before responding to any important email, "to be sure that you are understanding the other party." Slowing down and reflect-ing before sending anything can prevent conflict or at least keep one from escalating. When this happens, we find ourselves using our skills to clean up a mess *we* made, instead of solving the original problem.

Misunderstandings can occur when we read email in distracting envi-ronments.[29] I used to read email while waiting in line at stores or while my husband drove. But after overreacting to some messages and misin-terpreting others, I now wait until I can be fully present. I also found myself annoyed to be asked certain requests while at the supermarket. This, of course, makes no sense, as *I'm* the one who decided to open my email in the supermarket! We are highly irrational creatures.

When fully present, we can think through the content of the message and figure out the best approach. Tiffany read and reread a message from EZPass (a company that offers an electronic way to pay highway tolls) that denied her request for a waiver of unpaid tolls. She took time to write a message that "appealed to their empathetic side and I was able to walk away with a waiver that cut my cost in half from $800 to $400!"

In negotiations that require multiple email messages, continually restate what was agreed to in prior messages and list what remains to be decided. You can write something like "$10,000 sounds very reasonable. Thank you. Can we now just confirm payment options and the pickup date?"

Subject Lines

In ongoing discussions, update the subject line to reflect the status of the negotiation. For example, you do not want the subject line to read "Are you selling the 2018 Honda?" if you have moved to negotiating the payment options. This can be confusing and even slide the conversation backwards. Updating the subject line helps you guide the conversation. In other words, "Wrapping up: 2018 Honda" guides you both toward the completion of the negotiation. If you are not ready to commit, a subject like "Clarifying questions" alerts the party that they have some work to do before the sale will go through.

We tend to read email in opposite order, from the most recent message backwards.[30] So changing the subject line helps new joiners keep pace. Let's say you're planning a work conference, and two weeks into the email discussion someone adds Betty in accounting. Everyone finally settled on the Pearlstone Center for the event, but Betty writes, "What about having it in the Manassas Ballroom?" Everyone sighs, thinking, "Betty, we already picked the location. Catch up." Help Betty by updating the subject line.

Catherine, who read an early draft of this chapter, said, "I actually started doing this because of email threads with you! I noticed that you would always change the subject line to fit with the change in the conversation, so I started doing it with other people. I haven't seen other people doing this and now I find it really annoying [that they don't]." Catherine works in our university writing center, and she explained some confusion with the director when he sent her a message using an old thread titled "Adding you to the schedule next week." Catherine panicked, assuming that she now had to work during finals week. It turned out the director was working on *next year's* schedule. Reflecting on the mix-up, she said, "I didn't mind him using the same email thread, but it would have prevented me from feeling anxious and worried if he had used a different subject title!" If you use an old chain to find someone's email address, make sure you change the subject line to match the message content. Some email platforms, like Gmail, require you to expand the screen to see and change the subject line. It's annoying, but worth the extra step.

Write and Revamp

Write clearly and avoid mistakes. The other person will take you more seriously.[31] People may misinterpret mistakes as a sign that you are in a hurry and not giving them the time that they deserve. We're sensitive creatures. To avoid this, Mormon, an investigations analyst, says she likes to type out important messages first and then transfer them to email. She says, "This allows me to proofread and check my argument before sending it, and also eliminates the possibility of sending it before I am ready." Maryann adds, "I have found that reading something aloud helps too. I often catch mistakes and can correct them before sending them."

Watch out for email written on a smartphone. Catherine says, "When I look at those emails later, I tend to notice typos. This just gives me more anxiety because I think to myself, 'Now, I look unprofessional. I should've waited a few hours until I got home to respond on my laptop.'"

Writing While Angry

Writing while angry or upset can be as dangerous as texting while driving. It can kill a relationship. Our class watched it happen. Johanna tried completing a class assignment via text with Brent, a classmate at the hospital with his son, who had suddenly fallen into a coma. Brent's understandable grief transferred into an attack on his classmate. The two of them fell into a texting tailspin that killed their relationship. He could have simply written, "I'm at the hospital with a family emergency. Let's ask for an extension or get you another partner."

If you write while angry, please do not press send until you calm down and reread it.[32] Nafeesat writes her response out in notes, often finding that "the moment I get done typing and reading it, I never see the need to send it again." It's only a matter of time until artificial intelligence will scan our messages, warning us that our language sounds hostile and is likely to prompt a negative response in the recipient. Until then, prevent yourself from sending something you regret.

To prevent the tofu effect—the other person's mood affecting how *they* read your email—read your message as if you are a recipient who is angry or in a bad mood.[33] Also, read your email as if you are feeling vulnerable or insecure. A little bit of reassurance and respect can go a long way.

You want your message to maintain closeness and trust while giving others space to make their own decisions.[34] Negotiation expert Daniel

Shapiro says this is the key to healthy negotiations. Laneisha says, "I love this advice and definitely agree with it! In romantic relationships, for example, yes, you and your significant other are a couple but both of you are also individuals."

Because people often skim or skip the ends of email messages, convey the tone quickly and keep the content short. When in doubt, err on the side of being respectful and professional and imitate the other person's tone and length.[35] I find that the more powerful person often writes shorter email messages.

One topic per email works best. Catherine says, "Whether it's emailing financial aid about a billing problem or reaching out to an advisor or professor, I've learned to only *bring up one concern* or *ask one question* per email. If I bring up too many questions at once, individuals tend to only address my first and/or last concern—anything in the middle is usually overlooked."

To hear back more quickly, end your message with a question. Sometimes people do not respond because they are not sure exactly what you want from them. A question forces you to clarify what you're seeking and helps them as well. Does that make sense?

Email negotiations that go well can affect your life in profound ways. Shawn shared this success with the class:

> My wife was informed she would be taking a 20 percent pay cut at work that was going to start this past Monday. This couldn't have happened at a worse time. As you know, we are two weeks away from closing on our house. This cut could have caused us to lose the home and the money we spent so far. We thought about it and decided to send an email to the owner of the company.
>
> My wife started the letter thanking him for doing everything he did to save our jobs. In the email, we included that we are a few weeks away from closing on the house and this could cost us the home if the bank finds out. We asked if my wife could keep her full pay now and then start the pay cut after we close on the house. The owner of the company emailed back five minutes later saying, "Yes, I could do that." He told her to keep it confidential. The company would still verify her current pay when the bank called again to confirm that she still has a job.

Do not underestimate the power of a thoughtful email. Start practicing today.

Stranger Danger

Beware of any deal that sounds too good to be true, especially from strangers.

While taking a blood sample, a nurse asked me how to negotiate with someone who contacted her via email hoping to buy a virtual sword she had somehow acquired in a video game. She said, "They offered me $30,000 for the sword! It's not even a real sword. Is this legal? Can I sell this? Do I have to pay taxes on it?" We decided she should talk first to her accountant and be careful what personal information she shared.

Inbox Colonic

Many negotiations stall or fail because of an unread message, or a message lost in a spam folder. To demonstrate how often we all drop the ball, I assign an "inbox colonic." Colonics help unstick all the fecal matter trapped in your large intestine. In crasser terms, colonics clean out your shit. While medical experts debate the health benefits of colonics, students offer more unequivocal support for the inbox colonic, even if they at first cry in despair when asked to reduce their inboxes to fewer than one hundred messages. I encourage them to unsubscribe from anything they do not use or read. Then the results roll in:

Karim found a job offer, called the employer, and got the job.

Brendon found several large unpaid medical bills and set up a payment plan that allowed him to avoid late fees.

Veronica combed through six thousand messages. "I found a lot of missed opportunities to redeem coupons for restaurants and hair salons, and promo codes for tickets that I would have actually used."

Maryann said, "I realized that I was no longer on the free subscription for Sirius XM radio and have canceled that service. That saves me twenty dollars per month."

Gloria saw how the inbox colonic helps you stay on top of relationships: "I found an invitation to a bridal shower from 2018," she said. "It's funny because at the time I saw pictures from the event on Instagram and Facebook and wondered why I wasn't invited, since I was invited to the wedding. I came to find out that the invitation to the bridal shower was in my email." Gloria was not alone in these discoveries. Much of what we seek could be waiting in our inbox. That $100 a month you need to pay down your credit card may be sitting in your email in the form of coupons and invoices for unused services. Britni said, "I would recommend everyone do this, if not every week, then every two weeks. I find I'm more organized because of it." With less clutter, you can see the messages that matter.

INSTANT MESSAGING

The negotiation literature remains thin on best practices for instant messaging (IM), so this chapter draws lessons we learned the hard way (#Facepalm). First, don't assume that the other party wants to use IM. Ask them. If yes, pick a platform. (Current choices include WhatsApp, Facebook, Signal, Slack, LinkedIn, TikTok, Twitter, Instagram, and Snapchat.) Use platforms familiar to both parties. If you pick a platform that either of you never checks, this will slow the conversation and could lead to frustration. Always be careful when texting images of documents like your driver's license, birth certificate, or social security card.

Timing

Timing matters. During my advertising career, I met with the agency representing Coca-Cola. Their research found that people respond to advertising messages differently depending on what *role* they are in when they receive it. For example, if you receive an ad for diapers during work, you will not be as receptive as when you are in *parent* mode. In fact, you may be annoyed. Remember, the people you negotiate with have many roles (or wear many hats), such as parent, friend, employee, sibling, student, citizen, and so on. Aim to catch your counterpart when they are most likely to be receptive. For a work negotiation, that means probably not weekend mornings or off-hours. Nafeesat says, "If we are not family or close friends, texting me at the wrong time of the day is a deal breaker." Others agreed. On the recipient end, Catherine warned, "If you start responding to people outside of business hours, they continue to expect this from you."

On the upside, negotiation expert Noam Ebner likes that texting allows you to set your own pace. Those who think quickly can respond quickly. Slower thinkers can take their time to respond.[36] However, as a wise fortune cookie once told me, "Those who are late are happier than those who wait for them." I find that fast responders can become impatient with slower thinkers. Slower thinkers can calm faster thinkers by letting them know they need time.

Speed isn't always an advantage.

When selling clothing online, Catherine learned that responding more slowly worked in her favor. "I posted some new items in my Poshmark closet this morning, and I had one potential buyer "heart" one of the items, send me an offer on the item (ten dollars less than my listing price), and then send me several messages saying things like "I'm really interested in this item," "I'm trying to keep my total under sixty dollars," and "Can you offer discounted shipping?" After sending me all these messages, the interested buyer bought the item for what I listed it for before I could even respond to her! The sad thing for her is that I totally would have accepted her [initial] offer on the item, but she didn't give me the chance to respond!"

Give your offer a chance to breathe.

Texting through the Ages

Remember that people use texting in different ways. On average, in the United States, the most active texters—those sending roughly fifty messages each day—have not graduated from high school, make less than $30,000 a year, and are nonwhite.[37] Our elders, while increasingly tech savvy, may be less comfortable than you with IM and may struggle with shorthand (abbreviations, etc.).[38] Ebner urges older texters not to be offended when younger people use informal expressions, emojis, and strange punctuation or send curt messages.[39]

Think of emojis, images, and GIFs as emotional assists, helping you convey a mood. With people you do not know well, though, these tools can make you seem unprofessional or confusing. Misunderstandings readily follow from lack of familiarity with texting shorthand, as in the following:

Mom: Your great-aunt just passed away. LOL.

Son: Why is that funny?

Mom: It's not funny, David! What do you mean?

Son: Mom, LOL means Laughing Out Loud.

Mom: I thought it meant Lots of Love. Now I have to call everyone back.[40]

When texting with strangers, use your words to convey emotions— rather than pictures or abbreviations that, to the uninitiated, may look like flirting or lead to an uncomfortable or dangerous misreading.

Even punctuation matters. Go easy on each other, because not everyone agrees on best practices. Shanae says, "Depending on how you use it an exclamation point can make it seem like you are being way too demanding or extra." Psychology professor Danielle N. Gunraj and her research team at Binghamton University studied how undergraduates interpreted text punctuation and came to a different conclusion. Their participants found text messages with exclamation points *more* sincere than those end-ing with a period. For whatever reason, periods seem to freak people out over text, so avoid it.[41] Laneisha discovered this too: "I was an avid user of the period. People would call me out and say that I sounded too serious all the time. I just recently stopped using it when texting." For Lexy, it's generational: "I tend to use periods in text only when texting older generations concerning more serious matters." Be mindful of your choices.

Texting Negotiation Example

Sam: What price are you asking for the TV?

Angie: Well, it's still brand new in the box. What did you want to spend? I paid $165 for it on sale.

Sam: I was looking to pick up a TV for less than a hundred bucks.

Angie: I'll take ninety for it.

Sam: If I pay cash, how about eighty-five?

Angie: Sure.

Sam doesn't know if Angie would have accepted less, and Angie doesn't know if Sam would have paid more, but they both walked away happy.

Nastygrams

Keep messages clean and simple over text. When it comes to professional texting, experts Andrea Kupfer Schneider and Sean McCarthy advise using text to say you are running late, for example, but not to ask for a raise.[42] Avoid "nastygrams," meaning snarky or critical messages. I also recommend against using IM to communicate complex or negative emotions, which rarely get resolved via text.

Texting Gurus

With so few negotiation studies on texting, I turned to the real texting experts—dating coaches. Their advice rings true for negotiation as well. First, they disparage meaningless messages like "hey" or "hello" that offer no more content. When negotiating with someone via IM, do not over-give. Dating coach Matthew Hussey—who has advised Christina Aguilera, Eva Longoria, Ryan Seacrest, and Tyra Banks, among others—specializes in these texting matters. He says, "Meet him where he is. If he's barely investing, don't invest more back in your response.

If he says 'Hey' and you say 'Hey!', then walk away. Don't over-invest, but don't sever the relationship. Match the investment."[43]

How soon do you reply? This can be a delicate question. Natassja says, "If my boyfriend takes a long time to respond to my messages, then I'm slow to respond to him." Dating expert Matthew Hussey says that this kind of game playing erodes relationships. His advice? If you receive a text and you're available to respond, reply. Waiting four to five hours might lose the momentum, especially if they want to tell you about something that just happened.[44] Laneisha agrees: "I think most people avoid replying quickly because they don't want to look 'thirsty' [desperate]. This is how I used to think, but as I got older, I just realized that I didn't have time to fake like I was busy. If my phone is in my hand, I will most likely reply in seconds to minutes with no shame."

If you do not hear back, avoid monologues like the one below.[45]

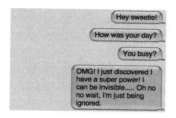

Seeing this text chain, Laneisha said, "For me, this is the type of thing that will get someone blocked very quickly." Nafeesat responded, "I agree, there's not going to be a second conversation after this." What kills relationships kills many negotiations. If you don't hear back, be careful about sending a barrage of messages that come off as aggressive and reveal your impatience.

Finally, when walking away from a negotiation, please tell your counterpart. Ghosting (disappearing) erodes relationships and trust. Be classy and thank them for their time. Plus, you never know when you might need them again. This is as true for employers as it is for potential employees.

Texting as Care

I want to acknowledge the beneficial power of texting. To strengthen your relationships, you can use texts to check on people without asking for anything. Laneisha says, "I actually have a group chat with two of my best friends and we made a rule that all of us must check in to the chat at least once a day." Research shows that this practice can improve our well-being. Adrian Aguilera, a social welfare professor at the University of California, Berkeley, and a clinical practitioner, supports low-income Latinos struggling with depression and other forms of mental distress. He and fellow researchers studied the effectiveness of texting check-ins between sessions. The results have been positive.[46] People's compliance with taking medicine improved, and so did their mood. Who can you check on right now?

Texting Summary

Instant messaging is a great negotiation tool for connecting and clarifying. But IM is not the forum to test a relationship or play mind games. One student bragged to the class that he likes to taunt people by starting to text but never finishing. They see the three bubbles and keep waiting for the full message. His classmates were not impressed. Successful texting (and care of the relationships involved) requires sensitivity to how others receive your messages. Here are a few simple guidelines for text negotiations:

- If you can respond, please do.
- Mirror the other party's message length and punctuation.[47]
- Avoid text monologues.
- Avoid emotionally charged texts.
- Communicate simple ideas.
- Tell people if you need time to respond.
- Use text to check in on family and friends.

Following these points will help lower anxiety and avoid tailspins. Caring about the other party's emotions builds the foundation for a longer-term relationship and increases your chances of a mutually satisfying outcome.

VIDEO CONFERENCING

Video negotiations sidestep many texting and email challenges but have their own pitfalls. The first challenge is stable internet access. Test your connection before an important call, especially if in a new location. As Andrew told the class, "The last thing you would want to happen is for you to be on the verge of closing a discussion and your internet fails. Also, if your network connection isn't stable, you can come off as unprofessional, or unprepared."

Video conferencing reveals class differences and inequities. So ask tactfully if the other party has a stable connection. If either person struggles with connectivity, switch to the phone. Repeated disconnections during a conversation can irritate participants, leading them to confuse their frustration with the internet with a frustration with you!

Unconscious biases (age, gender, ethnicity, class) return on video. Negotiation expert Noam Ebner suggests speaking to these differences by saying something like "Isn't it nice that we can come together from such diverse places?"[48] Highlighting these differences can be an asset, but I find that relationships flourish when we focus on commonalities and our shared purpose, rather than on what separates us. The equality of box size and fewer visible indicators of wealth and status on video can help diminish status posturing.

Your Movie Set

For an important negotiation or meeting, test your background and control your environment (as much as possible). You may recall the lawyer who, during a judicial hearing, appeared as a cat due to a Zoom filter he could not undo. He told the judge, "I don't know how to fix it. I'm not a cat." Then there are the kids, animals, and housemates caught on camera at an inopportune moment.

Whether or not they mean to, people will judge you on your setting. Vlogger Ally Long offered these tips:[49]

- Place the camera at eye level to make it feel like an in-person meeting.
- Test the audio and check background noise.
- Keep a cup of water nearby, but no food. Eating looks and sounds bad.
- Turn off notifications.
- Use a headset.
- Ensure good lighting.

Natural light works best, so ideally sit in front of a window. Otherwise, use artificial light with care. I prefer full-spectrum lights (happy lights), which can boost your mood and help you relax so that you can focus.

Now for your background. If you feel embarrassed about your environment or want privacy, use a blank wall, blur your background, or use a virtual background. A fun background can be a good conversation starter. Choose thoughtfully, however. If you are negotiating a lower rate or a raise, avoid images of your fancy vacation destinations. Also, avoid colorful backgrounds that wash you out. The same applies to virtual backgrounds that cut off your head when you move.

Remember posture. Researchers from Harvard and Columbia University found that sitting in open, erect postures decreased cortisol and helped people feel more powerful.[50] When people feel powerful, they advocate better on their own behalf. Slouching or letting your shoulders collapse cedes power and can give the impression that you are disengaged. Students studying online may find a slouchy semester working against them when they negotiate for a grade increase or an extension. Colleagues told me of students cuddling with partners during class, brushing each other's hair, and cracking open beers. Unless you just had back surgery, sit up.

Now for what to wear. Dressing "professionally" is politically charged because it usually means dressing like the dominant group. Historically marginalized groups and others may understandably want to push back on these cultural expressions of power. You need to decide if, when, and how you want to challenge structural norms. One student used the entire class to win a negotiation with her employer, Johns Hopkins Hospital, over her frequent change of hair color. They forbade these constant changes for a variety of reasons. She made no progress with them and eventually quit. Pick your battles and remember, even powerful people have their clothes controlled. I know a huge software company that chooses the clothes of their employees who present at their annual conference. They understand that appearance affects how people receive information. Make sure the colors work on camera, and watch out for jewelry that hits microphones.

Dress for the context. If you will meet with a loan officer at a bank, dress "bank." For a meeting with a web designer, a nice t-shirt might be okay. When in sales, I followed the rule of dressing just a touch better than the potential client, but not so much better that it looked like I was trying to get rich off them. In sum, dress appropriately while honoring your personal style and/or heritage.

So, before the meeting, check your internet, video setup, and outfit, then clear your work space and hide your phone. During the meeting, turn off "self-view" to keep your focus on the other party, rather than on your hair or makeup.

The Conversation

Harvard Business School's Deepak Malhotra sees people giving up too soon during video negotiations.[51] When parties travel for a negotiation, everyone works harder to find a mutually satisfying solution. Sharing meals and laughing together during breaks builds the trust needed to find solutions. We lose this online. Without the breaks, people tend to move forward more linearly, Malhotra observes. However, you do better when moving between *different* issues. Malhotra calls this "log rolling," or moving from issue to issue and then returning. This helps everyone better understand priorities and trade things of unequal value. For example, you could discover that time may be more important to them than money. If you decide on the time before you decide on the money, you may miss an opportunity for increased value for both.

Malhotra offers these additional tips:

- Send an agenda beforehand that includes breaks every half hour or so. This prevents video fatigue.
- In advance, send the proposal to be discussed.
- Manage expectations and plan future meetings before the first one, which takes the pressure off having to solve everything at once.
- To preempt misunderstandings, commit to giving each other the benefit of the doubt and letting each other know if something sounds aggressive or off-putting.
- Leave time for silence. Participants need space to think and emotionally process information as well as share concerns.
- Afterward, send an email summarizing the conversation.

New Research

More best practices will emerge as people report results of various studies. For now, the most useful study I found came from my student Ben Rogers, who conducted the first known study of online community mediation.[52] Mediation is a form of conflict resolution often involving two parties and an individual trained to help them find a way forward. Ben surveyed mediation participants and interviewed professional mediators at Community Mediation Maryland. These mediators help people (regardless of ability to pay) with discrimination issues, neighborhood arguments (noise complaints, etc.), roommate disputes, love triangles, addiction-related conflicts, school disputes, and custody battles.

Although mediation differs slightly from negotiation, these findings can serve negotiators. The good news is that over 70 percent of the participants responded favorably to online mediation. The mediators saw several benefits of online mediation. First, mediators noticed fewer intimidation tactics between participants because body posturing and dirty looks became more difficult to notice. As a result, participants felt safer and spoke more freely. This became especially important in cases involving personal violence.

The video environment also increased transparency about the process. Mediator teams often signal to each other, using glances to guide the conversation. Without that ability, they discussed options directly with participants. This gave participants more say in how the process unfolded. The biggest advantage was access. Online mediation removed barriers to mediation services for those who lack adequate or reliable transportation, or who have child-care issues, little time for in-person mediation, physical limitations, or chronic illness that makes travel difficult.[53]

The challenge, as with negotiation, is ensuring that everyone has a strong internet connection and a place to meet. Some of the participants struggled to find a quiet, private space to have the mediation, leaving them distracted by noises in the background. Mediators reported different challenges. Trained in nonverbal communication, such as body language, they struggled to gauge participant satisfaction and sincerity. Online participants could more easily manipulate their reactions. Able to see their own expressions on video, they could alter visual cues. Online, people can check their poker face and remove any giveaways that reveal their feelings. So, you may need to ask more direct questions about how people are feeling about the options on the table.

DIGITAL NEGOTIATION FOR SOCIAL TRANSFORMATION

What about negotiating for social transformation? For starters, new technologies allow more people to document rights violations. In 2021, seventeen-year-old Darnella Frazier ignited massive protests through her video of George Floyd's murder. Around the world, people increasingly use smartphones to record war crimes, hate crimes, police brutality, and other forms of violence. Increasingly these videos make it into courtrooms.

When negotiating for social transformation, new technologies offer other advantages. Email requests for social change can be sent and responded to more easily than letters. Justice-seeking groups can launch social media campaigns to pressure companies and/or governments to change their policies. Online petitions circulate quickly, gaining momentum with every digital signature.

Unfortunately, huge numbers of digital supporters and the new ease with which large protests form do not yet translate into stronger movements. Authoritarian states, acutely aware of the power of new media, have developed countervailing technologies of censorship and surveillance. What is more, most digitally networked social movements lack the depth of connection and commitment needed to sustain themselves and advance social change, according to Columbia University sociologist Zeynep Tufekci.[54] Social change requires strong networks, with participants who know how to negotiate powerfully and persistently on behalf of others.

Part of your power comes from your credibility. So be careful what you share. Online, lies travel faster than truth.[55] A study found that on Twitter people retweeted false news stories 70 percent more often than true stories. Deb Roy, who worked on the study, encourages us to pause and think carefully before exposing our networks to potentially inaccurate news. False stories damage your credibility and the credibility of your movement.[56] So be careful what you share. Check your sources, then repeat solid facts as best you can. In class, when we reviewed the Baltimore homicide statistics database maintained by the *Baltimore Sun*, Latierra said, "I don't believe these numbers. I know someone who was shot ten times and left in Druid Hill Park. He's not listed here." It's painful to see someone excluded from these sources. Perfect data will be difficult to find, but do your best.

Before posting an article to advance a cause, ask yourself whether the post offers solutions or simply upsets people. Does it foment love or hate? Those negotiating for social transformation illuminate pathways forward rather than simply describing hell.

Finally, because many people engage in self-harm and violent behaviors out of loneliness and desperation, we can sometimes best strengthen communities and movements by getting free from technology. Great negotiators know how to be physically and emotionally present with the people around them.

SUMMARY

When negotiating online, be present and intentional, staying focused on the needs of both parties and the trust level. Adjust accordingly. If the deal starts to wobble or the relationship starts to feel insecure, meet in person or on the phone. If in-person meetings scare you, practice by having coffee meetings with people when nothing is at stake. Then you will be more comfortable when the meeting matters. In an era of digital networks, those who still know how to connect in person become increasingly valuable.

ACTIVITIES

The following activities will help you enhance your ability to thrive online.

Inbox Colonic

We can easily lose track of conversations when our inboxes are full. An inbox colonic helps you keep on top of your negotiations. The challenge: Get at least one of your primary email addresses down to under a hundred messages. Unsubscribe from anything you do not read.

Did you find money, pay bills, or respond to people waiting to hear from you?

Where You Thrive Online

Every day for one week, jot down what communication technologies you used and how you used them. What did you negotiate about? Plans? Money? Did you use the tools to connect with loved ones or to build your network? What did you post and what was the intention of the posts? Reflect on how useful you found the media and on any associated feelings.

Check-In Groups: Selena Method

In a shelter for victims of domestic violence, staff did morning check-ins with residents to discuss their feelings and goals for the day. This also encouraged people to seek help when needed. Selena, who worked at the shelter, started this practice with friends in a group chat.

Try it: with a group of friends, family, or colleagues start a group chat in which you check in regularly with

1. one word describing how you feel;
2. one goal for the day, along with who you could ask for help in achieving it; and
3. one thing that made you happy recently.

Messages That Contribute

Make sure that at least one out of three of your social media postings offers something to enrich the lives of others. For ideas, think about whose posts make you feel good, make you laugh, teach you something, or offer valuable information. This builds your reputation as a giver.

CHAPTER 6

Power

OVERVIEW

This chapter begins with a discussion of the forms of power that hinder people and how power can shift depending on context. I then demonstrate how negotiation skills can help you leverage three kinds of power—personal, organizational, and collective—to free yourself and others.

QUESTIONS TO CONSIDER

Think of the last time you negotiated successfully with someone more powerful than you. Maybe it was a parent, boss, teacher, landlord, or business. What did you learn from this experience?

Think of a time when you *avoided* negotiating with someone more powerful. Why did you back down?

After prison, Chris Wilson landed a job with Strong City, a Baltimore nonprofit that prepares adults to join the workforce. Many of these adults understood very little about working life. Chris said, "I can't count how many times people failed to show up for interviews because they didn't understand the importance of meeting obligations every time."[1] Some would later ask about that same job and be shocked to learn that the position was taken. When offered another interview, they would miss that one too. When I asked Chris how he convinced them to show up, his answer surprised me. He called their grandmothers. They would say things like "Yo, slick, why'd you get me in trouble with my grandma?" He did it because it worked about 80 percent of the time. So, if you want to get a forty-year-old man into action in West Baltimore? Try calling his grandma. What worked for Chris may not work for you. Find out how to leverage power in *your* environment.

When contexts shift, so do power and acceptable uses of that power. Selena noticed this working with victims of domestic violence. "Often clients from other countries would tell me, 'He [my husband] does things differently now that we're here [in the United States] because there are more protections for women. He had to adjust how he would abuse me or control me because of this.'"

WHAT IS POWER?

German sociologist Max Weber (1864–1920) defined *power* as an ability to assert one's will despite resistance from others.[2] Psychologist Deborah Gruenfeld, who has researched power for over twenty-five years, similarly defines it as "the capacity to control other people and their outcomes."[3]

Any time we influence ourselves or others to achieve our goals, we exert power.[4] We exercise power when we convince a child to play outside instead of bouncing a ball in the house, or convince customer service to waive a late fee. Those with power can inflict harm, impose a decision, or walk away because they have better alternatives.[5]

FORMS OF POWER

Numerous theorists have created typologies of power, which help us think through the power dynamics underlying our negotiations. French philosopher Michel Foucault (1926–84) describes the dominant forms of structural power, summarized below:

> *Sovereign:* state decisions over who lives and dies, how much one pays in taxes, and how much time is demanded by the state (i.e., abortion, death penalty, tax exceptions, essential workers)
>
> *Disciplinary:* policies designed to prevent or correct behavior the powerful determined to be deviant (e.g., asylums or the carceral system)

Biopower: policies that manage populations by controlling bodies (e.g., mask requirements, vaccine mandates, speed limits, abortion bans)

French sociologist Pierre Bourdieu (1930–2002) introduced the concept of *social power* to explain how people enforce power structures and class hierarchy. While the state exerts the forms of power discussed by Foucault, we police each other by enforcing norms and monitoring class boundaries. This means that even people who love us may try to put us back "in line," and we them. Those negotiating for social mobility, and those wishing to support them, will want to pay attention to subtle forms of class enforcement. In *Caste: The Origins of Our Discontents,* Isabel Wilkerson says that this enforcement of class hierarchy can show up in the form of arguments about divine will, natural superiority, family heritage, control over marriage and sex, values of purity, occupational hierarchy, and the use of terror.

Let's keep these forms of power in mind as we turn to the situational forms of power discussed by negotiation scholars. Peter Kim encourages us to consider four kinds of power common in negotiation:

Potential: the chance of getting what you want

Perceived: your assumptions about your and the other party's power

Tactical: your ability to change the dynamic

Realized: how much power you have claimed[6]

Each of these can be influenced by location, class, and status. As Selena's example of domestic abuse showed, a woman's power can depend on the country's laws and dominant values.

Expert Bernie Mayer encourages us to consider the following ten sources of power before negotiating.[7]

Formal authority: status or title

Expertise: what one knows

Associations: who one knows

Resources: control over time, money, and so on

Procedural: control over the system (e.g., ability to extend a deadline or move a request forward)

Sanctions: ability to inflict harm

Nuisance: ability to cause discomfort—being persistent can be this kind of power (lacking many other forms of power, children use this one often)

Habitual: the person arguing for the status quo (no change) has default power

Moral: you are advocating an ethical position

Personal: confidence, clarity, communication skills, resilience, emotional mastery

Administrative offices often have at least six forms: official power, power over resources, procedural power, sanctioning power, expertise, and habitual power. This usually leaves employees with four forms of power: personal (persuasiveness), nuisance (persistence), associative (who you know), and moral (if your argument is an ethical one).

Here is a personal example. A university employee photographed me for an article. When I asked if I could use the extra photos on my website, the administrator in charge said no. When I asked why she had refused, she said, "It's just not possible. The school owns the photos." Note that those in power often offer short explanations. They lean on procedural norms rather than rationality.

I switched to *persuasive* and *nuisance* power when explaining that this policy made no sense because

- the school would never use the photos again,
- they were of me, and
- they could help me promote my work and the school.

No success.

"Have you ever made exceptions?" I asked.

The woman responded, "We don't have a procedure in place for exceptions."

To which I replied, "I understand, but by definition exceptions don't have procedures."

She refused to budge.

I called upon another administrator to help me (associative power). I ultimately paid for the photos (resource power) and signed some forms. One of the photos now headlines my website. Know their power, know yours, and keep trying different strategies until you reach your intended outcome.

> Think about a recent conflict or negotiation. Which of these forms of power did you have? Which did you lack?

Those with power also control time. Javier Auyero studied bureaucratic abuses of time in a welfare office in Buenos Aires, Argentina. He met people who traveled long distances to spend the day in a waiting room. At the end of the day, officials sometimes told people to return on Sunday or on a holiday when the office would be closed. These ludicrous directives made some doubt their own sanity and left many feeling powerless. Noemi, a woman waiting, said to Javier, "I told my husband: 'I'm going to the welfare office . . . I don't know when I'm coming back.'"[8] Bourdieu would refer to such time manipulation as a tool of domination.[9] If you are unclear about who has power in a situation, consider who makes the other wait without consequence. Note that although we may associate men with power seeking, researchers find that women seek power equally—just in different forms.[10]

FINDING OUR POWER

Regardless of who wields power, it is not static. Even seemingly all-powerful dictators can fall from power. Conflict expert Samantha Hardy told me, "The trick is to identify the power that you have, the power that you can build on, and then decide how to use it for your (good) purposes." Finding your power increases more than your status and your wealth; it affects your health. In 1992, Nina Wallerstein published a landmark study showing that "powerlessness, or lack of control over destiny, emerges as a broad-based risk factor for disease."[11] Wallerstein concluded that finding your power may truly be a health-enhancing strategy.

I will now discuss three forms of power worth cultivating: *personal, collaborative,* and *political.*

PERSONAL POWER

After completing work on her kitchen, a contractor refused to reinstall Menyvette's microwave. Menyvette refused to pay until he put everything back. The contractor called his manager, who agreed to Menyvette's request. That's personal power.

Clarity

Finding your power starts with clarity. Without clarity, others influence you more easily and you can get sucked into conflict spirals. Let's say the contractor refused to reinstall the microwave and Menyvette took them to court. A lawsuit could bury everyone (herself included) in paperwork and legal fees. She wanted a completed kitchen. Remembering this helped her sidestep a mutually destructive approach to the conflict.

Exploring Emotions

Emotions tell us what matters to us, and when something feels off, and they can propel us to act. We become powerful in our negotiations when we understand and channel emotions. Negotiation experts Roger Fisher and Daniel Shapiro help us explore our emotions through their Core Concerns model. In many negotiations, at least one of these factors contributes to our distress:

- Our *autonomy* feels threatened.
- We do not feel *appreciated*.
- Our *status* feels challenged.
- We feel treated like an enemy rather than like an ally (*affiliation*).
- We dislike the *role* we've been given.[12]

Opening the hood on our emotions helps us understand the source and find the solution.

For example, after several months as a manager, Simone found herself angry and frustrated. At first, she thought her anger was about being under*appreciated* and not given the appropriate *status*. As she prepared to negotiate with her boss for a salary increase, she realized that increased *status* and *appreciation* would not make her happier. The real problem was that she did not enjoy her *role* as an administrator. Instead, she applied to jobs working with children, her first love.

When exploring the source of your emotions, keep in mind that they are not perfect indicators. While riding the subway, Rodney watched two young boys roughhousing, screaming, and running around the moving train. Another rider, frustrated with the ruckus, confronted the boys' father about their behavior. The dad asked her to please excuse them. His wife had just died, and the family was just returning home from making her funeral arrangements. The atmosphere in the whole subway changed. We can misread a situation.

Self-Control

Remembering our long-term goals and our values can help us keep destructive emotions in check. A study found that journaling about a cherished value and its role in our lives can lead to increased self-control.[13] Another study found that journaling helped close the GPA gap between European American students and African American students. The African American students engaging in value journaling also reported greater health, well-being, and fewer doctor visits.[14] Before a negotiation, set a timer for ten minutes and write about what you want and what values matter to you most in life. This will keep you grounded when negotiating with someone with more power.

Post reminders of your values and goals where you can see them. Gary, rated Baltimore's best massage therapist, tattooed "Love Conquers All" on his upper chest to help him begin each day with a reminder to bring love to the day's challenges. Growing up in the city, Gary had witnessed the violence and death that occur when destructive emotions take over. Today, with a wife, kids, and a thriving business, he will not allow anger to derail him. I use Post-its, but if you need a tattoo, get a tattoo.

Cooking Raw Emotions

To find lasting solutions, we may need to express our emotions. This helps the other party understand what matters to us and, in some circumstances, prevents repression that can turn dangerous. Earl says, "I've witnessed this in the African American households where emotions are suppressed until there is a lash-out."

Because contexts (and cultures) differ, I offer general guidelines. Please adapt them to your world. Begin by thinking of raw emotions as raw eggs. Few people like raw eggs. So, prepare your emotional eggs before serving them. Maybe you warm them up and add a touch of spice before presenting them to someone else.

Let's say your sister doesn't call on your birthday. Your raw-egg reaction may be "Screw her!" You may want to retaliate by withholding a call on *her* birthday. Then you breathe, journal, and realize that underneath your anger is hurt. How could she forget your birthday? A way to share that emotion is to say, "Tania, I love you, you're such an important person in my life. I know it's maybe silly to care about birthdays as an adult, but I found myself hurt not hearing from you. Are you upset with me or maybe there's something going on in your life?" In that emotional omelet, you expressed how much you value her, aired your feelings, and gave her a chance to express her own emotions. Since few people speak this way, give the person a chance to reflect. They may not be accustomed to this kind of communication. If the other person refuses to engage, you can try again and/or accept that things may never change. Either way, be proud of yourself for modeling a more productive way to express emotions.

Feeling Powerful

Negotiations can be nerve-racking. Will we lose the opportunity? Did we ask for too much or too little? Feeling powerful can help us stay calm and get the best deal possible. Otherwise, we may fold too soon. Research shows that *feeling* less powerful makes us less prone to act, in part because we deliberate more over pros and cons.[15] So, how can we *feel* more powerful when we lack confidence?

Athletes, performers, and public speakers use various techniques to amplify their confidence. Lexy, a former performer, said, "We used to do a prayer or spiritual circle right before going on stage for a show." Others visualize, listen to music, or move their bodies. One research-proven method is recalling a successful moment or a time when you felt in control of a situation. Doing this before a negotiation can help you speak up for yourself, be persistent, stay creative, and not settle for a bad deal. Try journaling for five minutes about a time when you crushed it. If you need to, close your eyes to recall the exact feelings, sights, and sounds. Who was there? What did you say? What did they say?

When negotiating with Amtrak executives, Joy Smith reminded herself that even they were just doing a job for which they received a paycheck. Sometimes I remind myself that no matter how much power the person has, they cannot be sure what happens when we die. Or you can remind yourself that they too have experienced grief, fear, and insecurity. Maybe it's morbid, but I prefer the death one.

One caveat: watch out for feeling so confident that you miss important information. The researchers also found that powerful people think less about the implications of their decisions. They also rarely consider alternative viewpoints and are prone to making risky moves.[16] Get yourself feeling good, but during the negotiation stay vigilant and engaged with the other party.

Knowledge Acquisition

Pursuing knowledge and acquiring skills builds our personal power and prepares us to be creative negotiators. We can do this almost anywhere. While incarcerated, Chris Wilson became what he called a "book crusher."[17] He read everything he could get his hands on and through this expanded his imagination and prepared himself for a successful future. Marcetta, who worked in the prison at the time and saw Chris pursue his education, said, "I saw a lot of people like Chris." Marcetta explained to us that many incarcerated people work to better themselves through education. When we feel stuck in life, we can always read and strive to make the best of our conditions.

Collaborative Power

Creating anything beyond ourselves requires working with other people, often in an organizational setting. Unfortunately, many people think that organizational leadership requires exerting power over others. Mary Parker Follett (1886–1933), a pioneer in social work and management theory, argued that organizational power need not mean domination (*power-over*), but instead can be jointly created (*power-with*). A power-with approach supports healthy give-and-take between members, strengthening the organization as well as its members.

Joy Smith, who in forty years rose from a dining-car service attendant to senior manager of customer service at Amtrak, saw many rising employees mistakenly think that management requires dominating others. She would see people out of high school get a job, say, in a dining car and do a good job. The boss is happy, "now you want to be in charge," she says, "and you're terrible. You have no respect for the people under you. When you think power is about kicking ass and taking names, you're off base. You're paid to be a supervisor. It's not your company, you're not signing paychecks, so how are you in charge?" As manager, Joy *served* those under her so that they could do *their* jobs. To become a beloved and respected manager as a Black woman in the heavily male-dominated industry of rail transport was no small accomplishment.

Power-with is also a powerful negotiation approach within families. When Mel's teenage daughter wanted to see a movie with friends, they figured out how she could see the movie *and* complete her schoolwork. Mel, formerly Baltimore's jury commissioner, advises parents to avoid exerting power over kids and instead "encourage your child to have an opinion and express an opinion. [Help them] to feel confident and to make decisions that will benefit both of you." While some people worry that power-with approaches take longer, Mel finds that the power-with approach saves time by maintaining a happy household and helping kids learn how to make good decisions. When discussing something nonnegotiable with children, she encourages parents to be clear about the limit, rather than pretend there is wiggle room.

Clothing

Negotiations are a performance, which means that your costume matters, but not necessarily in the ways you may think. Yossi Maaravi and Boaz Hameiri studied the effects of looking wealthy by asking participants if they would be more likely to give a carwash discount to a man with a Mercedes or one with a Mitsubishi. Their answer? The Mitsubishi man, presumably because he needed the discount more. In another study, they asked people to imagine themselves as event planners offering a quote for a fifty-person event. When faced with two potential clients— one in jeans and one wearing a suit—they gave the better deal to the person in jeans.[18]

Clothing choices matter when we seek to achieve *power with* communities in need. Nafessat, who worked with Nigerian farmers, said: "In rural community development practice, you want to bring yourself to the level of the rural farmers. Only then will they listen to you. . . . Looking too formal and sophisticated doesn't depict the rural farmers' reality. Understanding farming entails getting your hands and clothes dirty. . . . When you're in a suit, they can never take you seriously. Because you obviously come from the city, they believe they have a lot to teach you." When looking to connect, reduce the visual disparity between you and those with whom you're working.

Anthropologist Brian Thom thinks about his clothing choices when meeting with Indigenous people in British Columbia, Canada, who are seeking a greater political voice, resources, and land sovereignty. He struggles between wanting to look professional and looking too much like hated government officials. For Indigenous spokespersons, traditional dress can increase negotiating power in some official settings, such as the United Nations. Thom recalls the beautiful traditional clothing worn by members to a UN event and how it contributed to their presence during the meeting and afterward through the circulating pictures. Think through how you present yourself, especially in the first meeting.

Titles

Some people negotiate precisely to *enhance* their power or to *feel* more powerful.[19] So err on the side of formality by beginning with titles like *Mr., Ms., Doctor,* or *Professor,* as appropriate. In Nigeria, Nafeesat says, people show respect for elders by using *Sir* or *Ma.* In the Yoruba and Igbo tribes, addressing people by their first names is offensive, she says. "Even customer care representatives will always address the caller as Sir/Ma."[20]

Use of your own title and credentials can help you in a situation with an unfavorable power differential. My friend Paul shared this example: "My surgeon entered my name into the hospital system as 'Dr. Hirsch' because of my PhD in history. So everyone—even the doctors—address me as 'Dr. Hirsch.' I love it. Finally, I'm not being condescended to by every medical person." Play up your qualifications when it's useful. If you started a small company, put "Founder and CEO" in your email signature.

Language

During a negotiation, the person with the greatest command over the language has an advantage. In the nineteenth century, Indigenous peoples of North America negotiated significant treaties using trading languages that had just several hundred words. In other treaty negotiations, the language of the settlers—often English or French—was dominant. Misunderstanding the meanings of the terms, many Indigenous leaders signed contracts they never would have agreed to had they comprehended them. Poet Adrienne Rich expresses their experience well: "This is the oppressor's language, yet I need it to talk to you."[21] When possible, negotiate in the language of your greatest comfort. If you cannot do that, find a reliable translator and/or go slowly to make sure that you understand the terms.

Many people *code-switch* during negotiations—that is, they change their dialect to adapt to the context. National Public Radio (NPR) correspondent Matt Thompson identified five reasons we code switch:

- Our brains do it automatically when we shift contexts.
- We do it to fit in.
- We do it to get something from someone.
- We do it to say something in secret.
- We do it to convey a thought not easily said in another dialect.[22]

Rosalind, a returning citizen who now teaches life skills, said, "Some people call it 'code-switching.' I call it communication." She says that access to multiple dialects gives her the power to reach more people. Nafeesat added how code-switching helped her connect with farmers in Nigeria: "Pidgin English is the only tool that helps me bridge the language barrier, as I cannot speak the local dialect of the northern farmers."

When the dominant culture treats one's native dialect as inferior, code-switching can feel oppressive. In 1897, sociologist W. E. B. Du Bois introduced the concept of "double consciousness," referring to the work African Americans must undertake to see themselves through others' eyes. African Americans have often felt pressure to switch from African American Vernacular English (AAVE, also called Black English and Ebonics) to Standard American English. AAVE has a consistent structure and is as valid linguistically as any other language or dialect. Author bell hooks says that Black vernacular speech originated as a way for enslaved persons to simultaneously claim English while rebelling against it.[23]

Journalist Gene Demby of NPR's *Code Switch* team illustrated President Barack Obama's navigation of multiple worlds with this example: "In January 2009, then-President-elect Obama went to Ben's Chili Bowl, a famous eatery in a historically black D.C. neighborhood. When the (black) cashier asked him if he needed change, Obama replied, 'Nah, we straight.'"[24] Through modeling and direct advice, Obama tells people that being successful requires shifting dialects.[25]

Then we have *jargon,* terms used within a particular discipline, which is notoriously difficult for outsiders to understand. Medicine, law, finance, and other professions often use jargon when communicating with clients. Lisa, forced to take full responsibility for her finances after a divorce, said, "I often allow big terms and fancy phrases to trip me up."

When confronted with jargon during negotiations, remember:

- Ask as many clarifying questions as you need.
- Learn the terms you need to know.

Also watch out for vague terms such as *access, soon, acceptable, timely,* and *satisfaction,* and even simple words like *is.*

Meeting

> Working in retail you feel replaceable. It's hard to find your power.
> —Leigh, student

Your power during a negotiation depends on how much the other person depends on you. In competitive fields or ones with high turnover, you need to make the case for why *you* specifically are an asset. Annie, who has spent over twenty years in the competitive museum industry, says, "I never negotiated, and when I did, I never got what I asked for. I told myself, 'I guess it *was* kind of hard to get this job, so maybe I shouldn't negotiate.' Employers seemed to share that attitude." Even after she was established within an institution, she found it difficult to negotiate on her own behalf. After four years of working at one museum, her boss announced that Annie would train a new person, with ten years less experience and without a degree, for her same position. Annie agreed to train the new person but asked to renegotiate her position and salary. When her boss refused, she quit and started a (now successful) consulting business. When other staff left soon after, the organization had to rethink its approach to staffing. But these shifts may not occur when you need them. Annie's proposed salary and position went to someone else a year after she had left.

Annie learned not to assume that a meeting signaled a negotiation. Some higher-ups will meet with you to placate you or acquire information. Even leaders with so-called open-door policies often use those same doors to shuffle you out. And watch out for human resources (HR) departments, whose mission is to protect the company, not the employee. You can make use of these meetings to explore their openness to your requests, but gauge their receptiveness before making your asks.

Advice

If you have a superior who seems resistant to your input, try asking for advice. Katie Liljenquist's research found that "soliciting advice is an especially useful strategy for navigating hierarchies when people feel they are in a position of weakness or need to cultivate advocates."[26] In longer-term relationships, Liljenquist found that seeking advice "can enhance warmth, sincerity, humility, promote cooperation, induce perspective-taking, and inspire commitment."[27]

When making such requests for help, Liljenquist offers these tips:

- First, allude to *your* competence.
- Say why you seek *their* advice (what skills/experience they have).
- Ask them *how* to do something rather than what to do.

Who could you ask for advice?

Advice seeking can even turn adversaries into allies. Let's say you are negotiating with an airline agent to refund a ticket. Ask the agent something like "Given your knowledge of the company, what advice do you have for me?" This moves the conversation in a problem-solving direction while treating the agent as a potential ally rather than an adversary.

When seeking advice, remember not to cede your power. You are reaching out, not presenting yourself as a victim in need of saving. Being a victim or sucking up to those in power will rarely serve you in the long term. Researchers Carsten De Dreu and Gerben Van Kleef found that when those in low-power positions framed their questions to match the perceived needs of the other party, they did not inspire cooperation. Selfish partners took advantage of them by becoming tougher and more demanding.[28]

BATNAS (BEST ALTERNATIVES TO A NEGOTIATED AGREEMENT)

You can increase your power by increasing your options. As discussed in earlier chapters, William Ury and Roger Fisher call these options BATNAs (best alternatives to a negotiated agreement). Acceptance into multiple universities, for example, can help you negotiate a great financial aid package. Options help us relax by reducing our dependency on one person's actions. You may share them with the other party during a negotiation if you think that this may motivate them to agree to your requests. But, negotiation experts say, "never share your BATNA with the other party if it is hopelessly weak."[29] In other words, if your best alternative to a raise is moving back in with your parents, keep that to yourself.

A word of warning: BATNAs are not for use in generating alternatives to an existing committed relationship. For instance, keeping a backup person in mind can prevent you from giving fully to this person and this relationship. I also advise against BATNAs when advocating the end of a moral evil, such as slavery, atrocity, or abuse. Stay committed and see it through. We will discuss this in the section on political power.

That said, in all situations we can develop our *inner* BATNAs, as William Ury encourages us to do.[30] You can do this by telling yourself that no matter what happens, you will respect and care for yourself. Joy Smith developed her inner BATNA during her four decades at Amtrak by saying to herself, "The job does not define me. It's only one facet of my life. No matter what happens, I can depend on me. I will always find work." Priming, journaling, mindfulness practice, and other techniques can deepen feelings of self-worth and help you stay steady in the face of anger tactics or deception.

Anger

Anger can derail a negotiation or be used to pressure one party into agreement. Studies show that people in positions of power tend to use anger to focus, toughen up, and claim more value.[31] Those with less power become flustered and soften their demands. So, if you are unsure who has more power in your negotiation, ask yourself:

· Who can express anger without negative consequences?
· Who, if they did the same thing, would be dismissed or reprimanded?

Former employees of Microsoft's Bill Gates, Apple's Steve Jobs, and Tesla's Elon Musk have discussed the emotional explosions, hissy fits, and foul language used by these tech CEOs. In fact, they even coach each other. When she became CEO of Pepsi, Indra Nooyi met with Steve Jobs, who coached her on how to throw a tantrum as a way to show people her passion about something.[32]

We see this behavior at the highest echelons of political leadership as well. Ilias Kapoutsis and Roger Volkema studied Donald Trump's negotiation style during his presidency.[33] Trump admits to using a competitive (rather than collaborative) approach to win at all costs. He bluffs, keeps himself in the spotlight, makes false promises, plays the good guy, plays the bad guy, self-flatters, and emphasizes status through his wealth, clothes, and family. For anyone other than dynasts and tycoons, however, tantrums rarely offer more than a fast track to the bottom. The same behaviors, when exhibited by people in the middle class, often lead to dismissal or ostracism.

I had a boss who slammed doors and threw fits when faced with challenges. When I once expressed being upset—behind closed doors, and only to the individual involved—my behavior was reported to headquarters as overly emotional and unprofessional. Yup, that's power, baby.

In sum, explosive anger and tantrums tend to work only if you're the boss or rule by domination. By "work," I mean they produce short-term gains and, maybe, some great products. Tantrum throwers can lose good people and even make themselves and others sick. Anyone who grew up with or lives with someone prone to fits of anger knows the cost.

In business, I never enjoyed dancing around these fits. The slamming doors, the red-hot faces, the shaming of others, the flailing arms—and over what? We didn't save lives—we provided software.

Although I do not prefer this style of persuasion, it exists and we must be prepared to confront it. So I asked students how they handle tantrums. Shanae shared this:

> I used to work for an attorney who would sometimes slack off. We received discovery requests from the opposing party and had thirty days to submit our answers. I completed the answers soon after I received the requests, emailed my drafts to my attorney, and placed the hard copy on her desk. I also set the deadlines and reminders on both of our calendars. Five days before our answers were due, I sent an email reminder. The day before, she came out of her office and asked me if I had filed the answers to discovery. I told her that she never gave me back her edits to file. She had a fit! It was almost like witnessing a two-year-old throw a temper tantrum! I couldn't believe it. She even went as far as complaining about me to our "big boss." I explained to our boss, and to my attorney, that I not only emailed her the drafts, but I placed a hard copy on her desk, set the deadlines on our calendars with reminders, and sent her a reminder via email five days prior. After that, I started to copy our big boss on every email status request and reminder I sent to her! I never had a problem after that. Ha ha.

Shanae learned to protect herself.

Rosalind took a different approach:

> I remember when I was on home detention and worked as a server at this restaurant. I gave the cook the wrong order for a steak, therefore had to discard a very expensive steak, and the owner cursed me out! I could not believe what this man said to me. I was hot on fire! Everybody just looked at me and I said, "I humbly apologize. It was my mistake." You could feel the

tension leave the building. I am grown and mature enough to admit when I am wrong, but know that I pulled him aside later and asked that he never talk to me like that again—and he apologized.

Rosalind owned her piece of the problem and, rather than challenge the restaurant owner in front of other employees, she spoke to him privately later. This helped him save face while giving her a chance to renegotiate his treatment of her.

Shanae and Rosalind knew not to negotiate with someone in the middle of a meltdown (also known as an amygdala hijack) that makes the person unable to process more data and rational arguments. People need to calm down before their neocortex can reengage. This part of the brain can hold conflicting ideas, distinguish right from wrong, and process new information.[34] A hot brain cannot engage productively, so timing matters. "When should people give up and walk away?" I asked. Lauren quit her job because of her boss's tantrums. She realized that things are unworkable "when you're sane and calm and your boss doesn't want to talk about it."

I Respectfully Disagree

Negotiating on our own behalf may require disagreeing or challenging someone with more power. How can we do this productively? Amy Gallo, a contributing editor at the *Harvard Business Review,* suggests considering the following before challenging those in power.

> *Risks:* What might happen if you disagree openly, and what might happen if you don't speak up?

> *Time and place:* Organize your thoughts and think about the best time and place to present your ideas. It might be one-on-one rather than in the presence of others.

> *Tact:* Let them know you have a difference of opinion, serve it to them gently and respectfully, ask their permission to share your ideas, and then present those ideas in terms of a shared goal.[35]

Gallo also suggests that we develop a process for working through disagreements in advance. When starting a new position, you can say something like "We're probably not always going to see eye to eye, and I was wondering how you want me to share my opinion if that happens."

As always, know your context. What works in one situation may not work in another. Understand how power works, navigate it thoughtfully, and know when to walk away.

Deception

Then we have deception. In 1804, the Chiefs of the Sauk Indian Tribe (as they were known) received an invitation to negotiate with the governor of Indiana, Henry Harrison, concerning the murder of several white settlers. The Chiefs came to the meeting and agreed, as their custom dictated, to pay damages to the family. They did not know, however, that Harrison had really called the meeting to convince them to sign a removal treaty that would give the United States modern-day Wisconsin and Illinois. Legend goes that Harrison used liquor to relax the Chiefs, who, even though they were unauthorized to sign such a treaty, did so.[36] They'd been thrown into a sham negotiation ill-prepared. The treaty was clearly unethical. Protect yourself from power plays by remembering that not everyone has your best interests at heart or plays by the same ethical rules.

Wharton professor Richard Shell teaches three schools of negotiation ethics:

Poker negotiators keep their cards close and see bluffing as part of the game.

Pragmatists believe that what goes around comes around. If you cheat, others will cheat you. So they act honorably.

Idealists act morally regardless of its impact on them.

A good example of the idealist approach can be found in the "paradoxical commandments" of Kent M. Keith, made famous by Mother Teresa. For example, "People are often unreasonable and self-centered. Forgive them anyway. If you are kind, people may accuse you of ulterior motives. Be kind anyway. If you are honest, people may cheat you. Be honest anyway."[37]

Which school of ethics do you belong to?

Students often asked about the difference between strategy and ethics. When negotiating, you don't need to share your alternatives, your walkaway point, or the highest amount you will pay. Nor do you have to respond to every question. For example, if a potential employer asks whether you have other job offers, you can say something general like "I'm exploring a number of possibilities, but if we can come to an agreement, I'd prefer to work something out with you." Frame the conversation the way you want, moving to points that you want to discuss or highlight.

If you must negotiate with someone you don't trust, protect yourself by doing your research, putting everything in writing, and saying as little as possible. To test someone's trustworthiness, ask them something you know the answer to, but that they might lie about.[38] For example, you could ask a realtor how often the management of a particular condo has raised its fees. If they say never, and you know that the fees went up last year, this tells you they are either lying or are (perhaps willfully) misinformed.

Good Treatment

While we want to protect ourselves from deception, we don't want to become cynical. In many cases, you can set the tone for transparency and mutual gain. When my husband and I needed to move, we called our landlady and told her how much we appreciated her and that we hoped to help find her a good replacement tenant. While we informed her of our decision to move within the legally acceptable timeframe, we chose a friendlier approach. This enabled us to discover numerous win-win solutions during the transition. She even invited us over to dinner.

> You can win more people over with honey than vinegar.—Lisa, student and pre-K teacher

Even if you cannot fulfill the other party's desires, how you treat them during a negotiation affects how they feel in the aftermath. Ginger, a former public defender in Baltimore, talked about the importance of process and perceived fairness. "When I think back to my practice, some of my most grateful clients were found guilty at trial." They often faced circumstances, such as parole violations, that rendered the state unwilling to negotiate. "As long as those clients felt they had a zealous advocate defending them, and as long as the judge gave me adequate opportunity to be heard and showed the defendants respect and courtesy, they generally accepted the outcome." We can always treat people with dignity and respect.

COLLECTIVE POWER

To change a broken system, we need to leverage our collective power. So I asked students, "How might negotiating for social justice differ from negotiating for a salary?"

Nedra, an elder-care advocate, said, "Negotiating for social change is different than negotiating for a salary, or a job, etcetera, because it requires changing attitudes, feelings, beliefs, values, perceptions and behavior for everyone, for humanity."

Ginger added: "Negotiating for social change often involves demonstrating the worth of an idea or set of values rather than the worth of an individual or set of skills. It involves navigating complex power structures and a myriad of entrenched interests."

Exactly.

Andrew, now a professional basketball player, challenged my question. "Why should I have to negotiate for something that's my basic human right?" he said. "Why should we have to negotiate to not be killed by the police? Why should we have to negotiate to get equal opportunities in education or housing? These are human rights issues that don't operate under the same set of circumstances as a business transaction."

"Andrew, I agree with you," said Toby, a security analyst from Nigeria. "These things shouldn't be negotiated in a utopian society, but unfortunately, we don't live in one. We need policies and laws to guarantee and protect the rights of all people. Throughout history, rights have rarely, if ever, been given without powerful asks by those affected. It is mostly forced through violent and nonviolent movements." Martin Luther King Jr. agreed with Toby. In his famous *Letter from Birmingham Jail*, King wrote: "We know through painful experience that freedom is never voluntarily given by the oppressor; it must be demanded by the oppressed."

But Andrew has a point. As Harvey Milk, the first openly gay politician in California, said, "It takes no compromise to give people their rights. . . . It takes no money to respect the individual. It takes no political deal to give people freedom. It takes no survey to remove repression."[39] Until all people treat each other with such dignity, negotiation skills help us change and enforce laws that protect rights.

Negotiators can also disrupt oppression through "win-win-win" thinking that considers the impact of our agreements on *everyone* affected. Many agreements ignore those not at the negotiating table. Here's an example first mentioned in the introduction: The City of Baltimore and New York developer La Cité signed off on a development project in West Baltimore without consulting the people of Poppleton, whose homes they planned to seize for the project.[40] The residents protested, but the project proceeded anyway. Mayor Brandon Scott came into office during the protests and facilitated a negotiation between the developer and the community, resulting in changes that satisfied more existing residents, even saving some homes.

Win-win-win thinking advances a practice promoted by John Rawls, a world-renowned justice theorist born in Baltimore. Rawls encouraged us to make decisions by use of a "veil of ignorance," through which we imagine we could be anyone affected by the decision. Would the developers be happy with the agreement if *their* homes were to be seized? Had the negotiating parties imagined themselves as Poppleton families, they might have engaged them earlier in the process. Instead, they made enemies. Through a win-win-win approach, the powerful avoid walking over those impacted by, but not invited to, the negotiation, whether they be a marginalized group of people, an endangered species, or even an old-growth forest.

Public Self

Becoming a negotiator who can advocate for others requires developing what political philosopher Hannah Arendt (1906–75) called a *public self,* which she distinguished from the *private* self.[41] Our private self uses negotiation to achieve independence, which can mean financial freedom, control over our time, fulfilling work, and a happy family. Finding our political (or collective) power, however, requires developing a *public* voice.[42]

How do you develop a public self? It starts with education. Krish Vignarajah's parents arrived in Baltimore as refugees from Bangladesh, believing that education could secure good and influential lives for their children. They made sure that their two children received a high-quality preliminary education and then encouraged them to keep going—and their daughter and son both attended Yale University, followed by top law schools. Krish's brother served as deputy attorney general of Maryland. Krish worked as an advisor to Secretary of State John Kerry and First Lady Michelle Obama. She is now the CEO of Lutheran Immigration and Refugee Service.

No matter what your education or position, negotiating for change requires working well with others. You amplify your influence when you do. In 2021, over thirty businesses in Baltimore leveraged their power by collectively threatening to withhold taxes if the city continued to allow public urination, public drinking, destruction of property, trash buildup, and drug dealing in their neighborhood.[43] They know they are stronger together.

Negotiating for structural changes also requires working with groups that disagree. Community mediator Renata Valree helps police, community members, and the Justice Department in her town near Los Angeles see themselves as "one community." She says, "Solutions are organic when you take away the identities and treat each other as human beings. The barriers that exist are those we create." Enduring agreements emerge when groups shift beliefs about each other and start working together for the collective good.

The Past

As noted in the introduction to this book, experts urge negotiators to focus on the future, not the past. They warn that looking back will entangle us in unresolvable issues. We cannot change the past, so why address it? While sometimes true, this perspective misses the point that many people cannot come to an agreement precisely *because of* an unresolved past. When historical upsets remain unspoken, agreements cannot be reached or may be short lived. Lasting agreements require trust. If parties cannot address historical betrayals, then even small future challenges can become cause to abandon an agreement.

The concept of Sankofa, a symbol of the Akan people of Ghana, offers another way to approach the past. Also popular among some African Americans and others of the African diaspora, Sankofa emphasizes the importance of drawing on wisdom from the past to create a strong future. Problems within marginalized communities originate in historical practices and attitudes imposed by a dominant group. If we negotiate for social change *without* this reach back, we develop incomplete solutions and miss where discrimination occurs today. We also deprive the harmed party the acknowledgment they deserve.

Stamina

Advocacy requires stamina. Ginger, a criminal defense attorney, warns that "the personal toll can be tremendous, particularly when there is a protracted movement with seemingly little progress." When negotiating for broader social change, Krish added, "you bring people along. Sometimes you have to coddle them a little." We must think beyond our immediate interests and even beyond the timeline of our own lives.

Successfully negotiating for larger social change involves working with larger teams, which helps with stamina and leads to better results.

Jacob, assistant director of a Quaker school, offered this: "In my own experiences with activism and organizing, it often feels quite helpless on your own but once you have like-minded people organizing with you, you can feel incredibly empowered." Collective action can create astonishing outcomes. As mentioned earlier, in 1977 Judy Heumann—bound to a wheelchair as a result of polio—led a twenty-eight-day sit-in with more than 150 disabled people in a San Francisco government building. This was the longest sit-in to date in a government building, one that successfully convinced the city government to sign into law two important pieces of legislation that became landmarks in the movement for the rights of persons with disabilities.[44]

When negotiating for social transformation, know your risks. When Egyptian activist Amal Fath posted a video about her treatment at a local bank and the poor quality of public services in her country, she was incarcerated.[45] Countries lacking journalistic freedom often respond harshly to protesters. The organization Reporters Without Borders identified the most dangerous places to speak up. They include China, Vietnam, Syria, Saudi Arabia, Cuba, North Korea, and Iran. As I write this, women in Iran and Afghanistan face incarceration, abuse, and even death for demanding the same rights that men in their countries have long enjoyed.

When You Get the Meeting, Stop Yelling

Because convincing people in power to take your cause seriously requires so much ferocity, some advocates struggle to shift into a collaborative frame once they get the meeting. Barack Obama experienced this, as a former president, when meeting with some of the leaders of Black Lives Matter. He advises: "Once you've highlighted an issue and brought it to people's attention and shined a spotlight, and elected officials or people who are in a position to start bringing about change are ready to sit down with you, then you can't just keep on yelling at them. And you can't refuse to meet because that might compromise the purity of your position. . . . The value of social movements and activism is to get you at the table, get you in the room, and then to start trying to figure out how this problem is going to be solved."[46] When you have the meeting, shift frames and get down to working together. To prevent anger from derailing your mission, ask yourself what approach best serves *the movement*. Sometimes it's too hard to be the person who yells *and* the one who reasons. In social movements, you can assign different people to different roles. This can advance the movement further.

The Power of a Letter

Don't underestimate the power of even a short meeting or a well-written letter. A Maryland legislator told me that he would like to meet with more constituents, but few people request meetings anymore. If you feel passionately about something, schedule a meeting.

Letters and emails can also result in powerful outcomes. In 1883, two years before his death, Victor Hugo, the author of *Les Misérables* and *Notre-Dame de Paris,* wrote one of the most important documents of his life. Addressing the municipal office in Paris, he made an impassioned request that the city *not* construct a street through the recently rediscovered Roman arenas that remained in Paris. Defending the preservation of the Arènes de Lutèce, he wrote: "The past brings the future. The arenas are the mark of antiquity on this notable city. They are a unique monument. A municipality that destroys them in effect destroys itself. Conserve the arenas of Lutèce at all costs."[47] Thanks to this letter, today you can see kids playing soccer in the ancient arena, and folks reading on the ancient bleachers. Locals even organize movie nights there. This piece of antiquity, preserved despite the value of its real estate, reminds us that we retain what the people say we must.

We don't all have the clout of Victor Hugo, but we can all write powerful letters. The results can be astonishing. I once wrote a letter—following the framework provided below for the "Letter to Someone in Power" activity—to Bay Area Rapid Transit (BART), a commuter rail company, which had sold advertising space to a hate group. A BART representative responded with a copy of their official advertising policy, asking me to comment. I wrote a review of the policy. BART's chief strategist responded: "Thank you for your response. We will forward this to the BART Board and staff." He later emailed to let me know that the board had voted unanimously to change the policy. The hate group could no longer advertise on the railway platform.

Well-written letters can also help you attain support from powerful people. Lisa says, "I wrote a letter to all the congressmen in my district asking for money to attend school. I shared how I would serve the community with my learned skills and expertise acquired through educational studies. The result: they sent me money for my AA degree through to my BA degree."

Because experiencing the power of your voice can be thrilling, I assign letter writing in class. Students shared their results:

- Grace scored a meeting with the provost at American University.
- Shelly received an invitation to meet with a state legislator.
- Kolby met with a senior member of the Baltimore Police Department.
- Natty received an invitation to join the board of an organization.
- Brittney received a call from St. Joseph's Hospital apologizing for her terrible experience and seeking to know how they could improve.

Sometimes we just don't realize how much power we have.

SUMMARY

Claiming our power begins with knowing what we want and then finding productive ways to pursue these goals. We must channel strong emotions so that they serve, rather than derail, us. We must strive to be conscientious about how we present ourselves and treat others. Having options strengthens us by decreasing our dependence on one person or outcome.

Before we make requests, we need to know how power operates in the relevant setting. Who has it? What forms does it take? Great negotiators know that if they lack one form of power (say, a fancy title), they may turn to their expertise or persistence to persuade others. They also know that what works in one space may not work in another. Negotiating for social change requires different negotiation skills, like learning to work in large groups and remembering that the timelines for social change can extend beyond our lives and will likely affect people we may never meet.

ACTIVITIES

Personal Power

Your Values

Remembering your values makes you harder to manipulate. Gather your personal power by writing one paragraph about something you value and three paragraphs with examples from your life that explain why you care about this.[48]

Priming

Before any negotiation, spend at least seven minutes writing about a time that you felt powerful and/or strong. This makes you more likely to advocate for yourself and less likely to accept conditions unappealing to you.[49]

Collaborative Power

Ask for Advice

Develop relationships with powerful people by asking them for advice. Most people like contributing to others. Think of someone in a position of power whom you admire and ask them advice about how to do something in their area of expertise. You may learn something and will likely improve the relationship.

Finding Your Sources of Power

When preparing for a negotiation, review Bernie Mayer's ten sources of power, listed earlier in this chapter.[50] As you do so,

- put a star next to the sources of power you have,
- put an arrow next to the sources the other party has, and
- circle the ones you could acquire.

If you and they share the same sources of power, ask yourself who has more of each.

Collective Power

Letter to Someone in Power

Pick an issue of importance to you and identify a person who has the power to respond to your request. Then write a powerful letter (or email). A powerful letter has several components:

1. *Introduction*—Include any relevant professional titles or experience that add authority to the request you will make.

2. *Compliment*—Acknowledge something that the organization or person has done right.

3. *Clear statement of the issue*—What do you want?

4. *Explanation of why this matters to you personally*—Tell a story.

5. *Appreciation and support*—Close the letter by thanking the person for their time. Provide your personal contact information, offering your assistance on this matter.

Send the letter via mail or email. If they respond to your request, please let me know at www.sarahfederman.com.

Note to teachers: If you assign this in class, consider using the honor system, whereby students tell you when they have sent the letter, without showing you the contents. Some have personal issues they do not want to reveal through exposure of the letter, or they may fear that you don't share their political outlook.

CHAPTER 7

Gender, Sex, and Race

OVERVIEW

Many negotiation books promise universally useful advice, but my students convinced me otherwise. The data support their claims. Women and men navigate different realities, as do women of color and white women. Age, gender, sexual preferences, ethnicity, body size, disabilities, marital status, parental status, education, religion, and health can influence how others respond to your requests. This chapter focuses on race and gender because my students struggled most with their immediate impacts and longer-term consequences and because we have ample research on them. The section on condom and marriage negotiations highlights an underdiscussed area that affects people's lives every bit as much as, if not more than, a financial negotiation.

QUESTIONS TO CONSIDER

Have you ever felt that a personal attribute, unrelated to the negotiation, affected how others responded to your request?

If so, what did they say or do that made you feel that way?

When was the last time someone's attributes affected *your response* to their request?

Everyone experiences some form of bias, and everyone judges others. In a negotiation, managers may not take young employees seriously and may treat older employees as irrelevant. Many people struggle to prove their commitment to work while juggling kids and elder care. Immigrants learning a new language fight assumptions to the effect that they lack intelligence. Even the rich and powerful cannot escape bias. In 2013, Oprah pointed to a handbag in a store in Zurich and the storekeeper told her, "No, no, no, you don't want to see that one, you want to see this one, because that one will cost too much, you will not be able to afford that one."[1] Speechless, Oprah walked out. This chapter addresses how to negotiate well amid the "-isms" (sexism, racism, ageism, ableism, etc.) and how to stop perpetuating them.

If you identify as a male, please don't skip this chapter. The discussion that follows includes challenges men face. Additionally, you may relate to more of this than you expect. Men can feel pressure to negotiate in a stereotypically masculine way to meet cultural expectations, even if this harms the outcome. Or a man may feel confident negotiating for a raise but, because of cultural messaging to be strong, may struggle to request emotional support.

WOMEN

Compared to women in many cultures, women in the Western world have tremendous freedom to choose their partners and their work and to live independently. This does not mean that working women have it easy. As Hillary Clinton once said, "It is *hard* to be a woman. You have to think [and communicate] like a man, act like a lady, look like a little girl, and work like a horse."[2]

While every group has its own struggles with negotiation, most subgroup research has been focused on women. The research does not adequately consider the intersection of gender with race, class, and other attributes. Most also focuses on the business sector. I'll fill in a bit of those blind spots here and in the section on race. For now, let's see what the studies on negotiation and gender can tell us.

Linda Babcock and her team studied 290 men and women and discovered that men negotiated (and made requests) *more than twice as often* as women and made bigger asks out of the gate.[3] The number and size of their asks enable men to get more of what they request. "Women should just speak up!" Peter offered in class one night. Seems logical. But first, let's explore what stops women from negotiating.

Women avoid negotiating because they feel anxious, whereas men more often reported enjoying negotiations, seeing them as a game.[4] But this just brings us to another question: Why are women anxious? Many women reported fears that negotiating would risk a relationship or make others think poorly of them. Do women care more about relationships because of their biology?

In her study of U.S. managerial professionals, Deborah Tannen found that socialization, *not* biology, explains women's reluctance to negotiate. American men are raised to express themselves in ways that others recognize as confident. Despite their advances in recent decades, many women in the United States are still raised to be demure, which can make them seem to be less competent or lacking in confidence.[5] If women break that mold and appear confident, both men and women tend to punish them for being "too demanding." Because women generally occupy lower-level positions, all people tend to see them as of lower status. These perceptions shape negotiation outcomes. Women feel more anxious about negotiating for good reason: self-advocacy *can*, in fact, expose them to ill will and lead to a loss of social capital, negative performance evaluations, and even threats of dismissal.[6]

Notice that I said that women suffer for their "self-advocacy." They suffer less, however, when advocating for others. In a study in which participants negotiated *on behalf of* others, women outperformed men.[7] Tiffany wasn't surprised by this finding, recalling her mother's fierce negotiation tactics, especially when it concerned her kids. She once called a store and said, "You told my son that he can't get his money back for these pants because it's past the thirty days, but . . . [she listed reasons]. So, he'll be back down to the store in a few minutes to get his money back." And he did. Hearing this story, Ashley laughed and said her mom did this kind of thing all the time.

Use "We" Language

How can women overcome this bias against self-advocacy? You see, men can often say to their boss, "I'd like to talk about the possibility of a raise/promotion," without risking any social capital.[8] According to Linda Babcock, Lei Lai, and Hannah Riley Bowles, women need a different approach to avoid harming their reputations. In a negotiation for professional advancement, they advise women to focus on:

- getting the raise/promotion; *and*
- making a positive impression by talking about how much they love the job, value their colleagues, and care about the company;[9] *while*
- using "we" language whenever possible.

Women can say something like "I'm so glad I decided to join this high-performing team, and, seeing the positive impact of my work, I believe I could support the company and team even more in a managerial position."

When negotiating for a promotion mid-semester, Lisa followed this advice. "I led the conversation with how I will contribute to the success of the agency to move the company forward." Her boss increased her salary and elevated her title.

Jennifer resisted using this strategy, saying, "Why do women have to do all this? Shouldn't society change?" Yes, but change takes time, and you presumably want the promotion ASAP. Plus, I think the advice is good for men too. Framing one's professional desires in terms of how they align with organizational goals supports healthy, functioning workplaces.

Highlight Your Talents

Negotiation researchers Emily Amanatullah and Catherine Tinsley found that women who cite work experience, achievements, titles, and other accomplishments during negotiations tend to be more successful and face less backlash.[10] So shine a light on your strengths. At the end of your workday, jot down what you contributed to the organization and keep your résumé up to date.

Find a Powerful Person Who Loves You

Increase your negotiation success by finding someone to champion your work. Linda Babcock found that "women thrive when they have someone powerful (male or female) to do a lot of their 'asking' for them."[11] To find powerful supporters, negotiation scholars Hannah Riley Bowles and Kathleen McGinn encourage women to build mixed-gender networks. They say that women "tend to be less well connected to networks of men in their workplace than other men. Because those who control resources within organizations tend to be men, these gender differences in social network configuration put women at a disadvantage in terms of gaining career-related resources and information."[12] We can all help out by advocating for someone who deserves recognition but is getting overlooked.

Role Models

Women who successfully navigate work and family from the margins can offer great advice. Graciela learned from her mother: "My mom, who is Puerto Rican, negotiates everything. She had to navigate working for the FBI, one of the first women from a minority to work as an agent. Even before that, her whole life she has had to negotiate, so she has taught my sister and me never to settle."

Robin invited one of her colleagues and mentors, Joy Spencer Smith, to our class. You may recall that Joy worked at Amtrak for four decades, starting as a service attendant and rising to senior manager of Customer Service. She earned four Presidential Safety and Service Awards for her leadership, dedication, and innovation. Joy told us, "Many men did not believe women needed to work in the railroad, never mind a Black woman, and never mind a superior." How did she handle it? She just kept showing up. At meetings, she would sit next to her supervisor and ask, "How are you?" She paid no mind to his grumbles, but instead

- gave senior men true compliments,
- asked their advice, and
- made her body language welcoming.

She told the students, "You buy the drinks next time. Show your human side." And she told them not to avoid all-male environments. "Sometimes, I'd rather be with the Old Boys than with a bunch of bitching women," she said. "Be careful not to substitute the Good Old Boys with the Good Old Girls. Women can be just as ruthless." Much of the class nodded in agreement.

Joy then offered several other tips to help you improve your work negotiations:

- Be consistent.
- Leave personal feelings at home.
- Don't be afraid.

- Let the quality of your work speak for you.
- Don't allow other people to control your behavior.
- Inquire about your coworkers' dreams and accomplishments.
- Remember that managers work for their employees.

Success Stories

Many students put this negotiation advice to good use. Shanae started out the semester saying, "I'm too nervous to negotiate after I've been given an offer. I'm afraid that if I make demands of what I really want, I will come off as aggressive and risk losing the job offer." She paid close attention in class and prepared for a negotiation with her boss. When he refused, she applied for another paralegal position and increased her salary by $20,000. That raise more than paid for her semester.

Barriers

Women face other barriers when trying to negotiate up. Tylis Cooper, a graduate student advisor and a public administration expert, explained that support staff and managerial positions are coded differently. If you land a job coded for support, "it's hard to jump tracks . . . [because] they might call you the 'gem of the office,' but they won't let you go manager." Unless someone (often a white person) in power "hand-picks" or repositions you, it won't happen, she said. In government administration, pick your job carefully, because no negotiation tactic may be able to change the track that you're on.

At a Ladies Get Paid event in Baltimore, I learned about a negotiation challenge faced by women in tech. Sharon, a programmer, shared her discovery that she earned thousands less than her male peers. "I'm far more skilled, have more experience, and developed the company's vision, yet I'm making so much less. What can I do?" Other women programmers shared similar experiences of denied or delayed requests for salary equity.

Unsure how to advise them, I asked someone who spent two decades in tech, first at Microsoft and then at Amazon. The tech field operates like an Old Boys Club, he explained. Women programmers advance until they become eligible for top management positions, then they find themselves ushered into marketing or project planning. Only men advance to the senior positions. Women who rose to the top despite these obstacles rarely helped other women. So, for the tech women out there: during a negotiation concerning your advancement, pay attention and try to discern whether management is moving you "up" or just sideways to another role.

The Motherhood Penalty

Parenthood adds new challenges for men and women in the workplace, but women more often experience a "motherhood penalty," meaning they are hired less often, receive lower starting salaries, and face higher expectations of competence and punctuality.[13] While men struggle with parenthood, too, at work they more often experience the "fatherhood bonus." Meaning that their careers benefit from parenthood.

Students fessed up to how they inflicted the motherhood penalty on others. Rodney admitted that despite being a Black man who understands discrimination intimately, while interviewing female candidates with children, he asked himself: "Will [she] be late more often than others? Will she miss time from work due to challenges with finding a sitter or for child illnesses? Can I depend on this candidate coming to work every day and being engaged in the tasks at hand?"

Tiffany admitted that even though she had experienced this bias when pregnant, she had since imposed it on other women. Matila, a mother who has trained other mothers, even confessed, "I can remember times where even I openly questioned a female candidate's ability to travel or fulfill some other work obligation when she brought up that she had a newborn or young child during a job interview." Recognizing this behavior in ourselves helps us interrupt it.

In fact, a working mother may be even *more* productive than her childless peers. When I asked the director of the Harvard Business School's executive education program whether I should pursue an MBA, she said, "Have a child. *That* will make you the most efficient."

Given the demands of school and family life, Hannah Riley Bowles says, "we should help women use negotiation not only to ask for more pay and benefits, but also to negotiate their roles and workloads to remain continuously employed and upwardly mobile."[14] To this list, Tylis encourages women to remember to negotiate for "training, travel, telework, loan forgiveness, mentorship, etcetera. We just don't know what to ask for. We don't ask for anything and often don't get anything." She's right. If we remain too fixed on money, we can too easily overlook other negotiable aspects of our lives.

Negotiating after Dark

Negotiations that take place after work may be the most important ones—especially those occurring after dark. Contracting a sexually transmitted disease (STD) or a surprise pregnancy will shake your world more than a $5,000 salary bump or a discount on snow tires. So let's talk about sex.

Condom negotiations affect everyone, even the rich and famous. Benito Mussolini, Ivan the Terrible, Al Capone, Napoleon Bonaparte, Vladimir Lenin, and the Tongzhi Emperor all allegedly suffered from sexually transmitted diseases—the great equalizer.

Before sharing the research on condom negotiation, I acknowledge how few of these studies focus on white participants. More research is needed across groups, but here's what the data show. A 2012 study on condom influence strategies among college students in Southern California had some interesting findings.[15] Researchers found that white, Black, Latino, and Asian and Pacific Islander American (APIA) students used multiple negotiation strategies, including withholding sex, providing risk information, making direct requests, using deception, or relationship conceptualizing, which means describing condom use as an act of care for the other person. White and Black students used direct strategies more than Latino and APIA students.

Other studies confirmed that negotiations go down differently depending on culture, but some even added variables including alcohol use, type of relationship (casual vs. committed), and history of sexual trauma.[16]

Sheryl Thorburn Bird and S. Marie Harvey studied college-aged Black women and reported in their article "No Glove, No Love" that their participants "(1) use strong, direct strategies such as threatening to withhold sex; (2) actively participate in condom use by making condoms available and initiating their use; and (3) use interactive strategies such as offering reasons for condom use." A few women reported educating their male partners about the benefits of condom use. The participants did not use tactics such as threatening to have sex with another partner, deception, pouting, touting the pleasurable benefits of condoms, or other incentives.[17] One respondent said, "It's almost like, to me, unprotected sex is like you having a gun and you shooting it at me, and you just shoot the gun, and I don't have no bulletproof vest on."[18] Pro-condom women saw demanding condoms as a sign of confidence and self-respect. For them, refusal to wear a condom became a deal breaker.

The women struggled, however, with how to start using condoms after already having unprotected sex. They feared their partner saying things like "Do you think I've been cheating on you? Why all of a sudden? We've been having sex without a condom for this long?"[19] These negotiations may require reassurance and care. Assure the person that the change reflects your own growing understanding of condoms' importance for everyone's safety, rather than a change in the relationship's status.

Despite having the knowledge, confidence, assertiveness, and negotiation skills necessary to influence men's behavior, Black women report low condom use. TyWanda McLaurin-Jones and her team wanted to know why, so they studied condom use among Black college women (around twenty years old).[20] The women surveyed reported various reasons for not using condoms. Some thought it was the man's responsibility or feared negative responses from their partners (as well as from other women), while others simply didn't like using them. The fear that a man would go find someone else was strong. For many women, condom negotiations are high-stakes. Many simply avoid negotiations over condom use, putting them at risk of a poorly timed pregnancy or STD.

Of course, cultures differ. Studies have found that Asian women and men use more *indirect* strategies, such as verbal hints and placing a condom within view. Even here, strategies differ by subculture: American college-aged women of Filipina and Chinese descent used more direct strategies than their peers at home.[21] A study of Latino youth saw gendered stereotypes. Women in Latin communities that prize sexually inexperienced women sometimes fear that demonstrating savvy around condom use tarnishes the idealized image. The Latino men, by contrast, were expected to be experienced and to have a high sex drive. Their drive could not always be controlled, it was storied, so condoms were often overlooked.[22] Lexy could relate. "I've even told my mom that I'm less inclined to date Hispanic guys," she said, "because many of them believe they have to fit into this [stereotype] or are so deeply rooted in it." Lexy identifies as mostly Latina, though her dad is African American and white and her mom is Puerto Rican, which, she says, makes her technically African, European, and Taino Indigenous.

Despite these norms among Latino youth, Jeanne M. Tschann and her team found that direct communication (whether verbal or nonverbal) about the risks of *not* using condoms increased condom use.[23] Young Latino men used direct negotiation strategies (just asking) more often than women. Some young women feared that their partner might end the relationship if they pressed for condom use, or feared physical retaliation by a partner prone to violence. Young Latina women reported hesitancy to insist on condom use—but, when they did insist, they were very effective in convincing the men to do so. Overall, the better the relationship, the better the outcome.

CONDOM NEGOTIATION TAKEAWAYS

- Don't negotiate while drunk (good advice for all negotiations).
- Plan your strategy before the heat of the moment (talk before).
- Keep condoms handy.
- Start using a condom the first time you have sex with the person.
- If you fear that the person will leave you or harm you for insisting on condom use, reconsider the value of this relationship.
- Survivors of sexual assault or intimate partner violence may struggle more with these conversations. Pick a quiet time to talk it over.
- Choose the negotiation strategy that works for you, but don't compromise on the outcome.
- Do your research: knowing the risks of sexually transmitted diseases helps you explain why condoms matter.

Lisa, now in her fifties, advised her younger peers, "This is one negotiation [in which] you must remain strong. Valuing yourself is the focus here, rather than seeking a few moments of pleasure. It's not worth it. Unfortunately, the woman is always the one who gets hurt the most." Wise words.

Negotiating Relationships

Some students shared struggles they'd had negotiating with family over their marital status. A Malian student declared that "my first marriage was for my parents, the next one will be for me," but found acting on that sentiment more difficult than she'd imagined. Her father might cut her off financially if she divorced her husband, leaving her without the funds to complete her master's program.

Matt Brim, a professor of poor queer studies at the College of Staten Island in New York, said that his undergraduates experienced marriage pressures from parents of many backgrounds—Catholic, Muslim, Hindu, Hispanic, and European. Some lesbian students, who had not come out to their parents, prolonged their academic studies to delay the inevitable marriage pressure that would arrive upon graduation.[24] How can students successfully negotiate with parents regarding their marital choices? While some families may never accept their children's choices, many others simply need time. Think of these negotiations as continued conversations rather than one-off meetings. Through patience, we can avoid destroying important relationships.

Those marrying the person of their choosing will still need to negotiate over matters related to the household, child rearing, and even gender norms. Matila says, "In the culture I was raised in, women are encouraged to adopt a strong personality outside of the home but submit to their male partners and relatives while operating within the family unit." These expectations can be discussed and negotiated, but as with parental negotiations, these shifts can take time.

When marriages end, couples negotiate the terms of a divorce. When Sam and his wife separated, they asked their lawyers to help them negotiate an agreement that would make their children proud. They knew they could find a way forward that would work for them both. By contrast, Martin saw his parents' lawyers making a mess of their divorce, so he intervened. They fired the lawyers, and Martin wrote the divorce agreement *with* his parents. Divorces may always be painful, but the negotiated terms don't have to destroy one or both parties. Increasingly, couples are uncoupling with kindness. Remember that you have a say in how negotiations unfold.

In sum, gender expectations affect how negotiations unfold. The studies and expert advice I have cited offer guidance on how gender norms affect our interactions with others. As I mentioned at the beginning of this chapter, much of the gender and negotiation research tends to overlook the impacts of race. This is the topic to which I now turn.

BLACK WOMEN/WHITE WOMEN

As noted in the introduction, the necessity of adding race to gender conversations became apparent in class when Aiysha discussed her work struggles. Marsha, a white student, suggested that Aiysha, a Black student, approach her boss and say something like "We need to find a better way of working together."

Aiysha replied, "Well, that might work for a white woman, but not for me."

As a Black woman, she would face harsh consequences for speaking up in that way. She told me, "I believe women of color and white women should be given different advice. Backgrounds, different colleges, and even your name can make a big difference when it comes to negotiating. There are a lot of stigmas and negative reputations put on women of color."

I brought the question to the class. I asked the class what differences they noticed between Black and white women in the workplace. From there we could determine the best advice. Chevonie said, "I have worked in corporate [offices] for over twenty years in human resources. . . . I realized late in my career that when I extend offers to white applicants, they ALWAYS ask for more money. However, when I extend offers to any other race, the likelihood of them wanting to negotiate is minimal. I'm not saying that everyone negotiates successfully, but typically those who do get at least $2,000 more." Here we see Black women accepting offers without negotiating.

Miss Emory, now in her seventies, noticed white women advance in other ways: "I've been in situations when I've had to train white women and watch them get promoted. When training people who did not deserve the grade or pay, I always told myself it wouldn't be long before I'd be earning my due increase, but the unfair disparities went on for many years." Here we see workplace bias, perhaps, accounting for the promotions of white women and/or for Black women not advocating for themselves.

Gloria, a younger student, added, "It's so important for Black women to remind themselves of their worth and remember that they are deserving of a salary that makes sense. . . . I would much rather go on a hundred interviews and be rejected by all than to settle for just anything."

From the ongoing discussion, it seemed that Black women needed more support and encouragement to negotiate on their behalf, and more people in power to support their advancement.

Black Women: The Research

The research shows that in 2019, Black women in the United States made roughly 40 percent of what white men earn. BIPOC men earn more than their female counterparts.[25] This is for the reasons shared above and because many Black women struggle to even get to the negotiating table. When Black women graduates of elite universities apply for jobs, they hear back less often than their white counterparts.[26] Why? Because employers too often discard strong applicants (male and female) with Black-sounding names.[27] The good news is that as of 2023, more organizations seek applicants from historically marginalized groups to demonstrate their commitment to racial equity. This means more applicants will find themselves contacted *because of* their ethnic-sounding names and offered attractive salaries.

The wage gap will not close quickly, in part because of career choices. No matter how well you negotiate, lower-paying sectors simply have less money to give. BIPOC women often pursue lower-paying careers than Asian women who often head to tech and finance or white women who often choose high-paying corporate jobs. In 2019, the Institute for Women's Policy Research reported that Black and Hispanic women work in "service" occupations twice as much as white women. Hispanic women are the least likely to work in the highest-paying sectors of business (financial and/or management) positions, followed by Black women.[28]

Why do even highly educated Black women avoid lucrative careers? Sociologist Maya Beasley wanted to know, so she interviewed Black women attending the University of California, Berkeley, and Stanford University. She saw more Black students veer toward lower-paying nonprofit work or other professions related to their ethnicity, like civil rights law or enhancing Black visibility through marketing or other fields.[29] Some Black students explained their choices as simply a desire to return to their communities. Others feared the racism in other sectors. Perhaps more Black students should be encouraged to pursue high-paying careers. Or maybe more white students want to follow Black women and use their education to serve others, rather than simply pursue wealth.

Negotiating in a Sea of Bias

Black women who choose corporate careers tend to negotiate well. Management consultants at McKinsey & Company reported that Black women in corporate jobs often negotiate for raises and promotions *as much as,* and sometimes *more than,* white men and women.[30] The challenge occurs, they found, when negotiating with racially biased people. Job evaluators who scored high for racial bias (people who buy into stereotypes of "laziness, incompetence, or poor job performance") often assume that Black candidates will not, or do not have the right to, negotiate for higher wages. When BIPOC candidates negotiated with these individuals, they received worse outcomes and greater backlash from biased managers who judged these candidates as negotiating "too much."[31]

Anticipate the backlash. As with the advice to women, focus on the value that you add to the organization and consider whether you want to continue working in a biased environment. Of course, bias may not be so easy to avoid. Many early-career Black women in the corporate sector, for example, report feeling pressure to be the model "Black" citizen, to change their speech, and to dismantle stereotypes. Meanwhile, they struggle to build social capital and find mentors.[32] Some felt excluded from cliques, ignored, and/or harassed and were compelled to combat assumptions about their incompetence. Some found themselves left out of informal events like lunch or reported being "accidentally" left out of meetings during which important information was exchanged.[33] Other degrading behavior included constant surveillance and having to disprove hostile stereotypes and demonstrate their intellectual competence.[34] Tylis Cooper, who worked in environments like these, reported feeling both invisible and hypervisible simultaneously.

Negotiation experts encourage people to make a personal connection with the other party. When people feel comfortable, they share more information, making a long-term mutually satisfying outcome more likely. Katherine Phillips and her team found that informal interactions (like lunch) that invite the sharing of personal information (like where you go on vacation) can *increase* the distance between employees of different backgrounds. Employees of color withheld information that confirmed stereotypes or avoided social interactions. That withdrawal can be misinterpreted as antisocial or aloof.[35] When negotiating with someone of a different background, resist judging them for their hesitancy to share personal information, and seek ways to connect without pressure to reveal personal details. Don't assume that you have nothing in common.

When applying to be the first Black woman writer at *Washington Post Magazine,* Jill Nelson won over then-editor Ben Bradlee during the job interview after she referred to her home at Martha's Vineyard. He had a home there too and was no longer concerned she would not fit in.[36] She got the job. I know, we don't all have houses on Martha's Vineyard. Play your angle. Brea told the class that she got a job by bonding with the hiring manager over Jeep Wranglers.[37] Seek commonalities.

Navigating Stereotypes

Talking about stereotypes can be dangerous. If we focus on them too much, we reinforce them. Yet if we deny their existence, we cannot defuse their power. As Linda Babcock says, "simply ignoring a stereotype or refusing to behave as expected doesn't solve the problem."[38] Yet, if we keep reinforcing negative stereotypes, we can harm people. Psychologist Claude Steele found that when male and female African American study participants were asked their ethnicity before taking a test, they performed more poorly than when asked nothing. Asians performed better, adhering to the stereotype that Asians are smart.[39]

Dawn Marie Dow interviewed mothers who help their Black sons avoid the "thug" stereotype, which can lead to more discipline and criminal charges.[40] Dow found that unfortunately, parents who coach their sons to be more deferential to avoid triggering the stereotype actually perpetuate the subordination of Black men. In the next section, I present the stereotypes that scholars and others make visible in order to defuse them. I share these labels to raise awareness of damaging ideas that we may carry unconsciously.

Black Women

When it comes to negotiation, more has been written about Black women. Ella Bell Smith, a management professor at Dartmouth's Tuck School of Business, identified two dominant stereotypes about Black women in the workplace:[41]

Mammy (or Big Momma): the caretaker who solves the emotional problems of the company (as opposed to doing the analytical work)

Sapphire: the always angry Black woman

Both stereotypes perpetuate myths that Black women belong only in support and not in technical or leadership positions. Being mindful of these stereotypes can help negotiators avoid being shuffled into boxes that feel safe for others.

Women of all ethnicities struggle with how to express anger in the workplace without damaging their reputations.[42] I know men who struggle with this too. In many work environments, however, women more often hurt their social capital by expressing frustration or anger. Black women face additional burdens. In their 2021 study, Daphna Motro and her team found that, indeed, when Black women express anger in the workplace, observers tend to interpret the anger as a personal attribute, rather than as situational. These stereotypical assumptions affect performance evaluations and confidence in these women's leadership abilities.[43] Black men, however, were *not* penalized for expressing anger. The study's authors put the onus on managers to counteract these stereotypes by training employees to understand how we may unconsciously buy into them.

How best to navigate when negotiating difficult subjects at work? Knowing the dangers of the Sapphire stereotype, Ella Bell Smith says, "I tell young sisters oftentimes, I need you just to lighten it up. Don't come in with your Black outfit on. Put some pearls on. Put a colorful scarf on and don't fold your arms. So, there's a whole way of talking to younger Black women so that they can open up in their body language because the assumption is that Black women are angry." Smith goes on: "I work very hard not to be the angry Black woman. Trying not to be the Sapphire. Because once you get the Sapphire role, it is hard to get that one off of you. It's really, really hard. And you lose points a lot with that one. So, I'm very strategic. When I do have something to say that's not necessarily all that positive, I have to be very careful about how I present it so that I'm not seen as the angry Black woman."

Tylis, in her role as academic advisor, shared how she crafts her professional persona around avoiding being seen as angry. She naturally has a low, commanding voice but notices that it becomes more girly and nonthreatening when she engages with more powerful people.

These stereotypes can be problematic when negotiating for promotions as well. Two students shared their struggles with balancing the need to demonstrate leadership skills without seeming aggressive. Britni said, "Management praised me for being 'aggressive' or firm with my team to get the job done, but when I applied for a higher-level role, they told me that I wasn't quite 'aggressive' enough. . . . These were the same managers both times, and it was very confusing for me."

Another student added: "Entering the corporate white-collar workforce has been an interesting experience to say the least. I find that often I am one of a handful of Black or brown bodies hired. . . . You become afraid to speak your mind because you don't want to be considered naggy or aggressive. You also don't want to say too little or you'll appear spineless or replaceable."

Fania Davis, founder of Restorative Justice for Oakland Youth (RJOY), says that the socialization of Black women begins early. She sees Black girls being "subjected to intersectional forms of stereotyping based on race and gender, such as being 'loud' and 'ghetto.' Black girls are especially penalized for deviating from gender norms and expectations of 'feminine' behavior, based on models of white womanhood."[44]

Imani agreed: "We are socialized to make white people feel comfortable." So did Chevonie, who has been in the workforce for decades. She says that "Black women want to come off as nonthreatening, collaborative, and grateful for the support and efforts of everyone around them."

Another challenge is that Black women can be *perceived* by others as angry when they are not. Justin Friesen's research found that white people and non-Black people of color wrongly perceive Black faces as angrier than they are. Friesen finds that white folks make this mistake because they don't look Black people in the eyes enough. If they did, they would see the emotion more clearly. He wonders whether not looking Black people in the eyes suggests something about status perceptions.[45] White readers, please look everyone in the eyes. It's a subtle but critical part of undoing the caste system. For the record, Black women are *not* angrier than white women. In fact, a 2012 study found that Black women report *less* anger than white women.[46]

Matila, a former student who reviewed this chapter, wanted me to balance these data and stories by including her positive experiences. She says, "I'm pretty demonstrative in personality. I tend to get credit for the work that I put in at the office. I am good with feigning confidence, even when I don't feel that way, and I tend not to be fazed by these social constructs around confidence and competence. Sometimes, though, I do wonder if I would come off as aggressive to some in the workplace if I were a male. More often than not, however, I think that people expect me to be aggressive in the workplace because I present as a Black woman." Many other Black students also succeeded in their workplaces. They just spent more time thinking about ethnicity than their white counterparts.

White Women

Ella Bell Smith says that white women negotiating their work space face stereotypes, too, such as being seen as the heartless *Snow Queen,* the *Iron Maiden,* or the *Miss Ann,* who is "there to do the work for the white male and will sabotage others, particularly women of color, in order to take care of the company." Stella Nkomo, a professor at the University of Pretoria, describes how this can play out. Sometimes a Black woman shares a reflection or complaint, and the Miss Ann brings the complaint to the person in power. These well-meaning efforts hurt the Black women who may be punished for the white person's advocacy.

Then we have the weepy, fragile white woman role. Mamta Motwani Accapadi studies responses to emotions expressed by women in the workplace. She found that white women sometimes score points for looking soft and often receive support for emotions like sadness, vulnerability, and despair. Tears can sometimes earn them sympathy and even protection from others.[47] By contrast, Accapadi found that nonwhite women rarely receive acceptance and support for their emotional pain. Tina Opie, a management scholar and owner of Opie Consulting, agrees: "If I cried as many times in the workplace as I've seen white women cry, I think I would be considered incompetent."[48] So what do we do about all these dynamics?

Love Them or Leave Them?

If you find yourself in a workplace where these dynamics affect your happiness and/or performance, you have a few choices:

- Leave.
- Make it better.
- Engage in activism outside of work.
- Climb to the top and be an inspiration to others.
- Fight! Lodge a complaint, take them to court, keep fighting.

In the early 1970s, Albert Hirschman distilled these choices into *exit, voice,* and *loyalty.*[49]

Exit, or leaving, may be the best decision. Discriminatory environments erode people's mental and physical health as well as their relationships.[50] Walking away is not always easy. Some people need to stay in a job for health benefits or uninterrupted income. If stuck for the moment, find allies, learn everything you can, consider how you might be making the situation worse. Do you gossip? Do you avoid opportunities to engage with others? If you can make the best out of a bad situation, you'll leave on a high note and can use the good reference for an even better position

What if you face outright discrimination? Lakeisha Mathews, director of the university's career services, educates our students about the Equal Pay Act, Title VII (Civil Rights Act), and the Americans with Disabilities Act. When I asked if she ever advises students to pursue enforcement of these rights, she said, "You can win the lawsuit and not bring more love into the world." We agreed that it's tricky territory. So get good advice if considering a formal complaint.

Negotiating Your Crown

Even though the Crown Act—active in several states, including Maryland—prohibits discrimination based on hair style or hair texture, students reported having negotiated with themselves and/or their employers over what constitutes "acceptable hair." As mentioned earlier, one student spent the semester using the class to win a negotiation with her employer, Johns Hopkins Hospital, over her changing hair color. Most students tangled up in hair negotiations found themselves caught between Afrocentric and Eurocentric styles. In the United States, Eurocentric styles are thought to be more professional than Afrocentric styles that show more natural, kinky hair texture. This privileges the natural hair of white people and treats the natural hair of Black people as problematic. Former Banana Republic employee Destiny Tompkins, for example, went viral with her story about wearing braids to work and her boss telling her that her hair was "unkempt" and "urban." The company offered a semi-apology.[51] Ironically, the epithet *banana republic* refers to an unstable country dominated by elites who exploit and dominate the working class.

If you think that this is a strange subject for a negotiation book, consider that Black women "spend nine times more than other groups on haircare."[52] Already facing the lowest salaries of all groups, this amounts to an enormous expense. But this is a high-stakes negotiation for other reasons. A 2022 study published by the *Journal of the National Cancer Institute* linked hair straighteners to uterine cancer.[53] Women can die because of the pressure to meet these standards.

It's not just white managers pressuring employees. Opie's study on hair in the workplace found that Black managers penalized Afrocentric hair *more* than white managers.[54] This may be because Black managers feel that their employees represent them and should therefore be more conservative in their appearance. Opie says that if organizations want to be inclusive and attract diverse candidates, they may need to revisit their appearance polices.[55]

Students shared their internal negotiations over hair expectations. Whitni said, "If your hair is puffy, you're suddenly akin to a wild child. If the bun is too messy . . . you're unkempt, and if the hair is not 'yours,' you're ghetto or unnatural." Tiffany added, "I was once told my braids were too long and the color was not natural, and it didn't fit in a leadership environment. But when I wore it in tight curls like an Afro, I was told it wasn't suitable for the work environment—but that was my natural hair! There is always some kind of policy. My son's father is from Haiti, with dreads all down his back. He couldn't get the job he wanted because they wanted him to cut his hair. He ended up working in a warehouse."

To prevent their hair from becoming an issue, many focus on finding a "safe" hairstyle. Mel, a jury commissioner, says, "I am bald-headed and blonde now, so no more hair stress for me! . . . This is a safe style for work, so I don't worry about offending anyone." Siham keeps her hair very simple in the interview stage; otherwise, "it brings up questions." She would rather talk about her expertise than her hair.[56]

Black women reported another hair negotiation: requests to touch it. Tiffany says, "People touch my hair. I think maybe they're interested because it's harder than it looks. But it's gross, I mean, I don't know where their hands have been. It doesn't feel very hygienic. I don't like it." Betty hated when someone touched her hair while on an elevator because to her, touching someone's hair is an intimate act done to someone you love. Requests to touch hair reflect racial power dynamics. Would you feel your boss's new toupee or poke at a white woman's Botox? It seems like a low bar, but let's step over it. Don't touch the hair.

Opting Out of White Spaces

Black women navigate workplace negotiation bias in a variety of ways. Some become entrepreneurs. In fact, Black women start businesses six times more than the national average.[57] Others opt to work from home in part because it's exhausting to change personalities (code switch), says Courtney McCluney, an organizational behavior scholar at Cornell University who studies race in the workplace.[58] Tylis urged me to add that home has its own challenges—especially, she says, if you're the only one with higher education, stable employment, and a car. This brings more responsibility to care for others, some of whom may even resent your achievements.

NEGOTIATION MENTORS

To negotiate well in your specific context, find someone who has already succeeded in doing so. Women can be hugely helpful to other women. When I mention this, students laugh nervously, grunt, and/or roll their eyes. They all have war stories.

While working as a criminal defense attorney, Ginger said, her best *and* worst mentors were women. One female judge attacked young female attorneys, especially those wearing makeup or high heels. "She chewed me up for eight years."

Tylis said, "I've only had male mentors and one or two women mentors, and they were all white. Never have I had a Black woman willing to mentor me."

Soolmaz Abooali, an Iranian refugee and World Karate Champion with a PhD focusing on sports diplomacy, says: "Women aren't great at cheering for other women. We just don't know what it's like to support each other in competitive spaces. . . . I would much prefer a male mentor over a female mentor, unless she's much older and in a different career." Senior women in karate withheld skills and knowledge to prevent the younger ones from unseating them. "They also made it feel like you should be serving them, instead of them working with you to bring you up." Male mentors, in contrast, gave her tangible steps toward improvement.

I was happy to hear from Selena about the wonderful mentorship she's received from senior women. We need more successes. Fortunately, the wider women's movement agrees on the importance of seeking better ways to support women *and* men. This fourth wave of feminism that emerged in 2012 focuses on empowerment, acknowledges marginalization, and stands up against abuses of power, no matter their source.

Individuals from the dominant group become vital negotiation mentors or allies. *Allyship,* meaning the support of marginalized groups, takes time and reflection, however. A 2020 survey of 7,400 employed American adults reported that 80 percent of white men and 80 percent of white women consider themselves allies of other ethnicities at work. However, only 45 percent of Black women and 55 percent of Latina women reported having work allies. When they find allies, rarely are they white.[59] Ella Bell Smith and Stella Nkomo, who studied over eight hundred women, found white women overestimating their closeness and underestimating their conflicts with Black women.[60]

To help women become better allies, Tina Opie and Beth Livingston introduced the concept of *shared sisterhood,* "a form of inter-relating that promotes trust, vulnerability, empathy, and risk-taking with the aim of collective advancement of women in the workplace."[61] Opie clarifies: "It's not always lovey-dovey, holding hands—it's not going to be that way."[62]

White colleagues can become stronger allies and mentors by watching documentaries and reading books about Black women's experiences, she says, and by following the lead of Black women: "We have had to navigate a landscape that requires that we hone emotional intelligence. We have to be sensitive to cultural signals and organizational cues. Or else, we are the first to be fired. So, when you see a woman of color who has made it to the top, you need to stop and pause and listen to her, especially when she tells you it's been a struggle."[63] That's why this book draws on the experiences of those who successfully navigate from a position of marginality. They know power better than those who wield it. When they make mentorship a priority, they can be the best.

WHEN YOU'RE IN CHARGE

This book is about social mobility as well as social transformation. Once you negotiate your way to the top, remember to use your power for good. Joceyln Frye, a senior fellow at the Center for American Progress and an expert on women's economic security, offers these recommendations:

- Strengthen legal protections for female workers.
- Encourage transparency in pay and benefits.
- Create a federal office that seeks ways to increase Black women's earnings.
- Offer paid family and medical leave, high-quality child care, and a caregiving stipend.
- Disseminate information on pay and benefits *before* a candidate accepts a job offer.[64]

Middle managers can help as well. Equity expert Iris Bohnet says that hiring managers improve equity when they

- conduct structured interviews that ask all candidates the *same* questions,
- advertise salary ranges for jobs (this became law in New York State in 2022),
- make sure that salary ranges reflect market value; and
- don't ask people what they earned before, which can replicate bias (in some states it's already illegal).[65]

When writing letters of recommendation for women, use superlatives like *outstanding, brilliant,* and *shows ambition.* One study found that softer compliments like *team player* or *kind* can hurt women's chances of getting a job.[66]

Speak up for great people. Stella Nkomo says, "I think white men and some white women are reluctant to go out on a limb for a Black person. . . . And I think the idea is that if I sponsor this Black woman, she may not make it."[67] A simple word of support can open doors for others. Finally, it is important to create inclusive environments, to give employees choice over how much they socialize with their coworkers.[68]

Our Men

> Men have nurtured me, mentored me, and supported me. Women, not so much.—Marcetta, student

Marcetta recalled multiple times when men served as crucial mediators when women treated each other poorly. During a book group on women and negotiation, everyone thanked Scott for attending. "We need our men too," Maria told him. Many students shared stories about men who supported them in a variety of ways. Tiffany, for example, talked about her mentor, who, before departing the company, said, "This is what I make, and this is what you should ask for when you go for my position."

Although men may typically enjoy negotiation more than women do, not every man enjoys negotiation or resonates with the alpha-male stereotypes. I have seen men in business crumble under pressure, cry, and become ill. Men suffer too. Our company wanted our Spanish business partner, Diego, to join our New York office. Diego arrived with his father, with whom he ran his company. When we offered him the job in Manhattan, they both teared up. To fulfill his dream of living in Manhattan, Diego would have to separate from his parents and extended family. Thank goodness they shared their true feelings instead of mimicking a New York businessmen stereotype. We never wanted to cause them such distress and said that if the idea caused them this much pain, then it was not an opportunity worth pursuing.

Several men at the top of their professional ladders have shared with me the terror they experience at work. One told me that he feared getting emotionally close to anyone because he built his business success by relying on his thick skin. If he were to become vulnerable, it could all come crashing down. Too often, men who kill off their emotions to survive tough negotiations kill their marriages along with them. Some turn to painkillers, sex, gambling, extramarital sex, or other destructive ways of discharging the tension. Professionally successful men often struggle to negotiate for their place in their families, including their role in child rearing.

Some male students bravely shared the vulnerabilities they carry both at home and at work. One young man came to me shaking. His uncle had just died in Nigeria, leaving him, at twenty-two, the family patriarch. This meant responsibilities to care for the large family and to negotiate conflicts within the extended family.

Great men in difficult contexts carry additional burdens. My husband and I work with a leader in the Sahel who negotiates with high-level tribal and political leaders to find nonviolent solutions to the problems in the region, helps villagers find missing cattle, and grieves with them after massacres. After a period of bloodshed, he flew to a small U.S. town to grieve alone. He told me he did not want to cry in front of his people.

Then we have the men on strike. Psychologist Helen Smith studied men opting out of marriage, fatherhood, and careers in response to anti-male sentiment expressed in various ways throughout American society.[69] When we discussed this trend, Ashley and Tiffany said that they know many men who feel insecure because they lack education. Tiffany said, "Women, more often, will take anything just to make it [life] work, to care for their kids. But if a man finds a low-paying job and tells himself 'I can't make enough here' he'll go sell drugs." Others confirmed this trend in Baltimore. One student told me during office hours, "No drug dealer I know would say it's better to sell drugs than to go to college. Everyone knows it's better to go to college. They just don't feel they could do it." Men cannot negotiate for social mobility when shame keeps them on the sidelines or engaged in activities that hurt them and/or other people.

Women can help. *Womanism,* a form of feminism introduced by Alice Walker, embraces men as part of its mission. We rise together.

SUMMARY

Drawing on research and interviews, this chapter has addressed the roles of gender and ethnicity in negotiations. Age, sexual preferences, body size, disabilities, marital status, parental status, education, religion, and health can also affect how others respond to your requests. I hope that this chapter inspires more negotiation research—by individuals of various backgrounds—about each of these sources of identity and disadvantage and their intersectionality.

Because so much existing research is focused on corporate environments, we talked about other contexts, such as social services, administration, and negotiations at home, including intimate conversations over birth control. Note that I did not address how adults face those most persistent of negotiators, their own children. Numerous books have been written about navigating those important conversations.

While specific advice differs for different contexts, here are some general negotiation takeaways:

- Frame what you want in a way that serves others as well as yourself.
- As a woman, watch out for being shuffled into support positions or project management instead of senior management or technical jobs.
- Find mentors and be one.
- Be mindful of bias, even within your own group.
- Negotiations over birth control and marriage may be the biggest in your life.
- Black women and white women navigate different stereotypes.
- Women can rise and bring other women *and* men with them.

Finally, in our ascent, we all risk replicating some of the oppressive dynamics we survived. Please use your negotiation savvy to support others, and leave the door open for those behind you.

ACTIVITIES

Accomplishment List

At the end of each workday, jot down what you did for the organization. When you negotiate a promotion, you will have a list that you can summarize and share.

Growing Up

Spend twenty minutes journaling about who made requests in your family and for what. Did the women negotiate for different things than the men? What kind of messaging do you recall receiving about being assertive?

Who Can Express It?

At work, who can express anger, rage, frustration, sadness, or fear without it damaging their reputation? Whose reputation might even be helped by expressing these emotions? What about at home?

Be the Change

What are three small actions that could make your workplace feel more inclusive? For example, if you and your colleagues grab a drink after work, who else could you invite?

How Much Do You Mold Yourself?

Consider whether you do the following (yes or no):

- Hide your personality or culture
- Change the way you speak
- Feel like you're under surveillance
- Think about how your hair will be perceived
- Hear people saying things that would get you fired or reprimanded
- Try to prove that you're not typical of your gender or ethnicity
- Easily find mentors in the workplace
- Find yourself invited to join social activities

For each statement to which you answered yes, how has it affected how you feel about yourself and your job?

Implicit Bias Test

No matter how "woke" or "wise" we believe ourselves to be, we all internalize messaging about the importance and attributes of different groups. The Implicit Bias Test helps us see our ethnic, gender, and other biases. When we see our biases, we free others and ourselves. Pick a category, do the test, and share your results. You can find the test here: https://implicit.harvard.edu/implicit/.

CHAPTER 8

Guns, Addiction, and an Orchestra

Defend your future, not your pride.

—Nawal Rajeh, cofounder, By Peaceful Means

OVERVIEW

This chapter considers perilous (and realistic) negotiations involving violence and drug addiction. If such negotiations are handled poorly, the involved parties can be incarcerated or horrifically wounded, harm others irreparably, or die. Drawing on the wisdom of those who have personal experience with violence and addiction (their own or that of others), this chapter discusses critical negotiation skills, including keeping your cool and knowing when *not* to negotiate. The final section, using an orchestra negotiation as a case study, discusses labor negotiations critical to the health of a community. The arts provide pathways to self-expression and growth. Without them, drugs and violence become poor substitutes. Negotiation skills can save individuals as well as the cultural life of our communities.

QUESTIONS TO CONSIDER

Have you used negotiation to avoid a dangerous altercation?

Have you ever tried to negotiate with someone addicted to drugs or alcohol?

If your community were to negotiate to increase support for the arts and arts education, what changes might you see?

Menyvette could not find her iPad, so she used the Find My Device app on her computer to locate it. When she saw it moving down a highway, she called the police. The operator connected her to an officer, who Menyvette directed toward the moving car. He caught up to the car and described it to her as a gray Toyota Corolla.

"Wait!" Menyvette said. "That's my car. Hang on, please do not approach it."

Her son had borrowed the car, and the iPad must have slipped under the seat.

Menyvette put the officer on hold and called her son. "If the police approach and ask for the iPad," she told him, "don't reach under the seat to grab it. It could look like you're reaching for a gun!"

Menyvette explained: "The cop was very nice and he was helping me, but I knew that if he approached my son and thought that he was pulling out a gun, the whole situation could quickly go bad." Slightly embarrassed at the time, she explained the mistake to the cop and thanked him for his assistance. Menyvette had skillfully negotiated a tense moment. Her knowledge of the potential for terrible outcomes when Black men interact with police helped everyone avoid an unnecessary confrontation. Until we change these racialized dynamics, people need to negotiate with the world as it is.

When negotiation experts talk about "tough negotiators" or "devils," they often mean those who bluff, mislead, feign emotions, lie, bully, shame, or use other manipulative tactics to get a deal. Preparing for these tactics can be useful. Those in marginalized, targeted, undersupported, polarized, armed, and/or impoverished communities, however, face a different kind of tough. Here, the devil can show up as a well-intentioned police officer, a prescription painkiller after a dental procedure, a friend asking for help to move a package (containing, as it happens, drugs) for a few bucks. The handgun in your brother's drawer or a manager trying to save their institution by making a few "small" salary cuts can quickly lead to devilish outcomes. These rivals cannot be defused by the same approaches used to stare down a bully in a boardroom. This chapter gives voice to those who succeed in dangerous and precarious situations, including those involving guns, drugs, and a category that may, at this point, seem out of place: threats to the arts.

NEGOTIATION SURVIVAL SKILLS

I'll begin this section with the witnessing words of a student, the Reverend Roy Axel Coats:

> Last year, four people were murdered within five blocks of where I live next to my church.
> Last year, six people were murdered within three blocks of the other church I serve.
> Last year, on Sunday, June 14, Michael Alston was shot right outside that church during our afternoon Mass.
> Over the years, I have attended and led numerous curbside vigils where everyone cries out that these things need to stop. A few months later, we do the same thing all over again.
> I look at the maps and I listen to the explanations and ideas.
> I also hear the weeping mothers, brothers, and sisters.
> I witness the slow decay of sidewalk shrines as the candles are extinguished, the flowers die, and the balloons deflate.

Keeping Your Cool

Fits of anger or tantrums might help you negotiate a flight upgrade, but in communities where a parking-space negotiation could turn violent, staying safe requires keeping your cool.

How do we stay calm when we feel threatened or when our dignity has been violated? Through education and practice—which starts young. Lisa trained preschoolers to negotiate: "I've implemented peacebuilding opportunities where children ages three to five sit at the table and talk about an issue they have. As a teacher, I get involved to offer options, but the choices are strictly theirs. One tool I used in the classroom is a Solutions Kit. When children fought over a toy they both wanted to play with, the Solutions Kit would have pictures of various choices; trading one toy for another, playing with the toy together, waiting for the child to finish. . . . It usually ends well."

By Peaceful Means, a free peace camp in East Baltimore, helps kids avoid danger by teaching them when to negotiate and when to disengage. The camp is in a neighborhood with many boarded-up buildings, where drugs, and those addicted to them, move throughout the community, along with guns and other weapons. On their walk from the camp building to the public pool, the campers sometimes pass people who make derogatory comments. Many kids want to mimic parents whom they see respond forcefully when goaded. The camp counselors offer a different approach. When kids want to respond, camp cofounder

Nawal Rajeh asks, "Do you know if that person is high? Do you know if they have a gun?" This pause helps the kids evaluate the risks of certain responses.

When the taunting becomes too difficult for the kids to resist, the staff invoke an invisible tube called "Mookie." When traveling inside Mookie, the kids must stay focused, quiet, and not respond to jeers. They love the game and it keeps them safe. I'm sure Nawal wouldn't mind if you borrowed Mookie for yourself or your kids.

Rebeccah trains young people (ages eight to eighteen) on parole and adults in prisons through the "Alternatives to Violence" program. "We have to bring them back to what emotions are. This isn't that easy," she explains. Even the simple question "How did you feel when Mark hit you in the head with a ball?" can elicit answers like "I feel that Mark's an asshole."

Violence becomes the language for some who can't express themselves any other way or who've learned that their emotions are of no interest to others. Alternatives to Violence helps people get leverage over their emotions by focusing on what they want for the long term. "The potential payoff of revenge in the moment," says Rebeccah, "robs them of their own future. This helps anchor the message that we're not trying to change people—we're just tapping into their dreams, and building communication skills that they never learned."

Window of Tolerance

We can all practice keeping our cool by first understanding how emotions operate. University of California, Los Angeles, psychiatry professor Dan Siegel writes about what he calls the "window of tolerance." Those operating within this window experience a healthy state of arousal, shifting easily between emotions such as frustration, boredom, excitement, serenity, and so on, without these emotions derailing their lives.[1] Arousal *above* the window leaves people too anxious, fearful, or overwhelmed to function well. Those experiencing a state *below* the window often feel too zoned out, disconnected, or depressed to take the necessary actions to change their condition. Negotiating while either above or below the window often yields poor results.

For those operating in dangerous and/or under-resourced communities, few can maintain a consistent sense of well-being. Even if someone creates stability at home and work, extended-family members or friends ensnared in drugs, violence, or self-sabotage cause them tremendous distress. When those you love struggle so acutely, it's hard to keep your peace.

PROFESSIONALS

Violence prevention requires guiding others into the window of tolerance. Violence prevention programs train participants in how to find this window, as do effective police departments. First you need to know when and where people spin out. When the Los Angeles Police Department received frequent critiques for their officers' excessive use of force, they asked for help. Phillip Atiba Goff, a psychologist and professor of African American studies at Yale University, studied their data and found that most of the violence occurred during foot chases. With this new understanding, Goff says, they started training their officers differently for how to handle themselves during a chase. They now tell them, " 'You're high on adrenaline, you slow it down, you count to ten, don't touch the person till the backup shows up.' They dropped their use of force by 23 percent the next month. And it stayed low, and it became a national model for training in foot pursuits," Goff explained.[2]

Individual officers can find creative ways to cool the moment. Knowing how upset people can be after a car accident, Philip, a police sergeant in our class, picked wildflowers on his way to the accident scene. He handed them to those experiencing shock to calm them and reassure them he was there to help. Michael Gardner, a police officer in Ohio, made a career out of finding ways to reduce violence during domestic disputes.[3] Affectionately known as the "Dork Police," he and his colleagues used humor and other techniques to bring down the emotions during domestic disputes—that most dangerous time for police. They say the danger came when the victim might turn on the police if they tried to arrest her partner. Emotions can run hot between couples.

Here is what they did. (Parents, take note: these strategies can also work with squabbling siblings!) First, rather than banging on the door upon arrival (BAM, BAM, BAM), they used playful rat-a-tat-tats. Door pounding, they said, simply stressed people out more. They realized that their uniforms further alarmed people, so they put their hats on sideways or untucked their shirts to look less severe.

They realized that the question "What's going on here?" put people on the defensive and invited a recitation of the whole story, which further entrenched them in the conflict. Instead they asked, "Since the time you called, what solutions have you found?" This pivoted them toward resolving their differences, rather than just explaining them. If the couple refused to stop arguing, the officers would sit down and start watching the television. When the couple looked perplexed, they would say something to the effect, "You're clearly not ready to talk it out. So, we'll wait." Their creative techniques successfully transformed the most dangerous encounters faced by their department. They began teaching others. Gardner says, "I can say confidently that I was involved in hundreds of peaceful resolutions that would have ended up in arrests or fights had we used traditional police procedure."[4]

Those who have suffered under the police can be the best negotiation trainers *for* police. Take another student, Kolby Brown. Growing up in Baltimore, Kolby experienced brutal altercations with the police, including once being thrown on the ground when school was let out early on an exam day. Yet Kolby doesn't blame the individual officers involved in these incidents. Rather, he sees the police as fearful, traumatized, and in need of support. To help provide that support to new cadets, Kolby interned within the training division of the Baltimore Police Department. Between sessions, the new cadets shared with him their fears of working in such a violent city, which few knew well. Environments where people can share their fears without shaming become critical to de-escalation, especially in paramilitary environments where force is taught as a principal response to conflict. Now Kolby works for the police full time as a data analyst.

WHEN NOT TO NEGOTIATE

When faced with paramilitary forces, *not* negotiating can save your life. In the United States, many Black parents coach their children on how to avoid negotiating with police. Los Angeles community mediator Renata Valree says that she first had "the talk" when her son was eight years old. "We didn't just have that talk at eight, we have it every day. We have it every time he leaves the house."

His training for these encounters shifted as he aged. As soon as he could drive, Renata bought him a special wallet for his car registration. This wallet stayed in the side door so that he could avoid reaching into his pockets if pulled over, which could look, to a cop, like he was reaching for a gun. Her son later added his own preparations, installing dashboard cameras behind the front and rear windows to record his interactions with police.

Renata and her son negotiate his activism as well. In the days following George Floyd's murder, two Black men in their community were found hanging from trees in public spaces. The police reported them as suicides. The community disagreed and rose in protest, calling the act a clear case of lynching. Renata's seventeen-year-old son, six-foot-one and over two hundred pounds, wanted to join the protest. The police were already in their riot gear. Renata held him back. "Wait, wait," she said. "I need to think. We need to figure out what to do."

"He wouldn't be seen as a kid," she explained. "They would see him as a threat."

After reading Renata's story, several students shared their fears for their Black sons and partners. Tiffany A. said, "I'm scared for my twelve-year-old son, who is pretty tall and big for his age. I don't even let him walk to the store alone." She added, "My fiancé is six-foot-five, and I fear for him every time he walks out the door. I call and text him frequently to just ease my anxiety." Karah agreed: "I feel fear every time my boyfriend leaves the house."

Immigrants of color can be shocked to hear that they need to offer this training to their children and youths. Lexy and her sister coordinated a community meeting to discuss racism. A woman who had recently immigrated from Africa expressed outrage that she should have "the talk" with her kids. Lexy explained, "She refused to compromise [on] the way she raised her son because of the state of our country." Who could blame her?

Is the answer to teach people to negotiate in the world as they wish it to be, or the world as it is? If we deny the immediate dangers, we leave people vulnerable. We need to acknowledge harsh realities without contributing to them.

Understanding how our brains work can help us make better decisions. In her book *Our Brains at War*, conflict expert Mari Fitzduff explains that when faced with someone in the "outgroup," the parts of our brains wired for empathy and self-reflection quiet down and the amygdala (fight-or-flight response) ramps up and takes over.[5] This means that even if you are not consciously biased against a group, your brain may be biased, thanks to media, films, podcasts, and the people in your life. These narratives and cycles become what social psychologist Peter Coleman calls "attractors."[6] They pull stronger in times of uncertainty, when people turn to beliefs and/or identities that bring comfort.

For those living in precarious environments like Baltimore, street violence and drugs serve as other kinds of attractors. Drugs, for example, offer a feeling of euphoria (or relief from suffering); guns provide a sense of power and control; and access to the cash-rich drug trade seems to provide a pathway to prestige and freedom from poverty. Gang participation can offer community and a sense of safety, however limited. Persuading someone with access to these apparent advantages to sign up for a minimum-wage job can be a tough sell. Even those who wish for something different find themselves drawn back in by peer pressure, lack of confidence, no support, or simple temptation. This dynamic plays out in Baltimore, but also in geographically disparate marginalized communities in such countries as Colombia, Mali, Afghanistan, Nigeria, and even Canada.

Those negotiating in these contexts understand that to many, death feels close, ever present, and even a possible way out. Richard, who worked in security, shared this story with the class: "Two weeks ago, I had a drunk homeless guy demand I shoot him, or he was going to attack me and take my gun and *force* me to kill him. He said he wanted to die because he was homeless and had lost his family and he doesn't want this life anymore." Richard talked to him about his troubles and gave him money to buy dinner. The man grumbled, took the money, and walked into a restaurant. These kinds of interactions—which may seem dramatic to those living in more stable environments—can be normal negotiations for those living amid the dangerous cocktail of drugs, guns, and poverty. Those who handle the moment well save themselves and others.

The rest of this chapter considers three of the most challenging negotiations, those involving guns, drugs, and institutional survival. Because no approach works every time, I will share a variety of strategies used by those who achieved positive results. These guiding principles, which form the basis of my discussion, are useful for all fragile moments. Just take the following steps:

1. Calm the parties down.
2. Find something they care about.
3. Help them find an enduring, peaceful way to protect it.

NEGOTIATING WITH A GUN

When weapons attend a negotiation, lose-lose-lose becomes the likely outcome. The shooter loses a piece of their humanity, the victim their sense of security (and maybe their life), and the community a sense of safety and trust.

Negotiation skills can help us de-escalate even an armed situation. For those navigating communities in which many people respond to conflict with violence, this topic is not hypothetical. Among the 335 homicides in Baltimore during 2022, bullet wounds killed 87 percent of the victims.[7] Briana said, "I know for a fact there were more homicides in my area." For every homicide, four people experience nonfatal shootings. This brings Baltimore to roughly a thousand shootings a year, or three a day. Those who survive often do so because of medical intervention at the Shock Trauma Medical Center. During a police ride-along, the officer I accompanied pointed to some of the medical staff standing in front of the hospital and said, "Whenever you see someone wearing pink scrubs, acknowledge them. *They* are the heroes in this city, saving kids every day."

How can negotiation skills help people intervene *before* the gun goes off? Many look first to law enforcement, but Phillip Atiba Goff—the Yale professor whose research findings have helped police departments stop contributing to the violence—reminds us that "law enforcement is not gonna prevent the violence. They're gonna respond to it. And if what you want is less violence, you want prevention."[8] If so, who can help prevent it?

VIOLENCE INTERRUPTERS

Many of the best street negotiators come from the streets. Epidemiologist Gary Slutkin launched a violence interruption initiative in Chicago called Cure Violence, which treats violence as a disease that outreach workers aim to contain and then eliminate. To create their team, Cure Violence sought out and mentored street-savvy individuals who were formerly gang-involved, deep in the drug trade, carrying criminal records or still incarcerated, with reputations for carrying weapons, or who had been shot.[9] The idea is that those who know the "code on the streets can best cure the streets."[10] Also known as *violence interrupters,* these intervenors mediate disputes, work toward long-term behavior change in individuals, and shift the street culture that normalizes (and even celebrates) violence. External evaluations of the program saw astonishing results in the form of "reduced levels of total violent crime, shootings, and homicides."[11]

Baltimore replicated the Cure Violence program under the name Safe Streets.[12] A study published in 2016 reported that interventions by Safe

Streets Baltimore (and even posters advertising cease-fires) significantly increased interest in nonviolent solutions among at-risk youth ages eighteen to twenty-four.[13] The Johns Hopkins Center for the Prevention of Youth Violence evaluated the effectiveness of Safe Streets by studying two hundred mediated disputes that had the potential to turn fatal. The study showed that Safe Streets resulted in "less acceptance for using guns to settle grievances. Program participants reported benefiting from their connections to outreach workers in numerous ways that could be protective against future involvement in violence. Three of the four program sites experienced large, statistically significant, program-related reductions in homicides or nonfatal shootings without having a counterbalancing significant increase in one of these outcome measures."[14]

Leonard Spain, a returning citizen and a victim of gun violence who has worked with Safe Streets, discusses what we need to know to safely negotiate these dangerous moments. First, he says, you need to know what triggers people, such as "perceived disrespect, personal altercations, and disputes over drug territory."[15] Drug territory disputes are serious. "Some people are making $30,000 to $40,000 a day," he explained.

"Wait, hold on," I said. "They're making up to $40,000 a day? No wonder they don't want to give it up!"

"Oh, they're going to give it up, one way or another," Leonard explained. "They'll go to prison, they'll get shot, but they're gonna lose it one way or another."

The hustle promises a pathway to glory but leads to short-term gains and often catastrophic long-term outcomes. Until the intervenors can convince people to leave this lose-lose-lose way of life, they must help negotiate them down from dangerous moments. Because no tactic works with everyone, they train in multiple negotiation strategies.

For his master's thesis, Leonard Spain interviewed Safe Streets workers to identify which strategies they found *most* useful. All pointed to these important steps:

1. separating the conflicting parties,
2. buying time for them to cool off, and
3. influencing them by bringing in key individuals.

While many people can implement the first two, the programs work because they train *key individuals,* already known and respected by those at risk. Police, by contrast, tend to move in and out of a community quickly. They rarely know people well enough to identify "odd" behavior in someone. By contrast, community members can better "observe unfamiliar patterns and secretive behavior," says Leonard.[16] He offers an example: you notice that someone who never wears their sweatshirt hood up is suddenly putting it up—on a hot day. You have to know the "normal" behavior to be able to identify a change. Insiders also have more information about when and where street conflicts might occur. They show up and do whatever it takes to interrupt the moment. Law enforcement and other outsiders misinterpreting signs can create a dangerous situation out of a benign moment.

To achieve this, the interrupter might show up and take the person out to eat. Interrupters have even been known to pull out a blunt and smoke it with the person who is threatening violence. While Leonard himself questioned the ethics of this, he decided that smoking pot with someone was better than having them shoot someone. Only when people calm down can alternative solutions be explored.

Anisha Thomas, deputy director of Safe Streets, and "Hamza" Gardnel Carter, a thirteen-year member of the organization, explain more about the problem-solving phase. For example, if people are fighting over an iPhone or a bike, Safe Streets might just buy a replacement item. Here are some other tactics used by outreach workers at Safe Streets and Cure Violence:[17]

Agreement	Arrange return of stolen goods/money. Help parties establish mutually acceptable boundaries for territory. Establish cease-fire or truce between groups.
Buying time	Invite individuals to get some food, go elsewhere, talk about the issue. Wait while the angry person calms down.
Blaming the violence interrupter	Encourage saying, "The violence interrupter asked me not to shoot," to save face.
Economics	Explain how shooting hurts business and will attract police attention. Emphasize the financial cost of going to jail.
Personal consequences	Point out the effect of violence on parents, children, siblings. Emphasize bad endings: jail or death.
Violence interrupter's story	Share personal experiences in jail or other negative outcomes.
Potential	Remind the person about goals and all the other things he could do with his life.
Third parties	Ask a friend or relative to convince the individual he doesn't need to shoot. Talk to the people the shooter wants to impress. Speak to gang leaders or other key individuals.
Questioning	Ask the individual to explain why he needs to do this. Together, think through actions.
Yelling	Yell at the individual: aggressively tell him not to shoot.

These tactics can be useful in a variety of dangerous situations. But be careful—even Safe Streets workers sometimes get shot.

THE BEST NEGOTIATORS AREN'T ALWAYS PERFECT PEOPLE

If you want negotiation help from people who know street life best, you cannot expect them to all be angels. As I write this, one worker who had finished serving a seventeen-year sentence returned to prison for using his Safe Streets role to disguise his involvement in the drug trade.[18] Safe Streets managers know they can't always pull workers back from street life's appeals. "You wouldn't ask an alcoholic to work in a bar," Thomas says, "but that's effectively what we do. We hire people because they have these histories and then take them back to the same neighborhood. You can't fire them or replace them for fucking up or take it personally . . . That's exploitation . . . to recruit people from the most vulnerable areas and then throw them in jail." Of course, you can't have your workers participating in the drug trade, but you need to work with lateness and other behaviors that might get someone fired in a normal job. Safe Streets workers are complicated heroes and not easily replaceable.

Hamza says they need people who will stick around and work odd hours: "After a mediation it's not enough just to end the violence in the moment. [The involved parties] will check up on you to make sure you're following through. Then *he* spreads the word that you're legit, [telling people] 'He allowed me to keep my dignity and the other guy his dignity, they just didn't want us to kill each other.'" They can get called on at any time. Anisha says, "A fight that happens at night started the day before. The hours of this job aren't regular."

Emotional rewards keep these community negotiators coming back to work. Hamza, who spent twenty years in prison, says, "Every time I help others, it helps me." They even become local stars, "Residents are happy to have them in the neighborhood. They see smiles on people's faces. It's reassuring that they're there," explains Anisha. This reinforces their new identity. One of the brightest stars of Safe Streets was Dante "Tater" Barkesdale, who worked with the organization for over a decade. Dante told those seeking revenge that "forgiveness is the most Gangsterish thing you can do." He redefined what it meant to be tough.

But training, street cred, and admirers cannot always protect violence intervenors from the dangers of negotiating in this environment. In January 2021, Dante was shot and killed for refusing to reveal his cousin's whereabouts to someone who wanted to harm him. In an apparent revenge killing, the woman who drove the getaway car was subsequently shot and killed.

Leonard, who was close to Dante, wants more people to have these negotiation skills. So he has expanded the training to others in the community. "Barbers can stop the war," he said, because "barbers have been cutting the hair of the involved parties since they were babies." During a recent workshop with a group of barbers, Leonard discussed a few traditional negotiation concepts:

Expanding the pie—helping people see there's more available than what they see.

Trade-offs—they can seek revenge, but what's the cost?

Problem solving—is there another way around this?

Separating the people from the problem—how can we solve the problem, without harming the people involved?

With this training and support, barbers can become master negotiators, helping their clients work through their problems in the chair, rather than on the street.

NEGOTIATING ALTERNATIVES TO STREET LIFE

When intervenors can't interrupt the violence and participants become sidelined by injury, other negotiation opportunities emerge. Leonard takes advantage of these opportunities through Johns Hopkins Hospital's Responders Program by visiting with recovering individuals throughout their hospital stay. Through multiple meetings, he builds trust, discourages retribution, and coaxes them to leave street life.

He establishes trust by sharing his story and showing his own wounds. Then, Leonard says, "you have to replace the revenge thought." He explained how he had approached this with a young man we'll call Sean. Imagine he had gone in and said, "Why don't you drop this fight?" Sean might have gotten defensive. Instead, Leonard drew on what he knew about Sean: that he had a child and wanted to be a good parent. Instead, Leonard opened with "How's your son?" This question positioned Sean as a father rather than as a street-involved individual. The question prompted Sean to think beyond the present moment and into the future. Encouraging this shift in thinking takes time and reinforcement. These conversations often return to the desire for revenge—and when that happened with Sean, Leonard used another form of perspective taking.

"When I get out of here, I'm going to show him. He has no idea who I am," Sean said.

Leonard pushed back: "You may have no idea who *he* is. You don't know if his father is a drug kingpin and will come down on you." Sean realized how little he knew about the person who shot him and reconsidered his capacity to respond.

When people feel violated physically and emotionally, the desire for revenge is an understandable response. Leonard helps them see how this impulse can lead to even more undesirable outcomes. These techniques work best, he says, when conducted by those who know street life and have a good reputation in those communities. When negotiating with individuals to choose a path other than revenge or hate, your hard-earned life lessons can be an asset.

WOMEN

Although conversations about gun violence often focus primarily on men as the attackers and the victims, women escalate and de-escalate violent conflict too. Leonard remembers when only one woman a year would be shot in Baltimore, but in 2022, twenty-two were shot to death. "It's mostly the guys they date," he explains. "Many times, they were sitting in the car when someone came for their boyfriend. Half the time when you ask them about it, the boyfriend is dead." Lisa, a student, said she knows a woman murdered the same way. "The killer was looking for the boyfriend and she was killed because she was in the car with him. It devastated the family and the church."

Women contribute to violence when they encourage revenge, demand luxury lifestyles, or "set up men against one another—to fight over them," says Anisha. They help prevent conflict when they do the opposite. Both Safe Streets and the Baltimore Police Department seek more women intervenors because they see how they can help defuse anger and negotiate nonviolent solutions. We all have a role to play.

NEGOTIATING ALTERNATIVES TO VIOLENCE

Many violence intervenors understand the deeper emotional needs people seek to fulfill through their violent acts. Philosopher William Irvine, who grew up in a poor mining town in Minnesota, once observed that "in our world, lots of people have given up on being loved, admired, and respected but nevertheless want other people to acknowledge their existence: 'If others won't love me, then let them fear me. If others won't respect me, then they will have to put up with my disgusting or belligerent behavior. I will not be ignored.'"[19] When one feels powerless, weapons become a great equalizer. For a moment, anyway.

People can get drawn into violence out of boredom. A man from Yemen told me, "You have to understand, our young men have nothing. They don't even have a movie theater. There's just dirt. What do you expect them to do?" This explains, he said, why many of them join jihadist groups who offer money, some amount of safety for themselves and their families, structure, belonging, and purpose.

Those supporting kids in violent neighborhoods understand the dangers of boredom. Tiffany says, "My mom always made us have different hobbies. She kept us so busy, we didn't have time to get into trouble . . . and it definitely helped!" Rebeccah, who works in Baltimore with kids on parole, sees what happens when there's nothing good to do: "The choices are hard. They can stay home and be bored and be called a 'loser' or be out with friends getting into trouble." She wishes they had more options.

Citizens can help by advocating the creation of positive places for kids to meet up. Melissa took on the challenge for a class assignment. When trying to plan her daughter's "sweet sixteen" birthday party, she discovered that Mustang Alley, a downtown bowling alley, prohibited entry to kids under twenty-one after 7 P.M. Melissa said, "I was so frustrated because there were literally NO other fun activities for my teens to do in downtown Baltimore, which ultimately led me to reach out to Councilman Costello of the downtown district . . . He personally reached out to the bowling alley and secured us three lanes until 7:30 . . . It was an amazing experience, and I am so glad I asked for some help from the councilman." Negotiations initiated by engaged residents like Melissa can transform whole communities. Don't underestimate the importance of your voice. You can inspire others.

When Melissa shared this story with the class, Rodney took notes. He wanted to bring up the idea of extending the bowling alley's hours to his colleagues at YouthWorks Academy, a government agency that provides internships for city youth aged sixteen to nineteen. In 2023, YouthWorks secured nine hundred summer positions for the city's youth. If you want less violence, engage people in meaningful activities organized by supportive people.

Persuading individuals once involved in armed conflict to choose another path requires even more engagement and support. Laura Baron

Mendoza does this work with former members of FARC, a guerrilla organization in Colombia. Through job training and placement, she and her organization help former combatants "reincorporate" into civil society. Some thrive, others struggle. One of the men she became close to returned to combat. When Laura asked him why, he said that he felt no purpose doing the jobs offered to him. The work bored him. Armed conflict, he said, was what he knew. Note that he returned to the violence *not* out of a desire for revenge, hatred of others, or a justice claim. He was bored and felt out of place. Some U.S. veterans may relate. Office work can seem deathly stifling after tours of active duty. We need to create compelling alternatives to foster willingness among combatants, and street-involved individuals, to leave the fight. Negotiation requires give and take. If you want to convince someone to change their way of life, what compelling alternatives can you offer?

DISARMING NEGOTIATIONS

I know that gun control is a dangerous tinderbox, yet I think that one would have to lack integrity, care, and common sense to deny that fewer guns means fewer shootings. Sometimes harm is accidental. Shanice told the class that her brother was killed by a friend playing with a gun. I then shared my story with the class. A former boyfriend insisted on showing me his handgun. He stood in front of me while I sat seated on the couch beseeching him to please put the gun away. He assured me that as a "weapons expert" he knew not to keep it loaded. Right after he said this, the gun went off, embedding a bullet in the floor next to me. He easily could have killed me. My boyfriend was a well-traveled, successful businessperson studying in one of Harvard's graduate programs. These incidents can occur anywhere guns are present.

Then we have intentional killings. During my three years in Baltimore, 1,147 individuals were shot to death. Some fatal shootings were close by. On March 25, 2021, across the street from my apartment and the university, Philip Blankenship, age twenty-nine, shot and killed Randolph Jones, thirty-nine.

Leonard says that back in the day when someone would get angry, it took them time to find a gun and seek revenge. Now, people have multiple guns. So, a flash of anger over a stolen cell phone, a perceived advance on one's territory, or jealousy over a girlfriend can end in death. Earl, born and raised in Baltimore, added that now younger kids have access to weapons, shooting others for "little to nothing."

We do not have to live like this. Montreal, a city with over four million people (compared to Baltimore's six hundred thousand) has impoverished areas and numerous residents living on the margins—yet, in 2022, Montreal had only 41 homicides, compared to Baltimore's 335.

Making guns harder to acquire and instituting buyback programs can help. Leonard laughs when I talk about paying people to turn in firearms with the promise not to press charges for unlawful possession. "It won't work," he says. "People have four or five guns." He knows the streets better than I, but to me one less gun is one less opportunity to grab something in a fit of fury. A study of the Australia buyback program found that it "significantly reduced Australia's homicide rate in the decade following the intervention (1997–2007)."[20] This program removed a specific type of firearm across the whole country. Other programs have had more difficulty correlating buyback efforts with reduced homicides.

By removing the guns, we can better address systemic problems instead of writing off violent places as people's personal failure. This is as true of Baltimore as it is of Afghanistan, the African Sahel, Yemen, and other regions flooded with arms. After living somewhere flooded with guns and seeing the results, I cannot understand why so many people advocate having more of them.

ADDICTION

How do you negotiate with someone who doesn't think there's anything wrong?—Maryann, student

Even more ubiquitous than guns, addictive substances create numerous negotiation challenges. I realized the importance of this section after a student, Sue, commented on our "high-stakes negotiation" readings:

My first reaction is to say I've never been involved in a high-stakes negotiation, but I'm wondering about the negotiations that took place with my ex-husband Mark and his mother in the aftermath of my discovery that he was addicted to heroin. These conversations felt like the stakes were very high—life and death even. . . . That first big negotiation was around whether Mark would stop using heroin, but that was just the tip of a very big iceberg of negotiations, including whether he would go into residential treatment, what would happen if he used, whether and how often he would go to Narcotics Anonymous meetings, how transparent he was about our shared history, and when he started using. . . . In the end, it was a process of engaged (and gradually more spaced out) negotiations, the last of which was getting him to sign separation papers.

Once I added addiction to the course topics, almost every student had a story to tell. Shanice said, "I lost four uncles to heroin. Everybody in my family was addicted to heroin. . . . We lost a whole generation." Karah admitted, "My father struggled with addiction his entire adult life until he passed in May of 2020."

> I could never bring up my mother's addiction when I was a kid because she was the parent. There was no negotiation.—Brenna, student

Together we explored whether negotiation skills can help those facing addiction and those who love them. To start, we noted that the addicted person remains in a constant negotiation with themselves: will they succumb or fight back? Those in recovery negotiate internally throughout the day to stay the course. Then, we have those negotiating with the afflicted. In such negotiations, we often find ourselves faced with *two* people: the sober person and the addicted person. The sober self may have little control over the addicted self, which, fearing the loss of the drug, avoids confrontation.

Hyland explored how negotiation strategies could help her strike a deal with her stepbrother, Nathan, who remained addicted despite going through six in-patient rehabilitation programs. After he showed up to Easter dinner intoxicated, Hyland wanted Nathan to agree to attend family events sober or not at all. He would take a sobriety test prior to events until she could trust him again. Hyland considered this negotiation "a total gamble" because when confronted in the past, he "denied his drug use completely and radiated an arrogant and defensive attitude."

She prepared first by examining her own feelings and behaviors related to his addiction. She said, "I need to stop blaming my stepbrother for hurting our family." Otherwise, he may pull away. She then prepared herself for whatever he might do or say. He shows up "a different person when he is under the influence compared to when he is sober . . . [and] I am prepared for him to manipulate, to schmooze, and to deceive."

In planning the meeting, Hyland considered how her age and gender might affect her ability to influence him. He saw her as "the little sister, not someone to be taken seriously." To mitigate this and to keep their emotions in check, she invited her mother and stepfather to attend. They agreed.

Together, they told Nathan that he could no longer attend family events intoxicated.

Nathan responded by saying, "I understand, and I will rebuild your trust, but it is unfair to exclude me from holidays when I am trying to better myself. How am I supposed to show you all that I am improving if I'm never around?"

After some discussion, Hyland and her parents agreed to give Nathan the opportunity to attend special holidays with this stipulation: "If he shows up to a holiday celebration under the influence, he must leave right away with no more chances to redeem himself." The family handled the conversation well, but time will tell if Nathan can hold up his end.

Often these agreements fail. Lisa shared, "I took my brother to a drug treatment program. . . . The family was so excited that he agreed to go, and I was very hopeful for his future. My husband even bought him a pair of new shoes, saying, 'This is the start of a new path for you, Joe' . . . [but four months later, in] March 2021, my brother left the program and went back out in the streets. By August 2021, he lost his life to drugs. It devastated the family." Drugs often lead to lose-lose outcomes for users and their families.

THE CHALLENGE OF ADDICTION

To learn about how to negotiate with individuals struggling with addiction, I spoke to Chris Novak. As of June 2021, Chris had been in recovery from heroin for two and a half years and now supported others. He began by emphasizing that addiction doesn't just affect the poor. He said he had good parents and attended a good school.

When I asked how best to support someone struggling with addiction, Chris said, "There's no negotiation with someone who uses. You can take drugs out, but if I don't change, I'll go back." People need to decide they want to recover.

Those committed to recovery often remain in a constant negotiation with themselves to stay clean. Chris described his own self-negotiations while managing the stress of his Baltimore-based construction company: "I get into a mood and worked up and I have to talk myself down. I want things to be fixed immediately with clients, with a job, with relationships and they can't always be fixed immediately." Seeing others return to drugs fuels his commitment to stay clean. He told me that a man he helped recover "was just found in an alley in Baltimore half-naked with a needle in his arm. That's not going to be me."

To help those in recovery uphold their agreements with you and with themselves, understand that success comes with challenges. Chris explains, "I have the money in my pocket. I live in Baltimore. I'm ten minutes away from getting any drug." Access and affluence become a dangerous combination. For this reason, he says, recovery and the associated personal work must remain the number one priority. Otherwise, anyone can end up like his friend Josh, a well-loved member of the recovery community. After he got clean, Josh became the owner of eight recovery houses and two treatment centers in Baltimore. He died two weeks before Chris and I spoke. "They said it was a heart attack," Chris said, "but it was an overdose. Josh didn't do his personal work. He got too big too fast. Money, power, and prestige are terrible for us."

Hopeful family and friends increase the pressure. "People are so proud of you, then you're depressed and feel like a traitor. You don't want people to see you relapsing, so you disappear. Then people don't feel like coming back."

"What can we do as family and friends?" I asked.

"You must create consequences," he said without hesitation. "The worst thing a family can do is turn away from the issue. It's a giant form of enabling." Chris recalled one Christmas when his brother left because he couldn't bear seeing Chris look so bad. This helped.

The consequences must be serious. Chris explained, "I stole jewelry from my mother once, and she just yelled at me. I figured I could handle getting yelled at again. . . . You need to give *hard love*. Give real guidelines about what's going to happen if the person keeps using. . . . If you say, 'I'm not going to talk to you while you're using,' then you must stick to it. Many people don't follow through." Lasting agreements between the addicted person and their loved ones require sustained effort and deep commitment. It may also require refusing to see your loved one for a period. Excruciating.

PAINKILLER NEGOTIATIONS

> It angers me that these pharmaceutical companies can't see all the deaths they've contributed to and what angers me is that they don't care.
> —Lisa, student

As with gun violence, the responsibility for drug addiction lies not just with those directly involved, but with those providing access. Many addictions begin with prescription drugs. Lisa, who lost her brother to drugs, hates watching her family's use of painkillers. "The first onset of pain, they are ready to pop a pill in their mouth. I tell them pain is an indicator. It tells you that something is happening in your body." This habit can become deadly. In 2020, more people died from prescription overdoses than from heroin overdoses.

Chris links many heroin overdoses to prescription drugs. He outlined this all-to-common trajectory:

1. People find pills in their parents' medicine closet or get prescriptions from doctors.

2. Once hooked, they try to buy pills on the street but find them too expensive.

3. They turn to heroin.

4. They may overdose, but Narcan revives them.

5. Many go into recovery but relapse once and die because their bodies can't handle the heroin anymore and especially not the fentanyl.

When I asked him about the pharmaceutical industry's responsibility, Chris said that he cannot pursue them because his recovery requires all his personal energy. His brother Jonathan, however, can and does. An alumnus of the University of Baltimore School of Law, Jonathan works for the Drug Enforcement Administration to expose the role of Big Pharma in the deaths of five hundred thousand people in the past two decades (his work can be seen in the 2021 HBO documentary *The Crime of the Century*). The pressure on complicit corporations to take responsibility became material in February 2022, when four major providers of prescription opioids agreed to pay $26 million in damages.[21] In November of the same year, Walmart added another $3 billion to the pot.

Lawsuits may slow down the providers, but what about medical professionals? Shelly told the class about negotiating with hospital staff during her husband's visit for a shoulder injury. She told the staff that he could not be prescribed narcotic painkillers. "We're recovering addicts," she explained.

The nurse insisted: "He needs to take these. Do you know how many people beg us for this prescription? And you're rejecting it!"

Shelly said, "I understand, but we cannot have those drugs. We're former addicts. We need something else." They had to simply refuse the drugs.

Hearing Shelly's story, others shared their negotiation experiences with medical professionals over a desire *not* to use painkillers for bone extractions, gall bladder surgery, and childbirth.

Alternatives exist. *JAMA*, a leading medical journal, published a study in 2017 that found no difference after two hours in the effectiveness of opioid and non-opioid painkillers for acute pain.[22] In other words, acetaminophen and ibuprofen work as well alone as they do when combined with codeine or oxycodone. Acupuncture provides yet another alternative. Knowledge like this can assist in negotiations with medical professionals.

In many ways, we all negotiate for our sobriety every day. Advertisers encourage us to turn to alcohol, pills, and, increasingly, marijuana to deal with pain. Staying sober requires negotiating first with ourselves, then with the system, and—at times—with loved ones who have fallen victim to addiction.

We can seek other outlets, such as the arts, to process and express, rather than supress, pain. Let's consider this pathway further.

AN ORCHESTRA

For the finale, appropriately enough, I call upon the orchestra. Discussing an orchestra negotiation may seem as out of place in this chapter as a world-class orchestra can seem in Baltimore. Most of the city's residents live less than five miles from the orchestra, though for many, the distance might as well be ten thousand miles. Seemingly inhabiting different worlds, their destinies are nevertheless intertwined: the Baltimore Symphony Orchestra (BSO) depends on the people of the city for support, and the people benefit from the music. Many believe that increased participation in the arts will enrich lives and reduce violence and drug use. To support this potential for positive change, the orchestra created OrchKids, which has provided thousands of children free music lessons after school. Music offers us all a pathway to the balanced emotional states (or the window of tolerance) needed to respond productively to challenges. Furthermore, the arts offer a means of self-expression and cultural commentary.

Many of the musicians bring their own dreams for Baltimore. Marin Alsop, OrchKids founder and former conductor of the BSO, said, "I'd love Baltimore to become known as the City of Music, rather than the City of Murder."[23] Who would disagree? Alsop's mentor, Leonard Bernstein, urged musicians who want to help, but don't know how, to consider music as their *response* to violence. Bernstein said, "This will be our reply to violence: to make music more intensely, more beautifully, more devotedly than ever before."[24]

The orchestra has done just that, even providing a soundtrack during some of the city's most difficult moments. In 2015, during local protests following Freddie Gray's death, BSO musicians played on the sidewalk. The orchestra's chief trumpeter, Andrew Balio, said that "our best response to such dismal darkness would be for us to turn on our brightest light—to perform an impromptu concert."[25] While National Guard helicopters circled the city, the orchestra performed to roughly a thousand listeners. Balio added that this is not new: "Throughout history, when entire societies have been at war, even at the very apex of conflict, people *want* to go to hear a concert of classical music." Sometimes orchestras have their own internal wars that threaten their survival. Those with experience running cultural institutions know the numerous negotiations needed to prevent dissolution.

The BSO: A Case Study

Baltimore Symphony Orchestra's struggles offer negotiation lessons for those committed to keeping arts institutions afloat. Founded in 1916, the orchestra almost collapsed soon after its one hundredth anniversary. On June 16, 2019, just days after the final spring concert, the BSO management announced to the musicians that, to save money, they had canceled the summer series and, with it, their summer salaries. Oh, and they would be locked out of the building. Musician cochairs Greg Mulligan (violin) and Brian Prechtl (percussionist) talked to me about this stressful time. Greg said that the lockout "felt truly bizarre." Brian recalled, "Things were very contentious. A lot of decisions were being made in a panic mode."

In September, the management, which saw cost cutting as the only solution to the BSO's financial crisis, offered the musicians a "take it or leave it" deal that included a 20 percent salary reduction. The players, who already made less than they had a decade before, refused the pay cut. Instead, they raised $1 million from community philanthropists to support their salaries. The management refused to accept the earmarked money. Enraged, the musicians demanded that the orchestra draw from its $60 million endowment trust to pay them.[26] The management refused, and the musicians protested on the sidewalks.

Yet, as of 2023, despite the additional challenges of COVID-19, the BSO is okay. What explains the turnaround? Greg and Brian discussed with me the negotiation strategies that saved the orchestra.

FINDING ALLIES

Find people to care about you. Get them to work on your behalf in a way that doesn't heighten the adversarial nature of the interactions.

—Brian Prechtl, BSO percussionist

Musician allies forced the management to find solutions other than cutting salaries and refusing to fill vacancies. Greg says the musicians began by "acknowledging the support we already had in the community. . . . We had significant allyship and I think that was absolutely huge." These allies included the Governing Members of the orchestra who supported the musicians' pleas. Several significant donors contributed by assertively questioning the management.

The musicians reached out to musicians at other orchestras, smaller donors, and legislators. Throughout the tense process, they supported one another. When the management cut the summer season, for example, they cared for those in dire financial need. They contacted MusiCares, the charitable arm of the Grammys, which supports professional musicians during troubled times.

Influential supporters help the musicians address the power imbalance throughout the negotiations. "We're just considered labor," Brian explained. "There's a caste system in this country, whether people want to admit it [or not]. We're not the same caste as the people on the boards." Board members who guide the orchestra's direction often ascend to these positions through business success, not artistic success. While musicians understand the importance of a balanced budget, says Brian, "we're not a business, we're a charity. We're here to make the world better." Supporters made this perspective audible to those in charge.

Mediator

In addition to allies, the musicians needed a good mediator. Brian called members of every orchestra that had faced similar challenges. "In almost every situation, some party stepped into the gap and helped the different parties. Sometimes it was a mayor, concerned businesspeople, board people, it seemed to be a pattern. One of the most influential conversations was talking to the folks in Detroit. . . . I talked to a real pivotal figure after their very contentious strike. They had so much bitterness, the parties couldn't be in a room together. I started to realize, we're not going to get anywhere like this, we need to start hearing each other and talking to each other."

With help, the Detroit orchestra and management team had transformed the tone and structure of the conversations between management and musicians. They had even included others affected by the board's decisions, such as the music director and even volunteers. "No one could bow out. They all had to be in," Brian explained. Once people could communicate, they could work together to solve the problems. The Detroit Symphony Orchestra flourished. Brian shared Detroit's story with Barry Rosen, the BSO board chair, who listened and created a Vision Committee to help them make similar changes.

The Right Expert at the Right Time

The musicians discovered that their lawyer's hardball tactics, useful in previous years, became a barrier to productive discussions. So they switched to Kevin Case, a lawyer who represents musicians and artists in labor disputes. According to Brian, "Kevin just lowers the temperature in the bargaining room. . . . Somehow, he makes everyone stay relaxed and work through problems."

The musicians sought additional experts to guide them toward a more unified approach to the negotiations. Greg explained that "when you're in a union, unity is hugely important and difficult. Just as Brian and I sometimes had different ideas about strategy, so did other intelligent musicians. That's no small thing to stay together." To help with this unity, they hired Randy Whatley, president of Cypress Media Group, a public relations firm. Greg said, "Randy was extraordinary as an advisor. He kept telling us the goal was 'to keep us from driving into the ditch on either side of the road.'" He advised them on how to speak to the press, the community, and the management. The consistent messaging kept their campaign focused and powerful. How did they afford this outside assistance? For the past ten years the musicians have deducted a small portion of their salaries to support any labor-related negotiations. Experts can be critical during crises, especially when trust dissolves between parties. Every labor union needs such a fund.

The board reached out to experts as well. Rosen contacted Michael Kaiser, the president of the John F. Kennedy Center for the Performing Arts. Kaiser, known as the "turnaround king" of the arts business, spoke to BSO management. Brain said, "He came with an arts-positive message, that you cannot cut your way to health in these organizations. You must invest in the artistic product and get people excited about it. . . . It's sort of a formula, but it really resonated here. . . . The musicians loved it.

They've been saying it for years." Sometimes people need to hear the message from someone else. When we can let go of pride and focus on finding the best carrier for the message, we can do more for our cause.

Kaiser won over the management and effectively wrote the BSO's current strategic plan. With a clear shared vision, they collectively raised $9.6 million in the first eight weeks of 2020. Success begat success. The state legislator approved more funding. Even in the middle of the COVID-19 pandemic, Greg reported, "the musicians got a progressive five-year agreement!" Create the culture for productive conversations, find the right massagers and key individuals, and focus on improvement rather than cuts.

LETTING IT GO

> There comes a time when you have to turn the page.
> —Greg Mulligan, BSO violinist

Greg acknowledged that the contention brought about critical change. The management needed to understand the distress of the orchestra members. A new vision and a healthier organization required that fight, Greg said. He added: "At some point, you have to switch from being oppositional to [orienting toward] some kind of an agreement. . . . It was hard for me to want to flip that switch. A certain amount of distrust has built up." Once parties reach an agreement, they many need to consciously shift from an adversarial to a collaborative way of approaching one another. While orchestra negotiations may not lead to life-or-death outcomes, when they fail, careers and important institutions die. The music can stop.

Long-term survival for the BSO requires continuing efforts to reach out to residents. The BSO already offers tickets to Baltimore's youth and more diverse programming than before. In addition, extra tickets could go to civil servants, medical staff, and other employed youth throughout the city. My husband credits his appreciation of classical music in part to the free tickets he received while working in a hospital kitchen as a young man. Fill every seat for every show through donations if necessary and everyone will thrive.

SUMMARY

This chapter considered some of the tough negotiations that are common where people and institutions operate in precarity. Those who thrive do so by bravely challenging the culture of violence, the drugs themselves, the money they generate, and cuts to the institutions that provide alternatives.

Many traditional negotiation principles are useful for those navigating a way out: knowing what you want, having alternatives, understanding the other party, and seeking a win-win outcome. But there are differences.

When weapons come to a negotiation, lose-lose-lose outcomes become likely. Those directly involved and the wider community all suffer when the guns go off. Weapons shift conversations from negotiations to ultimatums. Context-appropriate negotiation skills can, however, convince parties to drop the weapon. Violence interrupters teach the importance of

- separating the parties,
- finding something they care about, and
- discussing how violence will increase their chances of losing everything.

Only then can the conflict between the parties be addressed. Said another way, we remove the weapons and then guide people into a healthier emotional state before talking about the conflict. These conversations work best when led by individuals who are already trusted by the conflict parties. A former gang member or convicted felon can often influence a person at risk more than someone who never walked that path. The same may be true of a former member of Al-Qaeda, the Taliban, or the Islamic State. Once negotiators reduce the immediate threat, they can discuss alternatives to violence going forward.

Negotiating with someone who is suffering with addiction requires other skills. We need to understand that people must choose to recover. That said, those supporting family members or friends in recovery can push people toward that choice by setting limits. Your brother can say, for example, "No time with your nephew if you continue to use." Family and friends must stand by the terms they set, even when it means time apart. Seek recovery experts for advice when negotiating these boundaries.

While seemingly trivial compared to the loss of life, budget negotiations become high-stakes when communities lose resources that provide alternatives to violence and drugs. Music and other arts offer ways to process and express difficult emotions. Without them, people more often turn to harmful ways of processing fear, grief, feelings of insignificance, oppression, and even boredom. Keeping the arts alive requires finding allies, seeking expert advice, and using intermediaries who can change the tone of the conversation.

Experts in all three areas—guns, addiction, and the arts—need not be perfect people. In fact, those who have committed crimes, suffered addiction, or almost killed their orchestra are often best positioned to help others choose differently. They speak from experience. You need people with street cred who can navigate between conflict parties. Outsiders must support these experts and their programs that offer other pathways.

Finally, environments where people experience perpetual distress need trauma-informed negotiators with the skills to help parties find and maintain a "window of tolerance" in which they are not too agitated or too depressed to make good decisions. Helping people find their center is as important as generating solutions. It may be more important. When parties feel safe and heard, solutions often present themselves.

ACTIVITIES

Highest-Stakes Negotiation

In groups, share your highest-stakes negotiation. What did you learn about negotiating from the experience? What would you advise others to do?

From Mistake to Message

Our best negotiation advice to others can come from our biggest failures. Journal about a negotiation or a choice you made that you would now handle differently. How would you advise someone facing that situation?

Wisdom of Others

Interview a friend or family member about their highest-stakes negotiation. What happened? What did they do and, having survived, what advice do they have for others?

The Arts Can Heal

Find a cultural institution (art, music, dance, etc.) that almost folded but found a way to survive. How did they find their way forward? What resources, tactics, or negotiation savvy saved them?

Conclusion

"Not everything come down to how you carry it in the street. I mean it do come down to that if you gonna be in the street, but that ain't the only way to be," says Dennis, formerly street-involved, now a mentor.

"Around here it is," says Duquan, a recent high school dropout.

"Yeah, around here it is. World is bigger than that, at least that's what they tell me."

"Like, how do you get from here to the rest of the world?" asks Duquan.

"Wish I knew," says Dennis.[1]

This conversation from the quasi-fictional Baltimore drama *The Wire* speaks to the challenges of moving from one world into another. In a city where your zip code is correlated with your life expectancy, finding "the rest of the world" matters deeply. *The Wire*'s ability to depict such high-stakes conundrums earned it numerous accolades—the *BBC*, for example, called it the greatest TV show ever made.[2] But the on-air attention to the city and its problems did not result in positive change on the ground. Since *The Wire* first aired in 2008, the Baltimore homicide rate has increased by one hundred murders per year. Overdose deaths similarly continue to rise. The show's fame could not even save one of its most illustrious actors: Michael K. Williams, who played streetwise, homicidal, yet sympathy-inspiring Omar, died of an overdose on September 6, 2021.

Why did such a great and influential show lead to so little measurable change? Marcetta, who has worked in correctional institutions and psychiatric hospitals, offered this explanation: "The trauma of our lives has been played out on *The Wire* . . . None of the profits from my pain have made their way back to my community." The show missed some culpable players, she adds. "Corner boys are not manufacturing heroin. Heroin, disguised in other packages, is being brought into this port city by the corner store owners, nail salon owners, and restaurateurs. The owners work in Baltimore but live in the suburbs of Virginia, Pennsylvania, Montgomery County, and other non-Baltimore locations. They thrive off the narrative that death and crime are unapologetically Black."

Additionally, much of great fiction (and nonfiction) describes problems without offering solutions. Negotiation skills, by contrast, teach us *how* to make things happen in our lives. *Transformative Negotiation* offers context-appropriate training to support people navigating contexts rarely discussed in traditional trainings. Of course, a book cannot undo systemic challenges, the pull of drugs, corruption, or the ubiquity of guns, but it can open a conversation about how negotiation skills can serve people moving from precarity to stability.

Creating this book required input from those overlooked as negotiation experts. Take Rosalind, a formerly incarcerated graduate student who supports people in recovery: "You have to meet people where they are. I know all the bullshit," she said. When a client expressed anger at having to meet with her, Rosalind told him, "If you ain't a dragon and spittin' fire, I'm not afraid of you." His response? He smiled, shook her hand, and they worked out a meeting schedule. That's skill. In sharing their savvy, Rosalind, Marcetta, and the dozens of other contributors to this book expanded the field of negotiation and its reach.

Those navigating under-resourced, volatile communities know that what goals you pursue and how you pursue them has huge consequences for your life. Wes Moore, Maryland's 2022 governor-elect, knows the importance of choice. The day the *Baltimore Sun* announced his Rhodes Scholarship, the paper also announced a search for another Wes Moore, wanted for murder. Moore found and befriended the incarcerated Moore. They discussed how, despite their identical names and similar Baltimore upbringings, their choices had resulted in different lives.[3] *Transformative Negotiation* offers a variety of tips and stories to support people choosing a path other than the one most clearly laid out for them.

TRANSFORMATIVE NEGOTIATION IN REVIEW

Chapter 1: Imagine encourages you to take more time considering what you want and *why* you want it. Many of our desires emerge from our observations of others, family pressure, advertising, and the media. This chapter invites you to consider what will bring *you* the most stability and satisfaction in the long term. Those wishing to transition from one environment to another must make different choices than those around them. Because this can be lonely, the examples I provide offer ways to stay connected to families and communities of origin.

Chapter 2: Ask explores a simple observation, that you can have much of what you want by simply asking for it. This fact is often hidden from view. People from under-resourced communities or in discriminatory environments can absorb the message that they are undeserving. Historical trauma or upbringing can compound this messaging. We shake off at least some of these chains by merely reactivating our asking power.

Chapter 3: Give discusses the cycle of reciprocity. Askers who do not give become takers. Moreover, asking without giving contributes to feelings of victimization. The givers in this chapter teach us that no matter what our challenges, if we are being generous, we have value. That said, those who give everything while keeping nothing for themselves often suffer physically and emotionally. Many people navigating challenging environments are already huge givers. Women, for example, often engage in the unpaid labor of housework, child care, and elder care. Those with experience juggling these multiple caregiving roles share strategies for setting boundaries and saying no.

Chapter 4: Money talks about financial management. How can we know how much we can afford when we don't know what we owe or what we need now and in the future? Shockingly, negotiation books rarely help readers figure out what is an acceptable job offer. How much can they borrow, spend, or charge? These are not obvious calculations. Historically marginalized and under-resourced communities often lack good financial mentors. As a result, predatory businesses and individuals can take advantage. Some basic financial knowledge helps people stay anchored in negotiations and know their walk-away points.

Chapter 5: Digital considers how new technology upends old ways of negotiating and engaging with others. Digital communication can save time but also can destroy deals and relationships far more easily than face-to-face meetings. Drawing on the latest research and student examples, this chapter offers a series of best practices for negotiating online.

Chapter 6: Power offers negotiators and instructors a new way to think about power in negotiation. Beyond just time, money, and clout, negotiators want to consider structural power. When you're talking to the Internal Revenue Service about late fees on your tax bill, for example, it would be naive to ignore the power this organization can have over one's life. The IRS can make your life hell—the reverse is not true. This chapter talks about various forms of power and how to leverage yours.

Chapter 7: Gender, Sex, and Race draws on the latest research to explore how negotiation advice may differ for people with different backgrounds. In business, for example, women can lose social capital when asking for a raise, whereas men do not. The myth of white supremacy affects negotiations involving Black, Indigenous, and other people of color. This chapter discusses how to navigate a biased world while undoing that bias. The chapter even includes the under-addressed high-stakes negotiations surrounding condom use and marital pressure.

Chapter 8: Guns, Addiction, and an Orchestra takes on some of the most difficult negotiations faced by those navigating a community rife with guns and drugs and short on funding. What works in the boardroom will not necessarily work in the streets where drugs and guns take hold. In fact, those tactics can backfire in dangerous ways. Practitioners specializing in these types of negotiations offer their advice.

YOUR STORIES

A localized approach to negotiation requires more voices. I hope that this book encourages you to write about *your* world. Local guides, written in local languages that use regional examples, provide valuable advice. Negotiation guides can emerge from Indigenous reserves in Canada, from the urban centers of Honduras, even from refugee camps.

At the very least, please use this book to become a great negotiator and mentor. Neither requires being a perfect person or having a perfect life. In fact, your hard-earned lessons and current challenges will likely become your gifts to others. The book gathers insights from formerly street-involved individuals, those resisting the pull of opioids, homelessness, and debt, and those navigating complicated parenting situations, elder care, or abuse. Their striving, and yours, can support others.

EXPANDING NEGOTIATION

Your stories and advice will continue to expand the field of negotiation. This is a field that can too often suggest (or assert directly) that its advice works for "all readers." However, this book cites numerous studies showing how negotiations can play out differently depending on industry, age, gender, ethnicity, and even body size. So, in fact, the same advice does not work for all readers the same way. The challenge for the field is that nuanced and localized curricula require more work. Profitable trainings become less so if the instructor must redo the training to apply to the local context and find local individuals who know how things work. Unfortunately, new instructors too easily pick up a standard syllabus, as I did when I first arrived in Baltimore, and teach its unnuanced advice to a new set of students.

Pretending that advice works for all readers can do an immense disservice, especially for the most vulnerable. Telling a woman in Saudi Arabia to negotiate like a woman working on Wall Street is irresponsible and dangerous. Our faculty saw this up close when a Saudi doctoral student almost lost her children during her fieldwork. Her husband threatened to take them if she conducted the interviews needed to complete her degree. Fortunately, she found a way to conduct her research and keep her children. When we advise anyone without understanding such realities, we can put them in danger. Those of us in the negotiation and conflict fields want to be responsible when setting up satellite programs around the world. We can give bad advice and, in the process, disempower locals who have the knowledge to teach their own people how to navigate *their* world.

WHAT IS NEGOTIATION SUCCESS?

Negotiation experts can contribute to larger social change by expanding how we evaluate negotiation success. Like those of many negotiation instructors, my students end the term with raises, work flexibility, improved relationships, new jobs, and progress toward paying off debt. These are all good things. But when measuring the results of our trainings, we tend to look at the short-term gains of our students, not their long-term happiness or the effect of their negotiations on others.

Doug, a student, helped me think beyond the financial results students achieved. He used a negotiation assignment to get $450 back from a family member who had stolen it from him and said, "After I received it, I thought 'Do I really need it? No, it was about the principle of it.' So, I gave it to a homeless man. . . . His eyes opened wide. He didn't bother to count it and gestured me to sit down. We carried on a conversation. During the conversation, he broke down. He appreciated the conversation more than the money itself. He said it felt good to be recognized as a person." Doug learned more than how to negotiate and get money; he learned how to use money in a meaningful way.

Five years after our trainings, we can inquire: Are you happier? Have you stayed connected to your communities? How are your relationships? When they tell us that they negotiated a multi-million-dollar deal, we can ask whether all stakeholders were given a voice. When promoted into high-level positions, we can encourage them to use their power wisely. I'd love to know your short- and long-term outcomes. Please let me know at www.sarahfederman.com.

WIN-WIN-WIN

We would be wise to evaluate negotiation success on the agreement's ability to achieve a *win-win-win* outcome. That third win requires a conception of success beyond the satisfaction of the negotiating parties at the time of their agreement: we must think about those affected by our actions, even if they are not present. To help us with this, I propose adopting John Rawls's approach to fairness, which asks us to imagine ourselves as any party affected by the agreement. Would we still think it's fair? Another thought exercise is to adopt the Haudenosaunee (Iroquois) Seventh Generation Principle, which requires members to ponder how their decisions could play out seven generations into the future. Incorporating either of these practices will shift how we negotiate.

CARE, DIGNITY, AND TRUST

A win-win-win approach asks more than whether everyone received fair financial compensation. This approach to practice and evaluation asks how much care, dignity, and trust the process generates.

Care

Medical anthropologist Arthur Kleinman would tell us to approach our negotiations with an ethos of care: "Amid the hardness, hate, violence, and cynicism that fuel politics today, an anti-caring ethos prevails . . . Care is the human glue that holds together families, communities, and societies."[4] Care is not, he says, about being soft or sentimental, but rather is the key ingredient to functioning human networks. In many places where people struggle, the absence of care takes multiple forms. In Lowndes County, Alabama, lack of care shows up as residents are forced to live with raw sewage in their yards. With no sewage treatment provided by the state, this largely Black community must live in excrement. Emma Scott works six days a week in a chicken plant and cannot afford a septic tank. Alabama refuses to help. Journalist Bill Whitaker asks her, "Do you feel forgotten?"

"Yes sir," Emma replies.[5]

A politics of care would transform Ms. Scott's sewage system. You cannot care about someone and leave them in sewage. The poultry plant could pay her better and the state could step in. A politics of care could transform the carceral system, schools, and every aspect of our society. Without care at the center, no policy change will be sufficient. Negotiators who place care centrally in their work will find their relationships and communities enriched.

Dignity

Along with care, we can evaluate the dignity with which each party was treated. The violations against people are not just physical, but psychospiritual, says conflict expert Donna Hicks. Her book *Dignity: Its Essential Role in Resolving Conflict* considers different forms of dignity violations and how we can respond to and prevent them.

Our negotiated outcomes can also *interrupt* ongoing dignity violations. When Baltimore police officers refused to help prostitutes reporting abuse, they violated the dignity of those individuals. The Baltimore Police Department took a step toward restoring their dignity when it required new cadets to take *every* call, even those from prostitutes. In our daily negotiations, we can demonstrate dignity much more simply: by thanking people, looking them in the eye, responding to requests, and listening to what matters to them. If we attend to the emotional core of our negotiations, we can generate this dignity and help rebuild the trust that has been broken.

Trust

We can evaluate our negotiation success by the amount of trust each party earned in the process. Wharton negotiation professor Stuart Diamond says that trust makes life work.[6] Without trust, people focus on win-lose outcomes.

Political trust in Baltimore is extraordinarily low. Two of the last ten police commissioners stepped down, and the rest were forcibly removed on charges ranging from domestic abuse to tax fraud—a few are serving prison sentences.[7] In 2019, twenty Baltimore police officers were arrested, sentenced, or suspended.[8] Baltimore is not alone. Corruption has eroded trust in many U.S. cities, including Wichita, Cleveland, Richmond, New York, Los Angeles, Philadelphia, Chicago, and Washington, D.C. Judges accepting bribes, police officers selling drugs, and city officials taking kickbacks have earned Crystal City, Texas, a reputation as the most corrupt little town in America.[9]

Diamond says that in low-trust environments, one should build commitment incrementally. Avoid people who lie, and verify information when you can. In making contracts, he suggests adding contingency clauses that say a contracting party will pay more if they do not honor their word. "Second chance" language in agreements creates an opportunity for each side to try again.

Safe Streets Baltimore knows that trust-building requires long-term investment and many second chances. The organization of violence interrupters manages ninety formerly street-involved individuals. Safe Streets director "Hamza" Gardnel Carter, who served a twenty-year sentence, says that "building trust takes constant follow-up." The workers and those they serve in the streets all need multiple opportunities to change their behavior.

Only when trust exists can other life paths be discussed. Leonard Spain, who visits people recovering from bullet wounds, says that it can take weeks to build a relationship with someone, before getting to the point where Leonard will encourage the person to leave street life. Negotiating for larger social change requires more than a one-off meeting. We need to show up again and again. Those negotiating in or with war-torn, violence-inflicted, poor, or conflict-fatigued communities know this. They shift the landscape in which people negotiate by generating contexts of care, trust, and dignity.

RECLAIMING COMMUNITIES

When used for social transformation, creative use of negotiation skills reclaims communities. Here are some examples: Erricka Bridgeford cofounded Baltimore's Ceasefire weekends in 2017. Her organization negotiates with gang members to call a truce during several weekends throughout the year. She has drawn thousands to the cause and succeeded in interrupting deaths during some of these weekends.

Karim is helping reclaim Pennsylvania Avenue—known today for its gun violence. He and other involved community members now call it Baltimore's Black Arts District (B.A.D.). They commemorate the neighborhood's rich history while also negotiating successfully for property tax credits for developers who create spaces for artisans. Serving communities in this way requires what Karim calls "good anywhere people," meaning people who can talk to anyone and go anywhere without fear. Those who can negotiate productive outcomes across subcultures can rebuild fractured connections and restore trust.

Even kids can be taught the negotiation skills needed to reclaim their territory. By Peaceful Means, a free peace camp in East Baltimore, teaches kids how to resolve interpersonal conflict and engage in peacebuilding efforts at home and worldwide. One year, the kids protested the closing of a neighborhood pool and won.

Dan Stevenson, a resident of Oakland, California, reclaimed his community in a most unusual away. Though not a Buddhist, he bought a two-foot statue of Buddha and placed it where his community suffered the most crime, aggravated assault, and graffiti. Curiously enough, people stopped dumping their trash there.[10] These are all examples of what Daniel Shapiro would call creating the sacred. By making our communities sacred, even if others have forgotten them, we can shift the environment, physically and mentally. Creativity and commitment can transform these spaces.

Star negotiators of these communities succeed because they take ownership of and responsibility for the world in which they find themselves. So let's listen. In that spirit, I will give student Marcetta Young the last word:

> Baltimore is my city. The city with the first Health Department and the first Roman Catholic church in the Americas. The birthplace of David T. Abercrombie, Nancy Pelosi, Tony Evans, Chick Webb, Thurgood Marshall, and me. I add my name to this illustrious list because I can make as much of a difference in people's lives as they have. Not in spite of where I am from, but because of it.
>
> The ability to nurture our talents and overcome our obstacles is evidenced in the fact that we seek education. . . . We want to be seen as not just salvageable but sacred gods and goddesses in our own rights as opposed to children of a lesser god. . . . We triumph through our trauma because someone has to do it and today in Baltimore, it is not they, it is us.

Notes

INTRODUCTION

1. MacGillis, "The Tragedy of Baltimore."
2. Kram, "The 2019 Orioles Might Be the '27 Yankess of Awful?"
3. Pietila, *The Ghosts of Johns Hopkins: The Life and Legacy That Shaped an American City.*
4. I follow the Associated Press, which now capitalizes *Indigenous* and *Black.* See Associated Press, "Explaining AP Style on Black and White."
5. Rodricks, "Mike Busch, Catherine Pugh and That Thing Called Integrity."
6. Motro et al., "Race and Reactions to Women's Expressions of Anger at Work." See also Bernstein, Green Carmichael, and Torres, interview with Opie and Caridad Rabelo.
7. McIntyre, *Participatory Action Research.*
8. Rock, Grant, and Grey, "Diverse Teams Feel Less Comfortable—and That's Why They Perform Better."
9. Ross, "The Intuitive Psychologist and His Shortcomings: Distortions in the Attribution Process."
10. Ingram, "The Forgotten Dimension of Diversity."
11. Ingram, "The Forgotten Dimension of Diversity."
12. Lipsky, *Street-Level Bureaucracy,* 3.
13. Yoshino, *Covering: The Hidden Assault on Our Civil Rights.*
14. Diamond, *Getting More: How You Can Negotiate to Succeed in Work and Life,* 46.
15. Enloe, *Bananas, Beaches and Bases: Making Feminist Sense of International Politics.*
16. Cobb, Federman, and Castel, *Introduction to Conflict Resolution: Discourses and Dynamics.*
17. See Cobb, *Speaking of Violence;* Enloe, *Bananas, Beaches and Bases.*

18. Battilana and Casciaro, *Power, for All: How It Really Works and Why It's Everyone's Business,* 29.

19. Only after the Florentine Republic fell and Machiavelli suffered torture at the hands of the Medici family did he write *The Prince.* He wrote it under duress.

20. Hicks, *Dignity: Its Essential Role in Resolving Conflict.*

21. Diamond, *Getting More,* 79.

22. Niezen, *Defending the Land: Sovereignty and Forest Life in James Bay Cree Society.*

23. Organize Poppleton, "Save Our Block in Poppleton, Baltimore."

24. Ury, *Getting to Yes with Yourself (And Other Worthy Opponents).* John Elkington's "Towards the Sustainable Corporation" (1994) also encourages a win-win-win negotiation approach to balance the needs of customers, companies, and the environment.

25. Rawls, *A Theory of Justice: Original Edition.*

26. Stevenson, *We Need to Talk about Injustice,* 16:20.

27. Pressman, "The Decline of the Middle Class: An International Perspective."

28. Payne, *The Broken Ladder: How Inequality Affects the Way We Think, Live, and Die.*

29. Miller, *Halfway Home: Race, Punishment, and the Afterlife of Mass Incarceration.*

30. Halpern-Meekin, *Social Poverty: Low-Income Parents and the Struggle for Family and Community Ties.*

CHAPTER 1. IMAGINE

1. Irvine, *On Desire;* Schopenhauer, *The Essays of Arthur Schopenhauer.*

2. Irvine, *On Desire,* 101.

3. Babcock and Laschever, *Women Don't Ask: The High Cost of Avoiding Negotiation—and Positive Strategies for Change.*

4. Umoh, "Black Women Were among the Fastest-Growing Entrepreneurs."

5. Irvine, *On Desire.*

6. "20-Year Gap in Life Expectancy between Richer, Poorer Areas of Baltimore."

7. Williams, Lawrence, and Davis, "Racism and Health."

8. See Gone, "Redressing First Nations Historical Trauma"; Niezen, *Rediscovered Self.*

9. Westerhof et al., "The Influence of Subjective Aging on Health and Longevity."

10. Pontzer et al., "Daily Energy Expenditure through the Human Life Course."

11. Sale, *Let's Talk about Hard Things.*

12. Pinsker, "We're Learning the Wrong Lessons from the World's Happiest Countries."

13. Brooks, "How to Buy Happiness."

14. Callan et al., "Gambling as a Search for Justice."

15. Irvine, *On Desire,* 16.

16. Bohler, *Le bug humain.*

17. Irvine, *On Desire.*

18. Wilson and Witter, *The Master Plan: My Journey from Life in Prison to a Life of Purpose.*

19. Wilson and Witter, *The Master Plan,* 117–18.

20. Wilson and Witter, *The Master Plan.*

21. Babitz, *Slow Days, Fast Company: The World, The Flesh, and L.A.*

22. Fitzduff, *Our Brains at War: The Neuroscience of Conflict and Peacebuilding.*

23. Wilson and Witter, *The Master Plan,* 291.

24. Wilson and Witter, *The Master Plan,* 351.

25. Oliver, *Wild Geese.*

26. Thank you to Suzanne Waldron and Robert Dilts for this practice.

CHAPTER 2. ASK

1. Wilson and Witter, *The Master Plan.*

2. Berger, *A More Beautiful Question;* Telegraph Staff and Agencies, "Mothers Asked."

3. Taylor, "The Neuroanatomical Transformation of the Teenage Brain."

4. Brown, *Daring Greatly: How the Courage to Be Vulnerable Transforms the Way We Live, Love, Parent, and Lead.*

5. Some names changed. Students receive extra credit if they effectively pay for the negotiation course through negotiations conducted throughout the semester.

6. Speed, Goldstein, and Goldfried, "Assertiveness Training."

7. Adams, "Judith Heumann."

8. Lenski, "Friction with a Colleague."

9. Babcock and Laschever, *Why Women Don't Ask.*

10. McCrory Calarco, *Negotiating Opportunities.*

11. McCrory Calarco, *Negotiating Opportunities.*

12. Baker-Bell, *Linguistic Justice.*

13. See Dwyer, "A Politics of Silences"; Lara, *Narrating Evil.*

14. Peterson and Seligman, "Learned Helplessness and Victimization."

15. See Smith, Chambers, and Bratini, "When Oppression Is the Pathogen."

16. Volkan, "Transgenerational Transmissions and Chosen Traumas."

17. See Beecher Stowe, *Uncle Tom's Cabin;* Kendi, *Stamped from the Beginning.*

18. Krish O'Mara Vignarajah, personal communication with author, July 29, 2020.

19. National Aeronautics and Space Administration, *NASA's Hispanic Astronauts.*

20. Amnesty International, "Saudi Arabia."

21. Anderson, *Code of the Street.*

22. *Śūnyatā,* often translated from Sanskrit as "emptiness," enables phenomenological analyses of reality.

23. Popper, *The Logic of Scientific Discovery.*

24. Fisher, Ury, and Patton, *Getting to Yes.*

25. Ury, *Getting to Yes with Yourself,* 45.

26. Eichler, "'Askers' vs. 'Guessers.'"

27. Coleman, *The Way Out.*

28. Fisher and Shapiro, "Emotions Are Powerful."

29. Shapiro, "Negotiating Emotions."

30. Hicks, *Dignity.*

31. Mummendey et al., "Strategies to Cope with Negative Social Identity"; Runciman, *Relative Deprivation and Social Justice.* Mummendey et al. say that this psychological stress occurs because our emotions of contentment and resentment often correspond to what we believe our life might have been, compared to our current situation.

CHAPTER 3. GIVE

1. See Fisher and Ury, *Getting to Yes*; Grant, *Give and Take*; Kolb and Porter, *Negotiating at Work*; Lewicki, Barry, and Saunders, *Negotiation: Readings, Exercises, and Cases*; Shell, *Bargaining for Advantage.*

2. Aknin et al., "Prosocial Spending and Well-Being."

3. Mauss, *The Gift,* 74.

4. Ermine, "Giving What You Treasure to Get What You Need."

5. Schneider, *Financial Empowerment.*

6. Grant, *Give and Take.*

7. *The Mask You Live In.*

8. Grant, *Give and Take.*

9. Reinhard et al., "Valuing the Invaluable."

10. Slaughter, "The Work That Makes Work Possible."

11. U.S. Bureau of Labor Statistics, "May 2020 National Occupational Employment and Wage Estimates."

12. Organisation for Economic Cooperation and Development (OECD), *Enabling Women's Economic Empowerment.*

13. Wolff et al., "A National Profile of Family and Unpaid Caregivers."

14. Kleinman, *The Soul of Care.*

15. Sy and Romero, "Family Responsibilities among Latina College Students."

16. AARP and National Alliance for Caregiving, *Caregiving in the United States 2020.*

17. Sabia et al., "Association of Sleep Duration in Middle and Old Age with Incidence of Dementia."

18. Paradies et al., "Racism as a Determinant of Health." See also Williams, Lawrence, and Davis, "Racism and Health." This article claims that while everyone suffers, a surprising finding was that Asian American and Latino(a) American participants suffered the greatest emotional effects; Latino(a) American participants exhibited the greatest effects on their physical health.

19. Zaki, "'Self-Care' Isn't the Fix for Late-Pandemic Malaise."

20. Loughan and Perna, "Neurocognitive Impacts for Children of Poverty and Neglect."

21. Brefczynski-Lewis et al., "Neural Correlates of Attentional Expertise in Long-Term Meditation Practitioners"; Grewal, "Improving Concentration and Mindfulness."

22. Grosser, Kidwell, and Labianca, "Hearing It through the Grapevine."

23. Grosser, Kidwell, and Labianca, "Hearing It through the Grapevine."

24. Narayan, "Bonds and Bridges," 6.

25. Mazelis, *Surviving Poverty*, 10.

26. Companies such as McDonald's, Burger King, FedEx, UPS, Amazon warehouses, and some bakeries offer jobs that are critical for formerly incarcerated persons trying to build a new life.

27. van Eijk, "Does Living in a Poor Neighbourhood Result in Network Poverty?"

28. Sataline, "The Backlash against Tithing."

29. Ford, "Should the Poor Give?"

30. m1ority, January 8, 2011 (7:50 A.M.). Comment on African HYS team. "Can You Afford to Go to Church?" Midas is a legendary king in Greek mythology with the power to turn anything he touched to gold.

31. diones, January 7, 2011 (11:09 A.M.). Comment on African HYS team. "Can You Afford to Go to Church?"

32. Kelly, *Should the Church Teach Tithing?*

33. Kelly, "Here with Another View on Christian Tithing."

CHAPTER 4. MONEY

1. Aknin et al., "Prosocial Spending and Well-Being: Cross-Cultural Evidence for a Psychological Universal."

2. Chou et al., "Economic Insecurity Increases Physical Pain."

3. Perhach, "A Story of a Fuck Off Fund."

4. Reeves, McKee, and Stuckler, "Economic Suicides in the Great Recession."

5. Chatzky, "Do You Have a Complicated Relationship with Money?"

6. Horowitz, "Charles the Entrepreneur?"

7. Bell Smith and Nkomo, *Our Separate Ways.*

8. McCurn, "'Keeping It Fresh': How Young Black Women Negotiate Self-Representation and Controlling Images in Urban Space."

9. Brown, *Daring Greatly.*

10. Reid, "What's the Deal with Affirm, AfterPay, Klarna, and QuadPay?"

11. Perry et al., "The Devaluation of Assets in Black Neighborhoods"

12. Gourrier, "Banking the Black Community."

13. Wilson and Witter, *The Master Plan*, 300.

14. Callan et al., "Gambling as a Search for Justice."

15. Callan et al., "Gambling as a Search for Justice," 1526.

16. Allen, "Planning for the Unexpected."

17. Reynolds, "The Role of Mutual and Trust Funds in Caring for Grandchildren."

18. Caring.com, "2021 Wills and Estate Planning Study."

19. Byrd, "Importance of a Will."

20. Horton and Weisbord, "68% of Americans Do Not Have a Will."

21. Berger and Miller, "Why You Need to Make a 'When I Die' File."

22. Tretina and Curry, "How Fiduciary Duty Impacts Financial Advisors."

23. Mara Thee Reporter (@marascampo), "My daughter is asking the tooth fairy for $100, 'because I really liked that tooth,'" Twitter, January 31, 2021, 10:45 A.M.

24. Lowry, *Broke Millennial.*

25. Blanco, "Years after the Meltdown, Latinos Still Wary of Big Banks."

26. Shattock, "Focus on Unbanked Latinos."

27. Tessler, *The Art of Money.*

28. Shapiro, *Negotiating the Nonnegotiable.*

29. Ramirez-Fernandez, Ramirez-Marin, and Munduate, "Selling to Strangers, Buying from Friends."

30. Leonhardt, "60% of Women Say They've Never Negotiated Their Salary."

31. These states currently include Massachusetts, Maryland, Virginia, New York, Pennsylvania, and Washington, D.C.

32. Note that some human resources departments in government agencies, by law, give the job to the equally qualified person who asks for the lower salary.

33. See Salary.com, Glassdoor.com, Payscale.com, Vault.com, and Linke-dIn.

34. Daniel Shapiro, "Using Emotions as You Negotiate," presentation, Harvard Program on Negotiation, November 4, 2021.

35. Rangel, "5 Salary Negotiating Tips for Remote Jobs."

36. Volkema, Fleck, and Hofmeister, "Getting Off on the Right Foot."

37. Narula, "How Much Money Do Millennials Make?"

38. Fisher and Ury, *Getting to Yes.*

CHAPTER 5. DIGITAL (#FACEPALM)

1. Turkle, *Reclaiming Conversation,* 16.

2. Misra and Stokols, "Psychological and Health Outcomes of Perceived Information Overload."

3. Sherlock and Wagstaff, "Exploring the Relationship between Frequency of Instagram Use, Exposure to Idealized Images, and Psychological Well-Being in Women."

4. Gritters, "How Instagram Takes a Toll on Influencers' Brains."

5. Lovitt, "Death by Selfie."

6. Lup, Trub, and Rosenthal, "Instagram #Instasad? Exploring Associations among Instagram Use, Depressive Symptoms, Negative Social Comparison, and Strangers Followed."

7. Ward et al., "Brain Drain."

8. Misra et al., "The IPhone Effect."

9. Chotpitayasunondh and Douglas, "The Effects of 'Phubbing' on Social Interaction."

10. Al-Saggaf and O'Donnell, "Phubbing."

11. Turkle, *Reclaiming Conversation,* 14.

12. Hyman et al., "Did You See the Unicycling Clown?"

13. Centers for Disease Control and Prevention, "Distracted Driving."

14. Mark, Gonzalez, and Harris, "No Task Left Behind?"

15. Mark, Gudith, and Klocke, "The Cost of Interrupted Work."

16. Ebner et al., "You've Got Agreement."

17. Friedman and Currall, "Conflict Escalation"; Kupfer Schneider and McCarthy, "Choosing among Modes of Communication."

18. Gottman and DeClaire, *The Relationship Cure.*

19. Shonk, "Advanced Negotiation Techniques."

20. Ebner et al., "You've Got Agreement."

21. Wells and Dennis, "To Email or Not to Email."

22. Diamond, *Getting More.*

23. Thompson and Nadler, "Negotiating via Information Technology."

24. Shonk, "Online Negotiation in a Time of Social Distance."

25. Friedman and Currall, "Conflict Escalation."

26. Volkema, Fleck, and Hofmeister, "Getting off on the Right Foot."

27. Diamond, *Getting More.*

28. Forge, "How to Negotiate Car Price by Email."

29. Schneider, *Financial Empowerment.*

30. Schneider, *Financial Empowerment.*

31. Ebner et al., "You've Got Agreement"; Schneider, *Financial Empowerment.*

32. Diamond, *Getting More;* Friedman and Currall, "Conflict Escalation."

33. Diamond, *Getting More;* Schneider, *Financial Empowerment.*

34. Shapiro, "Negotiating Emotions."

35. Thompson and Nadler, "Negotiating via Information Technology."

36. Ebner, "Negotiating via Text Messaging."

37. McClain, "70% of U.S. Social Media Users."

38. Harvard Program on Negotiation Staff, "How to Negotiate via Text Message."

39. Ebner, "Negotiating via Text Messaging."

40. Adimsm5050, "Mom: Your great-aunt just passed away. LOL."

41. Gunraj et al., "Texting Insincerely."

42. Kupfer Schneider and McCarthy, "Choosing among Modes of Communication."

43. ABDd, "Matthew Hussey Gives Texting Advice."

44. ABDd, "Matthew Hussey Gives Texting Advice."

45. Wingko, "These 15 People Had the Perfect Responses."

46. Aguilera and Muñoz, "Text Messaging as an Adjunct to CBT in Low-Income Populations."

47. Kelly, "4 Tips to Send (and Receive) Better Texts."

48. Ebner, "Negotiating via Videoconferencing."

49. Long, "How to Ace Your Zoom Interview."

50. Carney, Cuddy, and Yap, "Power Posing."

51. Malhotra, "How to Negotiate on Zoom."

52. Rogers, "Community Mediation Online."

53. Rogers, "Community Mediation Online," 41.

54. Tufekci, "Does a Protest's Size Matter?"

55. Vosoughi, Roy, and Aral, "The Spread of True and False News Online."

56. Benkler, Faris, and Roberts, *Network Propaganda.*

CHAPTER 6. POWER

1. Wilson and Witter, *The Master Plan,* 296.
2. Weber, *Economy and Society.*
3. Gruenfeld, *Acting with Power,* 22.
4. Mayer, *The Dynamics of Conflict.*
5. Harvard Program on Negotiation Staff, "Power in Negotiation."
6. Kim, Pinkley, and Fragale, "Power Dynamics in Negotiation."
7. Mayer, "The Dynamics of Power in Mediation and Negotiation."
8. Auyero, "Patients of the State," 16.
9. Bourdieu, *Pascalian Meditations.*
10. Winter, "The Power Motive in Women—and Men."
11. Wallerstein, "Powerlessness, Empowerment, and Health."
12. Fisher and Shapiro, *Beyond Reason.*
13. Schmeichel and Vohs, "Self-Affirmation and Self-Control."
14. Walton and Cohen, "A Brief Social-Belonging Intervention."
15. Galinsky, Gruenfeld, and Magee, "From Power to Action."
16. Harvard Program on Negotiation Staff, "Power in Negotiation."
17. Wilson and Witter, *The Master Plan.*
18. Maaravi and Hameiri, "Deep Pockets and Poor Results."
19. Mayer, "The Dynamics of Power in Mediation and Negotiation."
20. "How do you greet someone in Nigeria?"
21. From the poem "The Burning of Paper instead of Children."
22. Thompson, "Five Reasons Why People Code-Switch."
23. hooks, *Teaching to Transgress.*
24. Demby, "How Code-Switching Explains the World."
25. Alim and Smitherman, *Articulate While Black.*
26. Liljenquist, LinkedIn message to author, May 8, 2021.
27. Liljenquist, "Resolving the Impression Management Dilemma."
28. De Dreu and Van Kleef, "The Influence of Power on the Information Search, Impression Formation, and Demands in Negotiation," 317.
29. Harvard Program on Negotiation Staff, "BATNA Strategy."
30. Ury, *Getting to Yes with Yourself.*
31. Harvard Program on Negotiation Staff, "Power in Negotiation"; Overbeck, Neale, and Govan, "I Feel, Therefore You Act"; Van Kleef et al., "Power and Emotion in Negotiation."
32. Elkins, "PepsiCo CEO Indra Nooyi."
33. Kapoutsis and Volkema, "Hard-Core Toughie." Martin Latz analyzed hundreds of Donald Trump's negotiations prior to the presidency in *The Real Trump Deal* and had similar findings.
34. Fitzduff, *Our Brains at War.*
35. Gallo, "How to Disagree with Someone More Powerful Than You."
36. King, *The Inconvenient Indian.*
37. Keith, "The Paradoxical Commandments." Reformatted into a poem by Mother Teresa entitled "Anyway."
38. Harvard Program on Negotiation Staff, "Tired of Liars?"
39. This quote comes from a Harvey Milk campaign speech in 1973.
40. Miller, "As Baltimore's Poppleton Neighborhood Braces for Change."

41. Arendt, *The Human Condition.*

42. Poppe, Leininger, and Wolff, "Introduction."

43. Anderson and Prudente, "Fells Point Businesses."

44. Education of All Handicapped Children under Section 504 of the Rehabilitation Act of 1973.

45. Associated Press, "Egypt to Free Lebanese Tourist."

46. Shear and Stack, "Obama Says Movements."

47. Deutsch, *Le metronome.* Note that Hugo's words are my translation.

48. Inspired by Payne, *The Broken Ladder,* 217–18.

49. Inspired by Galinsky, Gruenfeld, and Magee, "From Power to Action."

50. Mayer, "The Dynamics of Power in Mediation and Negotiation."

CHAPTER 7. GENDER, SEX, AND RACE

1. Gabbatt, "Oprah Winfrey Given Swiss Apology."

2. "Clinton, *What happened.*" She keeps this as a sign in her house.

3. Babcock et al., "Nice Girls Don't Ask"; Babcock and Laschever, *Women Don't Ask.*

4. Babcock and Laschever, *Women Don't Ask.*

5. Tannen, "The Power of Talk."

6. Bowles, Babcock, and Lai, "Social Incentives for Gender Differences"; Bowles and Babcock, "How Can Women Escape the Compensation Negotiation Dilemma?"; Heilman and Okimoto, "Why Are Women Penalized for Success at Male Tasks?"; Konnikova, "Lean Out."

7. Amanatullah and Morris, "Negotiating Gender Roles."

8. Bowles and Babcock, "How Can Women Escape the Compensation Negotiation Dilemma?"

9. Harvard Program on Negotiation Staff, "Women and Negotiation."

10. Amanatullah and Tinsley, "Ask and Ye Shall Receive?"

11. Babcock and Laschever, *Women Don't Ask,* 153.

12. Bowles and McGinn, "Gender in Job Negotiations."

13. Wong, "The Workplace Still Isn't Equal for Women."

14. Bowles, Thomason, and Bear, "Reconceptualizing What and How Women Negotiate for Career Advancement."

15. Holland and French, "Condom Negotiation Strategy Use."

16. Peasant, Parra, and Okwumabua, "Condom Negotiation."

17. Bird and Harvey, "'No Glove, No Love.'"

18. McLaurin-Jones, Lashley, and Marshall, "Minority College Women's Views," 6.

19. McLaurin-Jones, Lashley, and Marshall, "Minority College Women's Views," 8.

20. McLaurin-Jones, Lashley, and Marshall, "Minority College Women's Views."

21. Lam et al., "What Really Works?"

22. Tschann et al., "Condom Negotiation Strategies."

23. Tschann et al., "Condom Negotiation Strategies," 258.

24. Brim, *Poor Queer Studies.*

25. Hegewisch and Tesfaselassie, "The Gender Wage Gap."

26. Gaddis, "Discrimination in the Credential Society."

27. Hernandez et al., "Bargaining While Black."

28. Hegewisch and Tesfaselassie, "The Gender Wage Gap."

29. Beasley, *Opting Out*.

30. LeanIn.Org and McKinsey & Company, *Women in the Workplace 2020*.

31. Hernandez et al., "Bargaining While Black."

32. Dickens and Chavez, "Navigating the Workplace."

33. Livingston and Opie, "Even at 'Inclusive' Companies."

34. Hall, Everett, and Hamilton-Mason, "Black Women Talk about Workplace Stress."

35. Phillips, Rothbard, and Dumas, "To Disclose or Not to Disclose?"

36. Phillips, Rothbard, and Dumas, "To Disclose or Not to Disclose?"

37. De La Rosa, "[Melanated Scenes Podcast] Black Woman in the Workplace."

38. Babcock and Laschever, *Women Don't Ask*, 74.

39. Steele and Aronson, "Stereotype Threat and the Intellectual Test Performance."

40. Dow, "The Deadly Challenges of Raising African American Boys."

41. Bernstein, Green Carmichael, and Torres, interview with Bell Smith and Nkomo.

42. Victoria Brescoll and others have written about how women's anger is perceived negatively in the workplace. Most of these early studies do not consider ethnicity. See Brescoll, "Leading with Their Hearts?"; and Brescoll and Uhlmann, "Can an Angry Woman Get Ahead?"

43. Motro et al., "Race and Reactions to Women's Expressions of Anger at Work."

44. Davis, *The Little Book of Race and Restorative Justice*, 47.

45. Friesen et al., "Perceiving Happiness in an Intergroup Context."

46. Consedine et al., "The Affective Paradox."

47. Accapadi, "When White Women Cry."

48. Bernstein, Green Carmichael, and Torres, interview with Opie and Caridad Rabelo.

49. Hirschman, *Exit, Voice, and Loyalty*.

50. Woods-Giscombé, "Superwoman Schema."

51. Wu, "This Banana Republic Employee Was Allegedly Discriminated Against."

52. Schiffer, "Lagging in Diversity, Haircare Targets Black Customers."

53. Che-Jung et al., "Use of Straighteners and Other Hair Products and Incident of Uterine Cancer."

54. Opie and Phillips, "Hair Penalties."

55. Opie, "Let My Hair Be Me."

56. De La Rosa, "[Melanated Scenes Podcast] Black Woman in the Workplace."

57. *She Did That*.

58. Tulshyan, "Return to Office?"

59. LeanIn.Org, "White Employees See Themselves as Allies."

60. Bell Smith and Nkomo, *Our Separate Ways.*
61. Opie and Livingston, "Shared Sisterhood."
62. Bernstein, Green Carmichael, and Torres, interview with Opie and Caridad Rabelo.
63. Bernstein, Green Carmichael, and Torres, interview with Opie and Caridad Rabelo.
64. Frye, "Racism and Sexism Combine."
65. Bohnet, *What Works.*
66. Criado Perez, *Invisible Women.*
67. Bernstein, Green Carmichael, and Torres, interview with Bell Smith and Nkomo.
68. Dumas, Phillips, and Rothbard, "Getting Closer at the Company Party."
69. Smith, *Men on Strike.*

CHAPTER 8. GUNS, ADDICTION, AND AN ORCHESTRA

1. Siegel, *Mindsight.*
2. Pelley, "Reimagining Police Departments with Safety and Justice in Mind."
3. Gardner, "The Dork Police."
4. Gardner, "The Dork Police," 92.
5. Fitzduff, *Our Brains at War.*
6. Coleman et al., "Intractable Conflict as an Attractor."
7. "Baltimore Homicides."
8. Pelley, "Reimagining Police Departments with Safety and Justice in Mind."
9. Butts et al., "Cure Violence."
10. Webster et al., "Effects of Baltimore's Safe Streets Program on Gun Violence."
11. Henry, Knoblauch, and Sigurvinsdottir, "The Effect of Intensive Cease-Fire Intervention."
12. Slutkin's program was originally called "CeaseFire."
13. Milam et al., "Changes in Attitudes toward Guns and Shootings."
14. Webster et al., "Evaluation of Baltimore's Safe Streets Program," 4.
15. Spain, "Understanding Key De-escalation Resolution Strategies."
16. Spain, "Understanding Key De-escalation Resolution Strategies," 10.
17. Whitehill et al., "Interrupting Violence," 91.
18. Fenton, "Former Baltimore Safe Streets Worker Sentenced for Role in Federal Drug Case."
19. Irvine, *On Desire,* 37.
20. Bartos et al., "Controlling Gun Violence."
21. Mann, "4 U.S. Companies Will Pay 26 Billion to Settle Claims They Fueled the Opioid Crisis."
22. Chang et al., "Effect of a Single Dose of Oral Opioid and Nonopioid Analgesics."
23. "In Baltimore, Violins to Combat Violence."
24. Shank, *The Political Force of Musical Beauty.*

25. Balio, "Of Riots and Relevance."
26. McCauley, "Baltimore Symphony Orchestra."

CONCLUSION

1. *The Wire,* season 5, episode 5, "React Quotes."
2. Jones, "How *The Wire* Became the Greatest TV Show Ever Made."
3. Moore, *The Other Wes Moore.*
4. Kleinman, *The Soul of Care: The Moral Education of a Husband and a Doctor,* 6.
5. Whitaker, "60 Minutes Investigates: Americans Fighting for Access to Sewage Disposal."
6. Diamond, *Getting More.*
7. "Baltimore's Police Commissioners through the Years."
8. Jackson, "At Least 20 Baltimore Police Officers Arrested, Sentenced, or Suspended during Department's Ugly 2019."
9. Zapotosky, "This Might Be the Most Corrupt Little Town in America."
10. Johnson, "Buddha Seems to Bring Tranquility to Oakland Neighborhood."

Acknowledgments

Ten semesters of negotiation students, as well as other savvy individuals in Baltimore and Los Angeles, taught me about how they break through structural as well as personal barriers. They have enriched my life immeasurably, and I am delighted that you can meet some of them throughout the book. Those listed below allowed me to use their stories, offered advice, and/or provided significant moral support. Those in bold reviewed full chapters.

Soolmaz Abooali	Barry Brown	Earl Dobbs
Tusmo Ali	Kolby Brown	Katharine Dudley
Jennifer Allison	**Laneisha Brown**	Maryann Durst
Karim Amin	**Alexis Brownlee**	Elizabeth Eschholz
Jennifer Artis	Janice Campbell	Paul Eschholz
Tiffany Austin	Latierra Carter	Jamie Espinosa
Kevin Avruch	**John Contreras**	**Briana Foreman**
Lisa Beatty	April Cooper	Ashley Fox
Jody Ann Beckford	**Tylis Cooper**	Betty Fulmore
Selena Benitez-Cuffee	**Celeste Cortez**	Justin Gallo
Grace Blossom	Erica Crawford	Brittany Goings
Sue Borchardt	La'Monica Cummings	Staci Griffin
Britni Briscoe	Menyvette Curtis	Binta Hanne
Simone Briscoe	Wanda Dale	**Elton Harrison Jr.**

Roger Hartley

Shanae Henry

Mormon Hubbard

Karah Johnson

Alexandra Jones

Rosalind Jones

Chelsea Keane

Shantell Kendall

La'Nesa Kolody

Frances Laviscount

Vernon Leftridge

Annie Lundsten

Mimi Makowske

Talia Martinez

Lakeisha Mathews

Hyland McConville

Robin McDonough

Theresa Mina

Melissa Monroe

Janay Morant

Ronald Niezen

Chris Novak

Babatunde Olu

Krish O'Mara Vignarajah

Chevonie Oyegoke

Scott Paris

Marcus Ponder Jr.

Natassja Pupuma

Nafeesat Rabiu-ade-bayo

Nawal Rajeh

Natasha Ramsey

Andrew Robinson

Ginger Robinson

Takia Ross

Matila Sackor-Jones II

Daniel Shapiro

Ivan Sascha Sheehan

Alexandra Slick

Kegan Smith

Leonard Spain

Jenna Stallworth

Bonnie Stein

Richard Stuller

Gloria Tubene

Jacob Tuthill

Kelechi Uzochukwu

Renata Valree

Rodney Walker

Tiffany Walker

Brittany Ware

Senator Mary Washington

Brenna Williams

Chris Wilson

Whitni Wilson

Judy Wong

Lauren Wyatt

Marcetta Young

Britta Zang

Catherine Znamirowski

Karen Zuniga

The University of Baltimore and University of Maryland Women's Forum (USMWF) helped me compensate people for their time and wisdom. This includes Catherine Znamirowski, who served as a wonderful research assistant. Negotiation experts Daniel Shapiro, Donna Hicks, Kevin Avruch, Ivan Sascha Sheehan, Darren Kew, and Kathleen Coogan cheered on the project from inception to delivery while Caveday, the online co-working community platform, helped me focus.

Thank you to Maura Roessner and the University of California Press, who believed in this project and guided it into your hands. Many of the books I most treasure came from this press, including the works of Paul Farmer, Carolyn Nordstrom, Didier Fassin, Alex Hinton, and Nancy Scheper-Hughes. To have a book that sits anywhere near these authors brings me great joy.

And, of course, to Ronald Niezen, my husband, who kept me writing most days during the two-plus years of the COVID-19 pandemic and who read multiple drafts (mostly) with enthusiasm.

References

"20-Year Gap in Life Expectancy between Richer, Poorer Areas of Baltimore." *CBS Baltimore,* July 6, 2017. https://baltimore.cbslocal.com/2017/07/06/life-expectancy-baltimore/.

AARP and National Alliance for Caregiving. *Caregiving in the United States 2020. AARP,* May 14, 2020. https://www.aarp.org/ppi/info-2020/caregiving-in-the-united-states.html.

ABDd. "Matthew Hussey Gives Texting Advice in 'What to Text Him Back.'" *YouTube,* September 2, 2016.

Accapadi, Mamta Motwani. "When White Women Cry: How White Women's Tears Oppress Women of Color." *College of Student Affairs Journal* 26, no. 2 (2007): 208–15.

Ackerman, Diane. *Deep Play.* New York: Vintage Books, 1999.

Adams, Abigail, "Judith Heumann: 100 Women of the Year." *Time,* March 5, 2020.

Adimsm5050. "Mom: Your great-aunt just passed away. LOL." *Reddit* post, January 22, 2016. https://www.reddit.com/user/Adimsm5050/.

Aguilera, Adrian, and Ricardo F. Muñoz. "Text Messaging as an Adjunct to CBT in Low-Income Populations: A Usability and Feasibility Pilot Study." *Professional Psychology: Research and Practice* 42, no. 6 (2011): 472–78.

Aknin, Lara B., Christopher P. Barrington-Leigh, Elizabeth W. Dunn, John F. Helliwell, Justine Burns, Robert Biswas-Diener, Imelda Kemeza, et al. "Prosocial Spending and Well-Being: Cross-Cultural Evidence for a Psychological Universal." *Journal of Personality and Social Psychology* 104, no. 4 (2013): 635–52.

Alim, H. Samy, and Geneva Smitherman. *Articulate While Black: Barack Obama, Language, and Race in the U.S.* Oxford: Oxford University Press, 2012.

Allen, Elder Florence. "Planning for the Unexpected." Recorded on June 10, 2017. In Bettina Schneider, *Financial Empowerment: Personal Finance for Indigenous and Non-Indigenous People.* Saskatchewan, Canada: University of Regina, 2012. https://www.uregina.ca/oer-publishing/titles/financial-empowerment.html.

Al-Saggaf, Yeslam, and Sarah B. O'Donnell. "Phubbing: Perceptions, Reasons behind, Predictors, and Impacts." *Human Behavior & Emerging Technology* 1, no. 2 (2019): 132–40.

Amanatullah, Emily T., and Michael W. Morris. "Negotiating Gender Roles: Gender Differences in Assertive Negotiating Are Mediated by Women's Fear of Backlash and Attenuated When Negotiating on Behalf of Others." *Journal of Personality and Social Psychology* 98, no. 2 (February 2010): 256–67.

Amanatullah, Emily T., and Catherine H. Tinsley. "Ask and Ye Shall Receive? How Gender and Status Moderate Negotiation Success." *Negotiation Conflict Management Research* 6, no. 4 (October 2013): 253–72.

Amnesty International. "Saudi Arabia: Women's Rights Campaigner Loujain al-Hathloul Due in Court." March 9, 2020. https://www.amnesty.org/en/latest/news/2020/03/saudi-arabia-womens-rights-campaigner-loujain-alhathloul-due-in-court/.

Anderson, Elijah. *Code of the Street: Decency, Violence and the Moral Life of the Inner City.* New York: W. W. Norton, 1999.

Anderson, Jessica, and Tim Prudente. "Fells Point Businesses Threaten to Withhold Taxes If Baltimore Does Not Address Crime, Drug Dealing and Other Issues." *Baltimore Sun,* June 8, 2021. https://www.baltimoresun.com/maryland/baltimore-city/bs-md-ci-fells-point-letter-20210608-k3gjlrsnzbh-nzjrcnh6h2tcdii-story.html.

Arendt, Hannah. *The Human Condition.* Chicago: University of Chicago Press, 1998.

Associated Press. "Egypt to Free Lebanese Tourist Sentenced to 8 Years for Insulting Country." *Times of Israel,* September 9, 2018. https://www.timesofisrael.com/egypt-to-free-lebanese-tourist-sentenced-to-8-years-for-insulting-country/.

Associated Press. "Explaining AP Style on Black and White." *AP News,* July 20, 2020. https://apnews.com/article/archive-race-and-ethnicity-9105661462.

Auyero, Javier. "Patients of the State: An Ethnographic Account of Poor People's Waiting." *Latin American Research Review* 46, no. 1 (2011): 5–29.

Babcock, Linda, and Sara Laschever. *Why Women Don't Ask: The High Cost of Avoiding Negotiations—and Positive Strategies for Change.* London: Piatkus Books, 2019.

Babcock, Linda, and Sara Laschever. *Women Don't Ask: The High Cost of Avoiding Negotiation—and Positive Strategies for Change.* Princeton, NJ: Princeton University Press, 2003.

Babcock, Linda, Sara Laschever, Michele Gelfand, and Deborah Small. "Nice Girls Don't Ask—Women Negotiate Less Than Men—and Everyone Pays the Price." *Harvard Business Review,* October 2003.

Babitz, Eve. *Slow Days, Fast Company: The World, The Flesh, and L.A.* New York: New York Review of Books, 2016.

Baker-Bell, April. *Linguistic Justice: Black Language, Literacy, Identity, and Pedagogy.* New York: Routledge, 2020.

Balio, Andrew. "Of Riots and Relevance: An Orchestra in Baltimore." *Future Symphony Institute* (blog). Accessed March 19, 2023. https://www.futuresymphony.org/of-riots-and-relevance-an-orchestra-in-baltimore/.

"Baltimore Homicides." *Baltimore Sun.* Accessed March 17, 2023. https://homicides.news.baltimoresun.com/?range=2022&cause=shooting.

"Baltimore's Police Commissioners through the Years." *Baltimore Sun.* Accessed March 19, 2023. https://www.baltimoresun.com/news/crime/bal-baltimore-police-commissioners-through-the-years-20180515-photogallery.html.

Banks, Ingrid. *Hair Matters: Beauty, Power, and Black Women's Consciousness.* New York: NYU Press, 2000.

Bartos, Bradley J., Richard McCleary, Lorraine Mazerolle, and Kelsy Luengen. "Controlling Gun Violence: Assessing the Impact of Australia's Gun Buyback Program Using a Synthetic Control Group Experiment." *Prevention Science* 21 (2020): 131–36.

Battilana, Julie, and Tiziana Casciaro. *Power, for All: How It Really Works and Why It's Everyone's Business.* New York: Simon and Schuster, 2021.

Beasley, Maya A. *Opting Out: Losing the Potential of America's Young Black Elite.* Chicago, IL: University of Chicago Press, 2012.

Beecher Stowe, Harriet. *Uncle Tom's Cabin: Life among the Lowly.* Alexandria, Egypt: Library of Alexandria, 1909.

Bell Smith, Ella, and Stella M. Nkomo. *Our Separate Ways, with a New Preface and Epilogue: Black and White Women and the Struggle for Professional Identity,* revised ed. Boston: Harvard Business Review Press, 2021.

Benkler, Yochai, Robert Faris, and Hal Roberts. *Network Propaganda: Manipulation, Disinformation, and Radicalization in American Politics.* New York: Oxford University Press, 2018.

Berger, Shoshana, and B. J. Miller. "Why You Need to Make a 'When I Die' File—Before It's Too Late." *Time,* August 1, 2019. https://time.com/5640494/why-you-need-to-make-a-when-i-die-file-before-its-too-late/.

Berger, Warren. *A More Beautiful Question: The Power of Inquiry to Spark Breakthrough Ideas.* New York: Bloomsbury USA, 2014.

Bernstein, Amy, Sarah Green Carmichael, and Nicole Torres. Interview with Ella L. J. Bell Smith and Stella M. Nkomo. "Sisterhood Is Scarce." November 8, 2018. In *Women at Work,* produced by *Harvard Business Review,* podcast. https://hbr.org/podcast/2018/11/sisterhood-is-scarce.

Bernstein, Amy, Sarah Green Carmichael, and Nicole Torres. Interview with Tina R. Opie and Verónica Caridad Rabelo. "Sisterhood Is Power." November 19, 2018. In *Women at Work,* produced by *Harvard Business Review,* podcast. https://hbr.org/podcast/2018/11/sisterhood-is-power?registration=success.

Bertrand, Marianne, and Sendhil Mullainathan. "Are Emily and Greg More Employable Than Lakisha and Jamal? A Field Experiment on Labor Market Discrimination." *American Economic Review* 94, no. 4 (2004): 991–1013.

Bird, Sheryl Thorburn, and S. Marie Harvey. "'No Glove, No Love': Cultural Beliefs of African-American Women Regarding Influencing Strategies for

Condom Use." *International Quarterly of Community Health Education* 20, no. 3 (2000): 237–51.

Blanco, Octavio. "Years after the Meltdown, Latinos Still Wary of Big Banks." *CNN Business,* June 16, 2017. https://money.cnn.com/2017/06/16/news /economy/latino-financial-banks/index.html.

Bohler, Sébastien. *Le bug humain: pourquoi notre cerveau nous pousse à détruire la planète et comment l'en empêcher.* Paris, France: Robert Laffont, 2020.

Bohnet, Iris. *What Works: Gender Equity by Design.* Cambridge, MA: Harvard University Press, 2016.

Bourdieu, Pierre. *Pascalian Meditations.* Translated by Richard Nice. Palo Alto, CA: Stanford University Press, 2000.

Bowles, Hannah Riley, and Linda Babcock. "How Can Women Escape the Compensation Negotiation Dilemma? Relational Accounts Are One Answer." *Psychology of Women Quarterly* 37, no. 1 (March 2013): 80–96.

Bowles, Hannah Riley, Linda Babcock, and Lei Lai. "Social Incentives for Gender Differences in the Propensity to Initiate Negotiations: Sometimes It Does Hurt to Ask." *Organizational Behavior and Human Decision Processes* 103, no. 1 (2007): 84–103.

Bowles, Hannah Riley, and Kathleen L. McGinn. "Gender in Job Negotiations: A Two-Level Game." *Negotiation Journal* 24, no. 4 (October 2008): 393–410.

Bowles, Hannah Riley, Bobbi Thomason, and Julia B. Bear. "Reconceptualizing What and How Women Negotiate for Career Advancement." *Academy of Management Journal* 62, no. 6 (2019): 1645–71.

Brefczynski-Lewis, J. A., A. Lutz, H. S. Schaefer, D. B. Levinson, and R. J. Davidson. "Neural Correlates of Attentional Expertise in Long-Term Meditation Practitioners." *Proceedings of the National Academy of Sciences* 104, no. 27 (July 2007): 11483–88.

Brescoll, Victoria L. "Leading with Their Hearts? How Gender Stereotypes of Emotion Lead to Biased Evaluations of Female Leaders." *Leadership Quarterly* 27, no. 3 (2016): 415–28.

Brescoll, Victoria L., and Eric Luis Uhlmann. "Can an Angry Woman Get Ahead? Status Conferral, Gender, and Expression of Emotion in the Workplace." *Psychological Science* 19, no. 3 (March 2008): 268–75.

Brett, Jeanne M. "Culture and Negotiation." *International Journal of Psychology* 35, no. 2 (2000): 97–104.

Brim, Matt. *Poor Queer Studies: Confronting Elitism in the University.* Durham, NC: Duke University Press, 2020.

Brooks, Arthur C. "How to Buy Happiness." *The Atlantic,* April 15, 2021. https://www.theatlantic.com/family/archive/2021/04/money-income-buy-happiness/618601/.

Brown, Brené. *Daring Greatly: How the Courage to Be Vulnerable Transforms the Way We Live, Love, Parent, and Lead.* New York: Avery, 2015.

Burton, John. *Conflict: Human Needs Theory.* London: Palgrave Macmillan, 1990.

Butler, Paul. *Chokehold: Policing Black Men.* New York: The New Press, 2018.

Butts, Jeffrey A., Caterina Gouvis Roman, Lindsay Bostwick, and Jeremy R. Porter. "Cure Violence: A Public Health Model to Reduce Gun Violence." *Annual Review of Public Health* 36 (March 2015): 39–53.

Byrd, Elder Norma Jean. "Importance of a Will." Recorded on July 3, 2018. In *Financial Empowerment: Personal Finance for Indigenous and non-Indigenous People*, by Bettina Schneider. Regina, Saskatchewan, Canada: University of Regina, 2012. https://www.uregina.ca/oer-publishing/titles /financial-empowerment.html.

Callan, Mitchell J., John H. Ellard, N. Will Shead, and David C. Hodgins. "Gambling as a Search for Justice: Examining the Role of Personal Relative Deprivation in Gambling Urges and Gambling Behavior." *Personality and Social Psychology Bulletin* 34, no. 11 (November 2008): 1514–29.

Caring.com. "2021 Wills and Estate Planning Study." Accessed April 24, 2021. https://www.caring.com/caregivers/estate-planning/wills-survey/.

Carney, Dana R., Amy J.C. Cuddy, and Andy J. Yap. "Power Posing: Brief Nonverbal Displays Affect Neuroendocrine Levels and Risk Tolerance." *Psychological Science* 21, no. 10 (October 2010): 1363–1368.

Carpenter, C.C.J., Joseph A. Durick, Rabbi Milton L. Grafman, Bishop Paul Hardin, Bishop Nolan B. Harmon, George M. Murray, Edward V. Ramage, and Earl Stallings. Alabama Clergymen's Letter to Dr. Martin Luther King Jr., April 12, 1963.

Centers for Disease Control and Prevention. "Distracted Driving." March 2, 2021. https://www.cdc.gov/transportationsafety/distracted_driving/index .html.

Chang, Andrew K., Polly E. Bijur, David Esses, Douglas P. Barnaby, and Jesse Baer. "Effect of a Single Dose of Oral Opioid and Nonopioid Analgesics on Acute Extremity Pain in the Emergency Department: A Randomized Clinical Trial." *JAMA* 318, no. 17 (November 7, 2017): 1661–67.

Chatzky, Jean. "Do You Have a Complicated Relationship with Money? Read This." *Forbes*, August 22, 2016. https://www.forbes.com/sites/jeanchatzky /2016/08/22/has-money-ever-made-you-feel-confused-frustrated-guilty-shameful-read-this/.

Che-Jung Chang, Katie M. O'Brien, Alexander P. Keil, Symielle A. Gaston, Chandra L. Jackson, Dale P. Sandler, and Alexandra J. White. "Use of Straighteners and Other Hair Products and Incident of Uterine Cancer." *JNCI: Journal of the National Cancer Institute*, 2022.

Childre, Doc, Howard Martin, Rollin McCraty, and Deborah Rozman. *Heart Intelligence: Connecting with the Intuitive Guidance of the Heart*. Sherfield Gables, UK: Waterside Press, 2017.

Chotpitayasunondh, Varoth, and Karen M. Douglas. "The Effects of 'Phubbing' on Social Interaction." *Journal of Applied Social Psychology* 48, no. 6 (2018): 304–16.

Chou, Eileen Y., Bidhan L. Parmar, and Adam D. Galinsky. "Economic Insecurity Increases Physical Pain." *Psychological Science* 27, no. 4 (2016): 443–54.

Chris Rock: Tamborine. Directed by Bo Burnham. Written by Chris Rock. Jax Media. Aired February 14, 2018, on Netflix. https://www.netflix.com /title/80167498.

City-Data.com. "Crime Rate in Compton, California (CA): Murders, Rapes, Robberies, Assaults, Burglaries, Thefts, Auto Thefts, Arson, Crime Map." Accessed March 19, 2023. https://www.city-data.com/crime/crime-Compton-California.html.

Cobb, Sara B. *Speaking of Violence: The Politics and Poetics of Narrative Dynamics in Conflict Resolution.* New York: Oxford University Press, 2013.

Cobb, Sara B., Sarah Federman, and Alison Castel. *Introduction to Conflict Resolution: Discourses and Dynamics.* Landham, MD: Rowman & Littlefield International, 2019.

Coleman, Peter T. *The Way Out: How to Overcome Toxic Polarization.* New York: Columbia University Press, 2021.

Coleman, Peter T., Robin R. Vallacher, Andrzej Nowak A., and Lan Bui-Wrzosinska. "Intractable Conflict as an Attractor: A Dynamical Systems Approach to Conflict Escalation and Intractability." *American Behavioral Scientist* 50, no. 11 (2007): 1454–75.

Consedine, Nathan S., Carol Magai, David Horton, and William M. Brown. "The Affective Paradox: An Emotion Regulatory Account of Ethnic Differences in Self-Reported Anger." *Journal of Cross-Cultural Psychology* 43, no. 5 (2012): 723–41.

Criado Perez, Caroline. *Invisible Women: Data Bias in a World Designed for Men.* New York: Abrams Press, 2019.

Davis, Fania E. *The Little Book of Race and Restorative Justice: Black Lives, Healing, and US Social Transformation.* New York: Simon and Schuster, 2019.

De Dreu, Carsten K. W., and Gerben A. Van Kleef. "The Influence of Power on the Information Search, Impression Formation, and Demands in Negotiation." *Journal of Experimental Social Psychology* 40, no. 3 (2004): 303–19.

de Gaay Fortman, Bas. *Political Economy of Human Rights: Rights, Realities and Realization.* New York: Routledge, 2011.

De La Rosa, Tierra. "[Melanated Scenes Podcast] Black Woman in the Workplace Pt. 2." *YouTube,* March 1, 2021. Zoom call, 49:01. https://www.youtube.com/watch?v=mlDDxghqKB8.

Demby, Gene. "How Code-Switching Explains the World." *NPR,* April 8, 2013. https://www.npr.org/sections/codeswitch/2013/04/08/176064688/how-code-switching-explains-the-world.

DeOrtentiis, Philip S., Chad H. Van Iddekinge, and Connie R. Wanberg. "Different Starting Lines, Different Finish Times: The Role of Social Class in the Job Search Process." *Journal of Applied Psychology* (May 2021).

Deutsch, Loránt. *Le metronome: L'Histoire de France au rythme du metro parisien* [Metronome: A History of France through the rhythm of the Parisian metro]. Paris: Michel Lafon, 2015.

Diamond, Stuart. *Getting More: How You Can Negotiate to Succeed in Work and Life.* New York: Crown, 2010.

Dickens, Danielle D., and Ernest L. Chavez. "Navigating the Workplace: The Costs and Benefits of Shifting Identities at Work among Early Career U.S. Black Women." *Sex Roles* 78 (2018): 760–74.

diones. January 7, 2011 (11:09 A.M.). Comment on African HYS team. "Can You Afford to Go to Church?" *BBC,* January 6, 2011. https://www.bbc

.co.uk/blogs/africahaveyoursay/2011/01/can-you-afford-to-go-to-church
.shtml.

Dow, Dawn Marie. "The Deadly Challenges of Raising African American Boys: Navigating the Controlling Image of the 'Thug.'" *Gender and Society* 30, no. 2 (2016): 161–88.

Du Bois, W. E. B. *The Souls of Black Folk: Essays and Sketches*. Chicago: A. G. McClurg, 1903.

Dumas, Tracy L., Katherine W. Phillips, and Nancy P. Rothbard. "Getting Closer at the Company Party: Integration Experiences, Racial Dissimilarity, and Workplace Relationships." *Organization Science* 24, no. 5 (2013).

Dwyer, Leslie. "A Politics of Silences: Violence, Memory and Treacherous Speech in Post-1965 Bali." In *Genocide: Truth, Memory, and Representation*, edited by Alexander Laban Hinton and Kevin Lewis O'Neill, 113–46. Durham, NC: Duke University Press, 2009.

Ebner, Noam. "Negotiating via Text Messaging." In *The Negotiator's Desk Reference*, edited by Chris Honeyman and Andrea Kupfer Schneider, 113–50. Saint Paul, MN: DRI Press, 2017.

Ebner, Noam. "Negotiating via Videoconferencing." In *The Negotiator's Desk Reference*, edited by Chris Honeyman and Andrea Kupfer Schneider, 151–70. Saint Paul, MN: DRI Press, 2017.

Ebner, Noam, Anita D. Bhappu, Jennifer Gerarda Brown, and Kimberlee K. Kovach. "You've Got Agreement: Negoti@ting via Email." *Hamline Journal of Public Law & Policy* 31, no. 2 (Spring 2010): 427–58.

Eichler, Alex. "'Askers' vs. 'Guessers.'" *The Atlantic*, May 12, 2010. https://www.theatlantic.com/national/archive/2010/05/askers-vs-guessers/340891/.

Elkington, John. "Towards the Sustainable Corporation: Win-Win-Win Business Strategies for Sustainable Development." *California Management Review* 36, no. 2 (January 1994): 90–100.

Elkins, Kathleen. "PepsiCo CEO Indra Nooyi on Why Steve Jobs Advised Her to Throw Tantrums." *CNBC*, November 10, 2016. https://www.cnbc.com/2016/11/10/pepsico-ceo-indra-nooyi-on-why-steve-jobs-advised-her-to-throw-tantrums.html.

Enloe, Cynthia. *Bananas, Beaches and Bases: Making Feminist Sense of International Politics*, 2nd ed. Berkeley: University of California Press, 2014.

Ermine, Elder Willie. "Giving What You Treasure to Get What You Need. Part 2." Recorded on June 10, 2017. In *Financial Empowerment: Personal Finance for Indigenous and non-Indigenous People,* by Bettina Schneider. Regina, Saskatchewan: University of Regina, 2012. https://www.uregina.ca/oer-publishing/titles/financial-empowerment.html.

Federman, Sarah. "Holocaust Survival Stories: The Last Chapter." *Folklife,* November 8, 2021. https://folklife.si.edu/magazine/holocaust-survival-stories-last-chapter.

Fenton, Justin. "Former Baltimore Safe Streets Worker Sentenced for Role in Federal Drug Case." *Baltimore Sun,* September 21, 2021. https://www.baltimoresun.com/news/crime/bs-md-ci-cr-safe-streets-alexander-sentenced-20210921-orwxfq4m7rgwlpka7j6gwfp4gm-story.html.

Fisher, Roger, and Daniel Shapiro. *Beyond Reason: Using Emotions as You Negotiate*. New York: Penguin, 2005.

Fisher, Roger, and Daniel Shapiro. "Emotions Are Powerful, Always Present and Hard to Handle." In *Beyond Reason: Using Emotions as You Negotiate,* 3–14. New York: Penguin Books, 2005.

Fisher, Roger, and William Ury. *Getting to Yes: Negotiating Agreement without Giving In*. Boston: Houghton Mifflin Harcourt, 1991 [1981].

Fisher, Roger, William Ury, and Bruce Patton. *Getting to Yes: Negotiating an Agreement without Giving In*. New York: Penguin Books, 2012. First published 1981 by Houghton Mifflin Harcourt (Boston).

Fitzduff, Mari. *Our Brains at War: The Neuroscience of Conflict and Peacebuilding*. Oxford: Oxford University Press, 2021.

Ford, Craig. "Should the Poor Give?" *Money Help for Christians,* November 3, 2010.

Forge, Emmanuel. "How to Negotiate Car Price by Email (Exactly What to Say in 2021)." *YouTube,* February 26, 2020. Instructional video, 8:00. https://www.youtube.com/watch?v=pJxjHpcPQdM.

Friedman, Raymond A., and Steven C. Currall. "Conflict Escalation: Dispute Exacerbating Elements of E-mail Communication." *Human Relations* 56, no. 11 (2003): 1325–47.

Friesen, Justin P., Kerry Kawakami, Larissa Vingilis-Jaremko, Regis Caprara, David M. Sidhu, Amanda Williams, Kurt Hugenberg, et al. "Perceiving Happiness in an Intergroup Context: The Role of Race and Attention to the Eyes in Differentiating between True and False Smiles." *Journal of Personality and Social Psychology* 116, no. 3 (2019): 375–95.

Frye, Jocelyn. "Racism and Sexism Combine to Shortchange Working Black Women." Center for American Progress, August 22, 2019. https://www.americanprogress.org/issues/women/news/2019/08/22/473775/racism-sexism-combine-shortchange-working-black-women/.

Gabbatt, Adam. "Oprah Winfrey Given Swiss Apology for 'Racist Treatment' over Handbag." *The Guardian,* August 9, 2013. http://www.theguardian.com/tv-and-radio/2013/aug/09/oprah-winfrey-swiss-apology-racist-treatment.

Gaddis, S. Michael. "Discrimination in the Credential Society: An Audit Study of Race and College Selectivity in the Labor Market." *Social Forces* 93, no. 4 (June 2015): 1451–79.

Galinsky, Adam D., Deborah H. Gruenfeld, and Joe C. Magee. "From Power to Action." *Journal of Personality and Social Psychology* 85, no. 3 (2003): 453–66.

Gallo, Amy. "How to Disagree with Someone More Powerful Than You." *Harvard Business Review,* March 17, 2016. https://hbr.org/2016/03/how-to-disagree-with-someone-more-powerful-than-you.

Gardner, Michael. "The Dork Police." In *Sweet Fruit from the Bitter Tree: 61 Stories of Creative & Compassionate Ways out of Conflict,* edited by Mark Andreas. Boulder, CO: Real People Press, 2011.

Gee, Buck, and Denise Peck. "Asian Americans Are the Least Likely Group in the U.S. to Be Promoted to Management." *Harvard Business Review,* May

31, 2018. https://hbr.org/2018/05/asian-americans-are-the-least-likely-group-in-the-u-s-to-be-promoted-to-management.

Ginwright, Shawn A. *Black Youth Rising: Activism and Radical Healing in Urban America.* New York: Teachers College Press, 2010.

Goffman, Erving. *Stigma: Notes on the Management of Spoiled Identity.* New York: Simon and Schuster, 2009.

Gone, Joseph P. "Redressing First Nations Historical Trauma: Theorizing Mechanisms for Indigenous Culture as Mental Health Treatment." *Transcultural Psychiatry* 50, no. 5 (2013): 683–706.

Gottman, John M., and Joan DeClaire. *The Relationship Cure: A Five-Step Guide to Strengthening Your Marriage, Family, and Friendships.* New York: Three Rivers Press, 2001.

Gourrier, Al G. "Banking the Black Community: An Analysis of Banking among Baltimore's Predominantly Black Communities." *Public Integrity* (July 2021).

Grant, Adam. *Give and Take: Why Helping Others Drives Our Success.* New York: Penguin Books, 2013.

Gregory, Anne, Dewey Cornell, and Xitao Fan. "The Relationship of School Structure and Support to Suspension Rates for Black and White High School Students." *American Educational Research Journal* 48, no. 4 (2011): 904–34.

Grewal, Dalvinder Singh. "Improving Concentration and Mindfulness in Learning through Meditation." *IOSR Journal of Humanities and Social Science* 19, no. 2 (2014): 33–39.

Gritters, Jenni. "How Instagram Takes a Toll on Influencers' Brains." *The Guardian,* January 8, 2019. http://www.theguardian.com/us-news/2019/jan/08/instagram-influencers-psychology-social-media-anxiety.

Grosser, Travis, Virginie Kidwell, and Giuseppe (Joe) Labianca. "Hearing It through the Grapevine: Positive and Negative Workplace Gossip." *Organizational Dynamics* 41 (2012): 52–61.

Gruenfeld, Deborah. *Acting with Power: Why We Are More Powerful Than We Believe.* New York: Crown Archetype, 2021.

Gunraj, Danielle N., April M. Drumm-Hewitt, Erica M. Dashow, Sri Siddhi N. Upadhyay, and Celia M. Klin. "Texting Insincerely: The Role of the Period in Text Messaging." *Computers in Human Behavior* 55, Part B (2016): 1067–75.

Gürtin, Zeynep B., Lucy Morgan, David O'Rourke, Jinjun Wang, and Kamal Ahuja. "For Whom the Egg Thaws: Insights from an Analysis of 10 Years of Frozen Egg Thaw Data from Two UK Clinics, 2008–2017." *Journal of Assisted Reproduction and Genetics* 36 (2019): 1069–80.

Hall, J. Camille, Joyce Everett, and Johnnie Hamilton-Mason. "Black Women Talk about Workplace Stress and How They Cope." *Journal of Black Studies* 43, no. 2 (2012): 207–26.

Halpern-Meekin, Sarah. *Social Poverty: Low-Income Parents and the Struggle for Family and Community Ties.* New York: New York University Press, 2019.

Hanhimaki, Jussi M. *The Flawed Architect: Henry Kissinger and American Foreign Policy.* New York: Oxford University Press, 2004.

Harvard Program on Negotiation Staff. "BATNA Strategy: Should You Reveal Your BATNA?," *PON—Program on Negotiation at Harvard Law School* (blog), January 12, 2021. https://www.pon.harvard.edu/daily/batna/negotiation-research-you-can-use-should-you-brandish-your-batna-nb/.

Harvard Program on Negotiation Staff. "How to Negotiate via Text Message." *PON—Program on Negotiation at Harvard Law School* (blog), January 28, 2021.

Harvard Program on Negotiation Staff. "Power in Negotiation: The Impact on Negotiators and the Negotiation Process." *PON—Program on Negotiation at Harvard Law School* (blog), July 25, 2019. https://www.pon.harvard.edu/daily/negotiation-skills-daily/how-power-affects-negotiators/.

Harvard Program on Negotiation Staff. "Tired of Liars? Promote More Ethical Negotiation Behavior." *PON—Program on Negotiation at Harvard Law School* (blog), February 11, 2021. https://www.pon.harvard.edu/daily/negotiation-skills-daily/tired-liars-promote-ethical-behavior-negotiation-nb/.

Harvard Program on Negotiation Staff. "Women and Negotiation: Negotiating the Gender Gap." *Program on Negotiation at Harvard Law School* (blog), November 3, 2014. https://www.pon.harvard.edu/daily/conflict-resolution/women-and-negotiation-negotiating-the-gender-gap/.

Hegewisch, Ariane, and Adiam Tesfaselassie. "The Gender Wage Gap: 2019; Earnings Differences by Gender, Race, and Ethnicity." Institute for Women's Policy Research. March 2020.

Heilman, Madeline, and Tyler G. Okimoto. "Why Are Women Penalized for Success at Male Tasks? The Implied Communality Deficit." *Journal of Applied Psychology* 92, no. 1 (2007): 81–92.

Henry, David B., Shannon Knoblauch, and Rannveig Sigurvinsdottir. "The Effect of Intensive CeaseFire Intervention on Crime in Four Chicago Police Beats: Quantitative Assessment." Unpublished manuscript, September 11, 2014. https://cvg.org/wp-content/uploads/2019/09/McCormick_Crease-Fire_Quantitative_Report_091114.pdf.

Hernandez, Morela, Derek R. Avery, Sabrina D. Volpone, and Cheryl R. Kaiser. "Bargaining While Black: The Role of Race in Salary Negotiations." *Journal of Applied Psychology* 104, no. 4 (2019): 581–92.

Hewlin, Patricia Faison, and Anna-Maria Broomes. "Authenticity in the Workplace: An African American Perspective." In *Race, Work, and Leadership: New Perspectives on the Black Experience,* edited by Laura Morgan Morgan, Anthony J. Mayo, and David A. Thomas. Boston: Harvard Business Press, 2019.

Hicks, Donna. *Dignity: Its Essential Role in Resolving Conflict.* New Haven, CT: Yale University Press, 2011.

Hicks, Donna. *Leading with Dignity: How to Create a Culture That Brings Out the Best in People.* New Haven, CT: Yale University Press, 2018.

Hirschman, Albert O. *Exit, Voice, and Loyalty: Responses to Decline in Firms, Organizations, and States.* Illustrated ed. Cambridge, MA: Harvard University Press, 1972.

Holland, Kathryn J., and Sabine Elizabeth French. "Condom Negotiation Strategy Use and Effectiveness among College Students." *Journal of Sex Research* 49, no. 5 (September 1, 2012): 443–53.

hooks, bell. *Teaching to Transgress*. New York: Routledge, 2014.

Horowitz, Julia. "Charles the Entrepreneur? How the New King Built a Top Organic Food Brand." *CNN*, September 16, 2022.

Horton, David, and Reid Kress Weisbord. "68% of Americans Do Not Have a Will." *Conversation*, May 19, 2020. https://theconversation.com/68-of-americans-do-not-have-a-will-137686.

"How Do You Greet Someone in Nigeria?" *Answers Nigeria*, August 9, 2019. https://answersnigeria.com/how-do-you-greet-someone-in-nigeria/.

Hyman, Ira E., Jr., Matthew S. Boss, Breanne M. Wise, Kira E. McKenzie, and Jenna M. Caggiano. "Did You See the Unicycling Clown? Inattentional Blindness While Walking and Talking on a Cell Phone." *Applied Cognitive Psychology* 24, no. 5 (2010): 597–607.

"In Baltimore, Violins to Combat Violence." *Gulf Today*, April 25, 2019. https://www.gulftoday.ae/culture/2019/04/25/in-baltimore-violins-to-combat-violence.

Ingram, Paul. "The Forgotten Dimension of Diversity." *Harvard Business Review* 99, no. 1 (January/February 2021): 58–67.

Irvine, William B. *On Desire: Why We Want What We Want*. Illustrated ed. Oxford: Oxford University Press, 2007.

Jackson, Phillip. "At Least 20 Baltimore Police Officers Arrested, Sentenced, or Suspended during Department's Ugly 2019." *Baltimore Sun*, December 17, 2019. https://www.baltimoresun.com/news/crime/bs-md-ci-cr-20-baltimore-cops-sentenced-charged-2019-20191217-wtqklwhhqndk3hrgacufigczem-story.html.

Jan, Tracy. "1 in 7 White Families Are Now Millionaires. For Black Families, It's 1 in 50." *Washington Post*, October 3, 2017. https://www.washingtonpost.com/news/wonk/wp/2017/10/03/white-families-are-twice-as-likely-to-be-millionaires-as-a-generation-ago/.

Johnson, Chip. "Buddha Seems to Bring Tranquility to Oakland Neighborhood." *SFGATE*, September 16, 2014. https://www.sfgate.com/bayarea/johnson/article/Buddha-seems-to-bring-tranquillity-to-Oakland-5757592.php.

Jones, Emma. "How *The Wire* Became the Greatest TV Show Ever Made." *BBC*, April 13, 2018. https://www.bbc.com/culture/article/20180412-how-the-wire-became-the-greatest-tv-show-ever-made.

Kalenkoski, Charlene M., Karen S. Hamrick, and Margaret Andrews. "Time Poverty Thresholds and Rates for the US Population." *Social Indicators Research* 104, no. 1 (October 2011): 129–55.

Kapoutsis, Ilias, and Roger Volkema. "Hard-Core Toughie: Donald Trump's Negotiations for the United States Presidency." *Negotiation Journal* 35, no. 1 (January 2019): 47–63.

Keith, Kent M. "The Paradoxical Commandments." In *The Silent Revolution: Dynamic Leadership in the Student Council* [booklet for student leaders, 1968].

Kelly, MeMe. "4 Tips to Send (and Receive) Better Texts." *Wired,* June 7, 2021. https://www.wired.com/story/4-tips-to-send-and-receive-better-texts/.

Kelly, Russell Earl. "Here with Another View on Christian Tithing." *Wall Street Journal,* December 17, 2007.

Kelly, Russell Earl. *Should the Church Teach Tithing? A Theologian's Conclusions about a Taboo Doctrine.* New York: iUniverse, 2001.

Kendi, Ibram X. *Stamped from the Beginning: The Definitive History of Racist Ideas in America.* New York: Bold Type Books, 2016.

Killingsworth, Matthew A. "Experienced Well-Being Rises with Income, Even Above $75,000 per Year." *Proceedings of the National Academy of Sciences* 118, no. 4 (January 2021).

Kim, Peter H., Robin L. Pinkley, and Alison R. Fragale. "Power Dynamics in Negotiation." *Academy of Management Review* 30, no. 4 (October 2005): 799–822.

King, Thomas. *The Inconvenient Indian: A Curious Account of Native People in North America.* Toronto: Doubleday Canada, 2012.

Kleinman, Arthur. *The Soul of Care: The Moral Education of a Husband and a Doctor.* New York: Penguin Books, 2019.

Kolb, Deborah M., and Jessica L. Porter. *Negotiating at Work: Turn Small Wins into Big Gains.* Hoboken, NJ: John Wiley & Sons, 2015.

Kolb, Deborah M., and Judith Williams. *The Shadow Negotiation: How Women Can Master the Hidden Agendas That Determine Bargaining Success.* New York: Simon and Schuster, 2001.

Konnikova, Maria. "Lean Out: The Dangers for Women Who Negotiate." *The New Yorker,* June 10, 2014. https://www.newyorker.com/science/maria-konnikova/lean-out-the-dangers-for-women-who-negotiate.

Kram, Zach. "The 2019 Orioles Might Be the '27 Yankees of Awful." *The Ringer,* July 2, 2019. https://www.theringer.com/mlb/2019/7/2/20678381/baltimore-orioles-worst-teams-mlb-history.

Kupfer Schneider, Andrea, and Sean McCarthy. "Choosing among Modes of Communication." From *The Negotiator's Desk Reference,* edited by Christopher Honeyman and Andrea Kupfer Schneider. Marquette Law School Legal Studies Research Paper Series, no. 18–09 (2018): 107–14. https://ssrn.com/abstract=3123374.

Lam, Amy G., Amy Mak, Patricia D. Lindsay, and Stephen T. Russell. "What Really Works? An Exploratory Study of Condom Negotiation Strategies." *AIDS Education and Prevention* 16, no. 2 (June 2005): 160–71.

Lara, Maria P. *Narrating Evil: A Postmetaphysical Theory of Reflective Judgment.* New York: Columbia University Press, 2007.

Latz, Martin E. *The Real Trump Deal: An Eye-Opening Look at How He Really Negotiates.* Phoenix, AZ: Brisance Books Group, 2018.

LeanIn.Org. "White Employees See Themselves as Allies—but Black Women and Latinas Disagree." June 19–25, 2020.

LeanIn.Org and McKinsey & Company. *Women in the Workplace 2020.* https://wiw-report.s3.amazonaws.com/Women_in_the_Workplace_2020.pdf.

Lenski, Tammy. "Friction with a Colleague, Ask for a Favor." *Mediate.com,* October 2016. https://www.mediate.com/articles/LenskiTbl20161007.cfm.

Leonhardt, Megan. "60% of Women Say They've Never Negotiated Their Salary—and Many Quit Their Job Instead." *CNBC,* January 31, 2020. https://www.cnbc.com/2020/01/31/women-more-likely-to-change-jobs-to-get-pay-increase.html.

Lewicki, Roy, Bruce Barry, and David Saunders. *Negotiation: Readings, Exercises, and Cases.* New York: McGraw-Hill, 2006.

Liljenquist, Katie A. "Resolving the Impression Management Dilemma: The Strategic Benefits of Soliciting Others for Advice." PhD diss., Northwestern University, 2010. ProQuest (305215034).

Lipsky, Michael. *Street-Level Bureaucracy: Dilemmas of the Individual in Public Service,* 30th anniversary ed. New York: Russell Sage Foundation, 2010.

Livingston, Beth, and Tina Opie. "Even at 'Inclusive' Companies, Women of Color Don't Feel Supported." *Harvard Business Review,* August 29, 2019. https://hbr.org/2019/08/even-at-inclusive-companies-women-of-color-dont-feel-supported.

Long, Ally. "How to Ace Your Zoom Interview." *YouTube,* May 15, 2020. Instructional video, 6:19. https://www.youtube.com/watch?v=zRAHP7oWfMY.

Loughan, Ashlee, and Robert Perna. "Neurocognitive Impacts for Children of Poverty and Neglect." *CYF News* (American Psychological Association), July 2012. https://www.apa.org/pi/families/resources/newsletter/2012/07/neurocognitive-impacts.

Lovitt, Bryn. "Death by Selfie: 11 Disturbing Stories of Social Media Pics." *Rolling Stone,* July 14, 2016. https://www.rollingstone.com/culture/culture-lists/death-by-selfie-11-disturbing-stories-of-social-media-pics-gone-wrong-15091/.

Lowry, Erin. *Broke Millennial: Stop Scraping by and Get Your Financial Life Together.* New York: TarcherPerigee, 2017.

Lup, Katerina, Leora Trub, and Lisa Rosenthal. "Instagram #Instasad? Exploring Associations among Instagram Use, Depressive Symptoms, Negative Social Comparison, and Strangers Followed." *Cyberpsychology, Behavior and Social Networking* 18, no. 5 (May 2015): 247–52.

m1ority. January 8, 2011 (7:50 A.M.). Comment on African HYS team. "Can You Afford to Go to Church?" *BBC,* January 6, 2011. https://www.bbc.co.uk/blogs/africahaveyoursay/2011/01/can-you-afford-to-go-to-church.shtml.

Maaravi, Yossi, and Boaz Hameiri. "Deep Pockets and Poor Results: The Effect of Wealth Cues on First Offers in Negotiation." *Group Decis Negot* 28 (2019): 43–62.

MacGillis, Alec. "The Tragedy of Baltimore." *New York Times Magazine,* March 12, 2019. https://www.nytimes.com/2019/03/12/magazine/baltimore-tragedy-crime.html?searchResultPosition=1.

Malhotra, Deepak. "How to Negotiate on Zoom: Challenges & Solutions." *YouTube,* April 1, 2020. Instructional video, 11:12. https://www.youtube.com/watch?v=1uKKZfrddog.

Malhotra, Deepak, and Max H. Bazerman. *Negotiation Genius: How to Overcome Obstacles and Achieve Brilliant Results at the Bargaining Table and Beyond.* New York: Bantam Books, 2008.

Mann, Brian. "4 U.S. Companies Will Pay $26 Billion to Settle Claims They Fueled the Opioid Crisis." *NPR,* February 25, 2022.

Manzoni, Anna, and Jessi Streib. "The Equalizing Power of a College Degree for First-Generation College Students: Disparities across Institutions, Majors, and Achievement Levels." *Research in Higher Education* 60, no. 5 (2019): 577–605.

Mark, Gloria, Victor M. Gonzalez, and Justin Harris. "No Task Left Behind? Examining the Nature of Fragmented Work." Paper presented at SIGCHI Conference on Human Factors in Computing Systems, Portland, Oregon, April 2–7, 2005. https://www.ics.uci.edu/~gmark/CHI2005.pdf.

Mark, Gloria, Daniela Gudith, and Ulrich Klocke. "The Cost of Interrupted Work: More Speed and Stress." Paper presented at Twenty-Sixth Annual CHI Conference on Human Factors in Computing Systems, Florence, Italy, April 5–10, 2008. https://www.ics.uci.edu/~gmark/chi08-mark.pdf.

The Mask You Live In. Directed by Jennifer Siebel Newsom. Written by Jessica Anthony, Jessica Congdon, and Jennifer Siebel Newsom. The Representation Project, 2015. https://www.kanopy.com/product/mask-you-live.

Mauss, Marcel. *The Gift.* Chicago: HAU Books, 2016.

Mayer, Bernard. *The Dynamics of Conflict: A Guide to Engagement and Intervention.* New York: John Wiley & Sons, 2012.

Mayer, Bernard. "The Dynamics of Power in Mediation and Negotiation." *Mediation Quarterly* 16 (Summer 1987): 75–86.

Mazelis, Joan M. *Surviving Poverty: Creating Sustainable Ties among the Poor.* New York: New York University Press, 2017.

McCauley, Mary C. "Baltimore Symphony Orchestra, Musicians Endure First Work Stoppage in 31 Years. But They're Still Talking." *Baltimore Sun,* June 18, 2019. https://www.baltimoresun.com/entertainment/arts/bs-fe-bso-lockout-20190617-story.html.

McClain, Colleen. "70% of U.S. social media users never or rarely post or share about political, social issues." Pew Research Center. May 4, 2021.

McCrory Calarco, Jessica. *Negotiating Opportunities: How the Middle Class Secures Advantages in School.* New York: Oxford University Press, 2018.

McCurn, Alexis S. *The Grind: Black Women and Survival in the Inner City.* New Brunswick, NJ: Rutgers University Press, 2018.

McCurn, Alexis S. "'Keeping It Fresh': How Young Black Women Negotiate Self–Representation and Controlling Images in Urban Space." *City & Community* 17, no. 1 (2017): 134–49.

McIntyre, Alice. *Participatory Action Research.* Thousand Oaks, CA: SAGE, 2007.

McLaurin-Jones, TyWanda, Maudry-Beverly Lashley, and Vanessa Marshall. "Minority College Women's Views on Condom Negotiation." *International Journal of Environmental Research and Public Health* 13, no. 1 (2016).

Milam, Adam J., Shani A. Buggs, C. Debra M. Furr-Holden, Philip J. Leaf, Catherine P. Bradshaw, and Daniel Webster. "Changes in Attitudes toward Guns and Shootings Following Implementation of the Baltimore *Safe Streets* Intervention." *Journal of Urban Health* 93, no. 4 (August 2016): 609–26.

Miller, Hallie. "As Baltimore's Poppleton Neighborhood Braces for Change, Residents Liken It to a 'Family' Being Broken Apart." *Baltimore Sun,* July 23, 2021. https://www.baltimoresun.com/business/real-estate/bs-bz-poppleton-redevelopment-baltimore-20210723-7vvqfqekybdp7dkfxyeqcacn7i-story.html.

Miller, Reuben J. *Halfway Home: Race, Punishment, and the Afterlife of Mass Incarceration.* New York: Little, Brown, 2021.

Misra, Shalini, Lulu Cheng, Jamie Genevie, and Miao Yuan. "The IPhone Effect: The Quality of In-Person Social Interactions in the Presence of Mobile Devices." *Environment and Behavior* 48, no. 2 (February 2016): 275–98.

Misra, Shalini, and Daniel Stokols. "Psychological and Health Outcomes of Perceived Information Overload." *Environment and Behavior* 44, no. 6 (April 17, 2011): 737–75.

Mnookin, Robert H. *Beyond Winning: Negotiating to Create Value in Deals and Disputes.* Cambridge, MA: Harvard University Press, 2004.

Moore, Wes. *The Other Wes Moore: One Name, Two Fates.* New York: Spiegel & Grau, 2011.

Morton, Jennifer M. *Moving Up without Losing Your Way: The Ethical Costs of Upward Mobility.* Princeton, NJ: Princeton University Press, 2019.

Motro, Daphna, Jonathan B. Evans, Aleksander P. J. Ellis, and Lehman Benson III. "Race and Reactions to Women's Expressions of Anger at Work: Examining the Effects of the 'Angry Black Woman' Stereotype." *Journal of Applied Psychology* (April 2021).

Mummendey, Amelie, Thomas Kessler, Andreas Klink, and Rosemarie Mielke. "Strategies to Cope with Negative Social Identity: Predictions by Social Identity Theory and Relative Deprivation Theory." *Journal of Personality and Social Psychology* 76, no. 2 (1999): 229–45.

Narayan, Deepa. "Bonds and Bridges: Social Capital and Poverty." In *Social Capital and Economic Development,* edited by Jonathan Isham, Thomas Kelly, and Sunder Ramaswamy. Cheltenham, UK: Edward Elgar, 2002.

Narula, Svati Kirsten. "How Much Money Do Millennials Make? It's No Longer a Taboo Question." *Wall Street Journal,* May 3, 2021.

National Aeronautics and Space Administration. *NASA's Hispanic Astronauts.* Houston, TX: Lyndon B. Johnson Space Center, 2018.

National Institute of Drug Abuse. "Overdose Death Rates." National Institutes of Health, January 20, 2022. https://nida.nih.gov/research-topics/trends-statistics/overdose-death-rates.

Niezen, Ronald. *Defending the Land: Sovereignty and Forest Life in James Bay Cree Society.* New York: Routledge, 2016.

Niezen, Ronald. *#HumanRights: The Technologies and Politics of Justice Claims in Practice.* Palo Alto, CA: Stanford University Press, 2020.

Niezen, Ronald. *Rediscovered Self: Indigenous Identity and Cultural Justice.* Montreal: McGill-Queen's University Press, 2009.

Oliver, Mary. *Wild Geese.* Hexham, UK: Bloodaxe Books, 2004.

Opie, Tina. "Let My Hair Be Me: An Investigation of Employee Authenticity and Organizational Appearance Policies through the Lens of Black Women's Hair." *Fashion Studies* 1, no. 1 (2018): 1–27.

Opie, Tina, and Beth Livingston. "Shared Sisterhood: Harnessing Collective Power to Generate More Inclusive and Equitable Organizations." *Organizational Dynamics* (2021).

Opie, Tina, and Katherine W. Phillips. "Hair Penalties: The Negative Influence of Afrocentric Hair on Ratings of Black Women's Dominance and Professionalism." *Frontiers in Psychology* 6, no. 1311 (August 2015).

Organisation for Economic Cooperation and Development (OECD). *Enabling Women's Economic Empowerment: New Approaches to Unpaid Care Work in Developing Countries*. June 3, 2019. https://www.oecd-ilibrary.org/sites/4d0229cd-en/index.html?itemId=/content/component/4d0229cd-en#figure-d1e414.

Organize Poppleton. "Save Our Block in Poppleton, Baltimore." 2021. https://www.change.org/p/baltimore-city-council-save-our-block-in-poppleton-baltimore?recruiter=false&utm_source=share_petition&utm_medium=twitter&utm_campaign=psf_combo_share_initial&recruited_by_id=b8d7f650-e1ea-11eb-9e23-95a4f82d4c57_.

Overbeck, Jennifer R., Margaret A. Neale, and Cassandra L. Govan. "I Feel, Therefore You Act: Intrapersonal Effects of Emotion on Negotiation as a Function of Social Power." *Organizational Behavior and Human Decision Process* 112 (2010): 126–39.

Page, Sydney. "This Maryland Man Was a Sanitation Worker. Now He Is Accepted to Harvard Law School." *Washington Post,* July 1, 2020. https://www.washingtonpost.com/lifestyle/2020/07/01/former-sanitation-worker-this-maryland-man-was-accepted-harvard-law-school/.

Pager, Devah, Bruce Western, and Bart Bonikowski. "Discrimination in a Low-Wage Labor Market: A Field Experiment." *American Sociological Review* 74, no. 5 (2009): 777–99.

Paradies, Yin, Jehonathan Ben, Nida Denson, Amanuel Elias, Naomi Priest, Alex Pireterse, Arpana Gipta, Margaret Kelacher, and Gilbert Gee. "Racism as a Determinant of Health: A Systematic Review and Meta-Analysis." *PLoS One* 10, no. 9 (September 2015).

Payne, Keith. *The Broken Ladder: How Inequality Affects the Way We Think, Live, and Die.* New York: Viking Press, 2017.

PayScale.com. "Racial and Gender Pay Gap Statistics for 2021." *PayScale,* March 24, 2021. https://www.payscale.com/data/gender-pay-gap.

Peasant, Courtney, Gilbert R. Parra, and Theresa M. Okwumabua. "Condom Negotiation: Findings and Future Directions." *Journal of Sex Research* 52, no. 4 (2015): 470–83.

Pelley, Scott. "Reimagining Police Departments with Safety and Justice in Mind." *CBS 60 Minutes,* November 21, 2021. https://www.cbsnews.com/news/police-reform-austin-texas-60-minutes-2021-11-21/.

Perhach, Paulette. "A Story of a Fuck Off Fund." *The Billfold,* January 20, 2016. https://www.thebillfold.com/2016/01/a-story-of-a-fuck-off-fund/.

Perry, Andre M., Jonathan Rothwell, and David Harshbarger. "The Devaluation of Assets in Black Neighborhoods." Brookings Institution, November 2018. https://www.brookings.edu/research/devaluation-of-assets-in-black-neighborhoods/.

Peterson, Christopher, and Martin E. P. Seligman. "Learned Helplessness and Victimization." *Journal of Social Issues* 39, no. 2 (1983): 103–16.

Phillips, Katherine W., Nancy P. Rothbard, and Tracy L. Dumas. "To Disclose or Not to Disclose? Status Distance and Self-Disclosure in Diverse Environments." *Academy of Management Review* 34, no. 4 (2009): 710–32.

Pietila, Antero. *The Ghosts of Johns Hopkins: The Life and Legacy That Shaped an American City.* Landham, MD: Rowman & Littlefield, 2018.

Pinsker, Joe. "We're Learning the Wrong Lessons from the World's Happiest Countries." *The Atlantic,* June 27, 2021.

Pontzer, Herman, Yosuke Yamada, Hiroyuki Sagayama, Philip N. Ainslie, Lene D. Anderson, Liam J. Anderson, Lenore Arab, et al. "Daily Energy Expenditure through the Human Life Course." *Science* 373, no. 6556 (August 2021): 808–12.

Poppe, Annika Elena, Julia Leininger, and Jonas Wolff. "Introduction: Negotiating the Promotion of Democracy." *Democratization* 26, no. 5 (2019): 759–76.

Popper, Karl. *The Logic of Scientific Discovery.* New York: Routledge, 2005.

Pressman, Steven. "The Decline of the Middle Class: An International Perspective." *Journal of Economic Issues* 41, no. 1 (March 2007): 181–200.

Ramirez-Fernandez, Jaime, Jimena Y. Ramirez-Marin, and Lourdes Munduate. "Selling to Strangers, Buying from Friends: Effect of Communal and Exchange Norms on Expectations in Negotiation." *Negotiation and Conflict Management Research* 12 (2018): 281–96.

Rangel, Lisa. "5 Salary Negotiating Tips for Remote Jobs." *Firsthand,* July 14, 2020. https://firsthand.co/blogs/salary-and-benefits/how-to-negotiate-salaries-for-remote-jobs.

Rawls, John. *A Theory of Justice: Original Edition.* Cambridge, MA: Harvard University Press, 2009.

Reeves, Aaron, Martin McKee, and David Stuckler. "Economic Suicides in the Great Recession in Europe and North America." *British Journal of Psychiatry* 205, no. 3 (2014): 246–47.

Reid, Hilary. "What's the Deal with Affirm, AfterPay, Klarna, and QuadPay?" *New York Magazine,* August 13, 2020. https://nymag.com/strategist/article/how-to-use-affirm-klarna-quadpay-afterpay.html.

Reinhard, Susan C., Lynn Friss Feinberg, Ari Houser, Rita Choula, and Molly Evans. "Valuing the Invaluable: 2019 Update Charting a Path Forward." AARP Public Policy Institute, November 2019. https://www.aarp.org/ppi/info-2015/valuing-the-invaluable-2015-update.html.

Reynolds, Elder Margaret. "The Role of Mutual and Trust Funds in Caring for Grandchildren." Recorded on June 10, 2017. In *Financial Empowerment: Personal Finance for Indigenous and non-Indigenous People,* by Bettina Schneider. Regina, Saskatchewan, Canada: University of Regina, 2012. https://www.uregina.ca/oer-publishing/titles/financial-empowerment.html.

Roberts, Laura Morgan, Anthony J. Mayo, and David A. Thomas. *Race, Work, and Leadership: New Perspectives on the Black Experience.* Boston: Harvard Business Press, 2019.

Rock, David, Heidi Grant, and Jacqui Grey. "Diverse Teams Feel Less Comfortable—and That's Why They Perform Better." *Harvard Business Review,*

September 22, 2016. https://hbr.org/2016/09/diverse-teams-feel-less-comfortable-and-thats-why-they-perform-better.

Rodham Clinton, Hillary. *What Happened.* New York: Simon and Schuster, 2017.

Rodricks, Dan. "Mike Busch, Catherine Pugh and That Thing Called Integrity." *Baltimore Sun,* April 8, 2019. https://www.baltimoresun.com/opinion/columnists/dan-rodricks/bs-md-rodricks-column-busch-0408-story.html.

Rogers, Benjamin. "Community Mediation Online." Unpublished master's thesis, University of Baltimore, 2021.

Ross, Lee. "The Intuitive Psychologist and His Shortcomings: Distortions in the Attribution Process." In *Advances in Experimental Social Psychology,* vol. 10, edited by Leonard Berkowitz, 173–220. Cambridge, MA: Academic Press, 1977.

Runciman, Walter Garrison. *Relative Deprivation and Social Justice: A Study of Attitudes to Social Inequality in Twentieth-Century England.* Berkeley: University of California Press, 1966.

Sabia, Sabia, Aurore Fayosse, Julien Dumurgier, Vincent T. van Hees, Claire Paquet, Andrew Sommerlad, Mika Kivimäki, Aline Dugravot, and Archana Singh-Manoux. "Association of Sleep Duration in Middle and Old Age with Incidence of Dementia." *Nature Communications* 12, no. 2289 (2021): 1–10.

Sale, Anna. *Let's Talk about Hard Things.* New York: Simon and Schuster, 2021.

Sandel, Michael J. *The Tyranny of Merit: What's Become of the Common Good?* New York: Farrar, Straus and Giroux, 2020.

Sataline, Suzanne. "The Backlash against Tithing." *Wall Street Journal,* November 24, 2007. https://www.wsj.com/articles/SB119576921737201375.

Schiffer, Jessica. "Lagging in Diversity, Haircare Targets Black Customers." *Vogue Business,* November 6, 2020.

Schmeichel, Brandon J., and Kathleen Vohs. "Self-Affirmation and Self-Control: Affirming Core Values Counteracts Ego Depletion." *Journal of Personality and Social Psychology* 96, no. 4 (2009): 770–82.

Schneider, Bettina. *Financial Empowerment: Personal Finance for Indigenous and Non-Indigenous People.* Regina, Saskatchewan, Canada: University of Regina Press, 2018.

Schopenhauer, Arthur. *The Essays of Arthur Schopenhauer; Counsels and Maxims.* Glasgow, UK: Good Press, 2019.

Seema, Mody, and Harriet Taylor. "Egg Freezing Has Become the Go-To for Delayed Parenthood—and Companies Are Popping Up to Provide More Cost-Effective Solutions." *CNBC,* May 9, 2019. https://www.cnbc.com/2019/05/09/millennials-are-driving-down-the-cost-of-egg-freezing.html.

Shank, Barry. *The Political Force of Musical Beauty.* Durham, NC: Duke University Press, 2014.

Shapiro, Daniel. "Negotiating Emotions." *Conflict Resolution Quarterly* 20, no. 1 (September 2002): 67–82.

Shapiro, Daniel. *Negotiating the Nonnegotiable: How to Resolve Your Most Emotionally Charged Conflicts.* Illustrated ed. New York: Penguin Books, 2017.

Shattock, Julie. "Hispanics Don't Trust Banks and It's Costing Them." Consolidated Credit, June 1, 2016. https://www.consolidatedcredit.org/financial-news/unbanked-latinos-may-be-losing-out/.

Shear, Michael D., and Liam Stack. "Obama Says Movements Like Black Lives Matter 'Can't Just Keep on Yelling.'" *New York Times,* April 23, 2016. https://www.nytimes.com/2016/04/24/us/obama-says-movements-like-black-lives-matter-cant-just-keep-on-yelling.html.

She Did That. Directed by Renae Bluitt and Sterling Milan. Written by Renae Bluitt, Trizonna McClendon, and Brittany Stalworth. Featuring Luvvie Ajayi, Fifi Bell, and Renae Bluitt. Aired August 20, 2019. https://shedidthatfilm.com/.

Shell, G. Richard. *Bargaining for Advantage: Negotiation Strategies for Reasonable People.* New York: Penguin Books, 2006. First published 1991 by Viking Penguin (New York).

Sherlock, Mary, and Danielle L. Wagstaff. "Exploring the Relationship between Frequency of Instagram Use, Exposure to Idealized Images, and Psychological Well-Being in Women." *Psychology of Popular Media Culture* 8, no. 4 (2019): 482–90.

Shonk, Katie. "Advanced Negotiation Techniques: Negotiating Partnerships Online." *PON—Program on Negotiation at Harvard Law School* (blog), February 8, 2021.

Shonk, Kate. "Online Negotiation in a Time of Social Distance." *PON—Program on Negotiation at Harvard Law School* (blog), March 26, 2020.

Siegel, Daniel J. *Mindsight: The New Science of Personal Transformation.* New York: Bantam, 2009.

Slaughter, Anne-Marie. "The Work That Makes Work Possible." *The Atlantic,* March 23, 2016. https://www.theatlantic.com/business/archive/2016/03/unpaid-caregivers/474894/.

Smith, Helen. *Men on Strike: Why Men Are Boycotting Marriage, Fatherhood, and the American Dream—and Why It Matters.* New York: Encounter Books, 2014.

Smith, Laura, Debbie-Ann Chambers, and Lucinda Bratini. "When Oppression Is the Pathogen: The Participatory Development of Socially Just Mental Health Practice." *American Journal of Orthopsychiatry* 79, no. 2 (2009): 159–68.

Spain, Leonard. "Understanding Key De-escalation Resolution Strategies Used by Baltimore City Safe Streets Program Workers." Unpublished master's thesis, University of Baltimore, 2019.

Speed, Brittany C., Brandon L. Goldstein, and Marvin R. Goldfried. "Assertiveness Training: A Forgotten Evidence-Based Treatment. *Clinical Psychology: Science and Practice* 25, no. 1 (2018): 1–20.

Steele, Claud M., and Joshua Aronson. "Stereotype Threat and the Intellectual Test Performance of African Americans." *Journal of Personality and Social Psychology* 69, no. 5 (1995): 797–811.

Steflja, Izabela, and Jessica Trisko Darden. *Women as War Criminals: Gender, Agency, and Justice.* Stanford, CA: Stanford University Press, 2020.

Stevenson, Bryan. "We Need to Talk about Injustice." *TED,* March 2021. TED Talk, 23:25. https://www.ted.com/talks/bryan_stevenson_we_need_to_talk_about_an_injustice/transcript.

Sy, Susan R., and Jessica Romero. "Family Responsibilities among Latina College Students from Immigrant Families." *Journal of Hispanic Higher Education* 7, no. 3 (2008): 212–27.

Tannen, Deborah. "The Power of Talk: Who Gets Heard and Why." In *Negotiation: Readings, Exercises, and Cases,* edited by Roy J. Lewicki, David M. Saunders, and Bruce Barry, 323–36. New York: McGraw-Hill, 2007.

Taylor, Jill Bolte. "The Neuroanatomical Transformation of the Teenage Brain." *YouTube,* February 21, 2013. TED Talk for TEDxYouth@Indianapolis, 16:30. https://www.youtube.com/watch?v=PzT_SBl31-s.

Telegraph Staff and Agencies. "Mothers Asked Nearly 300 Questions a Day, Study Finds." *Telegraph,* March 28, 2013. https://www.telegraph.co.uk /news/uknews/9959026/Mothers-asked-nearly-300-questions-a-day-study-finds.html.

Tessler, Bari. *The Art of Money: A Life-Changing Guide to Financial Happiness.* Berkeley, CA: Parallax Press, 2016.

Thompson, Leigh, and Janice Nadler. "Negotiating via Information Technology: Theory and Application." *Journal of Social Issues* 58, no. 1 (January 2002): 109–24.

Thompson, Matt. "Five Reasons Why People Code-Switch." *NPR,* April 13, 2013. https://www.npr.org/sections/codeswitch/2013/04/13/177126294/five-reasons-why-people-code-switch.

Toosi, Negin R., Shira Mor, Zhaleh Semnani-Azad, Katherine W. Phillips, and Emily T. Amanatullah. "Who Can Lean In? The Intersecting Role of Race and Gender in Negotiations." *Psychology of Women Quarterly* 43, no. 1 (March 2019): 7–21.

Tretina, Kat, and Benjamin Curry. "How Fiduciary Duty Impacts Financial Advisors." *Forbes Advisor,* April 21, 2021. https://www.forbes.com/advisor /investing/what-is-fiduciary-duty/.

Tschann, Jeanne M., Elena Flores, Cynthia L. de Groat, Julianna Deardorff, and Charles J. Wibbelsman. "Condom Negotiation Strategies and Actual Condom Use among Latino Youth." *Journal of Adolescent Health* 47, no. 3 (2010): 254–62.

Tufekci, Zeynep. "Does a Protest's Size Matter?" *New York Times,* January 27, 2017.

Tulshyan, Ruchika. "Return to Office? Some Women of Color Aren't Ready." *New York Times,* June 23, 2021. https://www.nytimes.com/2021/06/23/us /return-to-office-anxiety.html.

Turkle, Sherry. *Reclaiming Conversation: The Power of Talk in a Digital Age.* New York: Penguin, 2016.

Umoh, Ruth. "Black Women Were among The Fastest-Growing Entrepreneurs—Then Covid Arrived." *Forbes,* October 26, 2020. https://www .forbes.com/sites/ruthumoh/2020/10/26/black-women-were-among-the-fastest-growing-entrepreneurs-then-covid-arrived/.

University of Southern California. "Racism Has a Toxic Effect: Study May Explain How Racial Discrimination Raises the Risks of Disease among African Americans." *ScienceDaily,* May 31, 2019. https://www.sciencedaily .com/releases/2019/05/190531100558.htm.

Ury, William. *Getting to Yes with Yourself (And Other Worthy Opponents)*. San Francisco: HarperOne, 2015.

U.S. Bureau of Labor Statistics. "May 2020 National Occupational Employment and Wage Estimates United States." Accessed March 19, 2023. https://www.bls.gov/oes/current/oes_nat.htm.

U.S. Census Bureau. "QuickFacts: Baltimore City, Maryland; United States." Accessed march 19, 2023. https://www.census.gov/quickfacts/fact/table/baltimorecitymaryland,US/PST045219.

van Eijk, Gwen. "Does Living in a Poor Neighbourhood Result in Network Poverty? A Study on Local Networks, Locality-Based Relationships and Neighbourhood Settings." *Journal of Housing and the Built Environment* 25, no. 4 (2010): 467–80.

Van Kleef, Gerben A., Carsten K.W. De Dreu, Davide Pietroni, and Antony S.R. Manstead. "Power and Emotion in Negotiation: Power Moderates the Interpersonal Effects of Anger and Happiness on Concession Making." *European Journal of Social Psychology* 36 (2006): 557–81.

Volkan, Vamik D. "Transgenerational Transmissions and Chosen Traumas: An Aspect of Large-Group Identity." *Group Analysis* 34, no. 1 (2001): 79–97.

Volkema, Roger J., Denise Fleck, and Agnes Hofmeister. "Getting off on the Right Foot: The Effects of Initial Email Messages on Negotiation Process and Outcome." *IEEE Transactions on Professional Communication* 54, no. 3 (2011): 299–313.

Vosoughi, Soroush, Deb Roy, and Sinan Aral. "The Spread of True and False News Online." *Science* 359, no. 6380 (March 9, 2018): 1146–51.

Wallerstein, Nina. "Powerlessness, Empowerment, and Health: Implications for Health Promotion Programs." *American Journal of Health Promotion* 6, no. 3 (January 1992): 197–205.

Walton, Gregory M., and Geoffrey L. Cohen. "A Brief Social-Belonging Intervention Improves Academic and Health Outcomes of Minority Students." *Science* 331, no. 6023 (March 18, 2011): 1447–51.

Ward, Adrian F., Kristen Duke, Ayelet Gneezy, and Maarten W. Bos. "Brain Drain: The Mere Presence of One's Own Smartphone Reduces Available Cognitive Capacity." *Journal of the Association for Consumer Research* 2, no. 2 (2017): 140–54.

Weber, Max. *Economy and Society: An Outline of Interpretive Sociology*. New York: Bedminster Press, 1968.

Webster, Daniel W., Jennifer Mendel Whitehill, Jon S. Vernick, and Frank C. Curriero. "Effects of Baltimore's Safe Streets Program on Gun Violence: A Replication of Chicago's CeaseFire Program." *Journal of Urban Health* 90 (2013): 27–40.

Webster, Daniel W., Jennifer Mendel Whitehill, Jon S. Vernick, and Elizabeth M. Parker. "Evaluation of Baltimore's *Safe Streets* Program: Effects on Attitudes, Participants' Experiences, and Gun Violence." Johns Hopkins Center for the Prevention of Youth Violence, Johns Hopkins Bloomberg School of Public Health, January 11, 2012. https://www.jhsph.edu/research/centers-and-institutes/center-for-prevention-of-youth-violence/field_reports/2012_01_11. Executive%20SummaryofSafeStreetsEval.pdf.

Weiner, Jonah. "Nicki Minaj: Hip-Hop's Hottest Sidekick Goes Solo." *Details,* May 2010.

Wells, Taylor M., and Alan R. Dennis. "To Email or Not to Email: The Impact of Media on Psychophysiological Responses and Emotional Content in Utilitarian and Romantic Communication." *Computers in Human Behavior* 54 (2016): 1–9.

Westerhof, Gerben J., Martina Miche, Allyson F. Brothers, Anne E. Barrett, Manfred Diehl, Joann M. Montepare, Hans-Werner Wahl, and Susanne Wurm. "The Influence of Subjective Aging on Health and Longevity: A Meta-analysis of Longitudinal Data." *Psychology and Aging* 29, no. 4 (2014): 793–802.

Whitehill, Jennifer M., Daniel W. Webster, Shannon Frattaroli, and Elizabeth M. Parker. "Interrupting Violence: How the CeaseFire Program Prevents Imminent Gun Violence through Conflict Mediation." *Journal of Urban Health* 91 (2014): 84–95.

Whitaker, Bill. "60 Minutes Investigates: Americans Fighting for Access to Sewage Disposal."

CBS 60 Minutes, December 19, 2021.

Williams, David R., Jourdyn A. Lawrence, and Brigette A. Davis. "Racism and Health: Evidence and Needed Research." *Annual Review of Public Health* 40, no. 1 (April 2019): 105–25.

Wilson, Chris, and Bret Witter. *The Master Plan: My Journey from Life in Prison to a Life of Purpose.* New York: Penguin, 2019.

Wingko. "These 15 People Had the Perfect Responses When Their Text Message Was Ignored" (blog), April 13, 2015. https://winkgo.com/15-perfect-responses-ignored-text-messages/.

Winter, David G. "The Power Motive in Women—and Men." *Journal of Personality and Social Psychology* 54, no. 3 (1988): 510–19.

The Wire. Season 5, episode 5, "React Quotes." Directed by Agnieszka Holland. Written by David Simon and David Mills. Originally aired February 3, 2008, on HBO. https://play.hbomax.com/page/urn:hbo:page:GVU2_OgSfB4NJjhsJAWRH:type:episode.

Wolff, Jennifer L., Brenda C. Spillman, Vicki A. Freedman, and Judith D. Kasper. "A National Profile of Family and Unpaid Caregivers Who Assist Older Adults with Health Care Activities." *JAMA Internal Medicine* 176, no. 3 (March 2016): 372–79.

Wong, Kristin. "The Workplace Still Isn't Equal for Women. Here's Some Advice to Navigate It." *New York Times,* June 17, 2019. https://www.nytimes.com/2019/06/16/smarter-living/the-workplace-still-isnt-equal-for-women-heres-some-advice-to-navigate-it.html.

Woods-Giscombé, Cheryl L. "Superwoman Schema: African American Women's Views on Stress, Strength, and Health." *Qualitative Health Research* 20, no. 5 (2010): 668–83.

Wu, Sarah. "This Banana Republic Employee Was Allegedly Discriminated Against for Her Box Braids." *Teen Vogue,* October 9, 2017. http://www.teenvogue.com/story/banana-republic-box-braids-discrimination-allegation.

Yoshino, Kenji. *Covering: The Hidden Assault on Our Civil Rights.* New York: Random House, 2006.

Yuan, Karen. "Black Employees Say 'Performative Allyship' Is an Unchecked Problem in the Office." *Fortune*, June 19, 2020. https://fortune.com/2020 /06/19/performative-allyship-working-while-black-white-allies-corporate-diversity-racism/.

Zaki, Jamil. "'Self-Care' Isn't the Fix for Late-Pandemic Malaise." *The Atlantic*, October 21, 2021. https://www.theatlantic.com/ideas/archive/2021/10 /other-care-self-care/620441/.

Zapotosky, Matt. "This Might Be the Most Corrupt Little Town in America." *Washington Post*, March 5, 2016. https://www.washingtonpost.com/world /national-security/this-might-be-the-most-corrupt-little-town-in-america /2016/03/05/341c21d2-dcac-11e5-81ae-7491b9b9e7df_story.html.

Index

Founded in 1893,
UNIVERSITY OF CALIFORNIA PRESS
publishes bold, progressive books and journals
on topics in the arts, humanities, social sciences,
and natural sciences—with a focus on social
justice issues—that inspire thought and action
among readers worldwide.

The UC PRESS FOUNDATION
raises funds to uphold the press's vital role
as an independent, nonprofit publisher, and
receives philanthropic support from a wide
range of individuals and institutions—and from
committed readers like you. To learn more, visit
ucpress.edu/supportus.